The Popular Front Novel in Britain, 1934–1940

Historical Materialism Book Series

The Historical Materialism Book Series is a major publishing initiative of the radical left. The capitalist crisis of the twenty-first century has been met by a resurgence of interest in critical Marxist theory. At the same time, the publishing institutions committed to Marxism have contracted markedly since the high point of the 1970s. The Historical Materialism Book Series is dedicated to addressing this situation by making available important works of Marxist theory. The aim of the series is to publish important theoretical contributions as the basis for vigorous intellectual debate and exchange on the left.

The peer-reviewed series publishes original monographs, translated texts, and reprints of classics across the bounds of academic disciplinary agendas and across the divisions of the left. The series is particularly concerned to encourage the internationalization of Marxist debate and aims to translate significant studies from beyond the English-speaking world.

For a full list of titles in the Historical Materialism Book Series
available in paperback from Haymarket Books, visit:
https://www.haymarketbooks.org/series_collections/1-historical-materialism

The Popular Front Novel in Britain, 1934–1940

Elinor Taylor

Haymarket Books
Chicago, IL

First published in 2017 by Brill Academic Publishers, The Netherlands
© 2017 Koninklijke Brill NV, Leiden, The Netherlands

Published in paperback in 2018 by
Haymarket Books
P.O. Box 180165
Chicago, IL 60618
773-583-7884
www.haymarketbooks.org

ISBN: 978-1-60846-046-5

Trade distribution:
In the US, Consortium Book Sales, www.cbsd.com
In Canada, Publishers Group Canada, www.pgcbooks.ca
In the UK, Turnaround Publisher Services, www.turnaround-uk.com
All other countries, Ingram Publisher Services International, ips_intlsales@
ingramcontent.com

Cover design by Jamie Kerry and Ragina Johnson.

This book was published with the generous support of Lannan Foundation
and the Wallace Action Fund.

Printed in the United States.

10 9 8 7 6 5 4 3 2 1

Library of Congress Cataloging-in-Publication data is available.

Contents

Acknowledgements

This book began as a doctoral thesis at the University of Salford, and I'm indebted to Ben Harker for his unfailingly painstaking and patient supervision. Many thanks are also due to Kristin Ewins, who has been an invaluable source of support and encouragement throughout. I must thank both Ben and Kristin, especially, for continuing to support the work after they had left Salford for new positions. The University of Salford's award of a Graduate Teaching Studentship enabled me to complete my doctoral research. This book was written in London, and I'm grateful to my new colleagues in the Department of English, Linguistics and Cultural Studies at the University of Westminster for providing such a supportive and welcoming environment in which to complete it. Thanks, for many things, are also due to Rob Clark, David Cunningham, Joe Darlington, Danny Hayward, David Meller, Stan Smith, Henry Stead, Awena Taylor, David and Ellie Taylor, Lee Walker, and Alex Warwick.

Materials from the papers of James Barke are ©CSG CIC Glasgow Museums and Libraries Collection: The Mitchell Library, Special Collections. I am grateful to The Mitchell Library for permission to quote from these materials.

Materials from the papers of Douglas Garman are quoted by permission of the Department of Manuscripts and Special Collections, University of Nottingham.

I am grateful to the staff of these institutions, as well as of the Working Class Movement Library in Salford, for making the archival work for this book possible.

This book is for my dad, Richard Taylor (1947–2006).

Introduction

The Popular Front means a struggle for a genuine popular culture, a manifold relationship to every aspect of the life of one's own people as it has developed in its own individual way in the course of history.

GEORG LUKÁCS, 1938[1]

∙ ∙ ∙

... the nauseous spectacle of bishops, Communists, cocoa-magnates, publishers, duchesses and Labour MPs marching arm in arm to the tune of 'Rule Britannia'

GEORGE ORWELL, 1938[2]

∙ ∙

Beleaguered by the intertwined malignancies of intractable economic crisis, insurgent fascism and Stalinism ascendant, the 1930s still stand in cultural memory as an economic and political nadir, a 'dark valley' of airless, accelerating catastrophe against which all subsequent crises must be measured.[3] The contemporary convulsions in the global capitalist system, bringing with them crises in representative democracy, economic devastation, and populist movements from left and right, are still read as signs of an impending or already occurring 'return to the thirties'.[4] British culture in the 1930s saw a widespread movement of intellectuals, artists and writers towards affiliation with left-wing politics, driven by the failure of democratic governments to either remedy the desperate conditions of the Depression or offer effective resistance to advancing fascism. The mobilisation of many prominent intellectuals in the cause of Republican Spain has come to stand both for the unprecedented extent of this commitment and for its failure: the failure, ultimately, to halt the Francoist

---

1 Lukács 2007, p. 57.
2 Orwell 1970b, p. 305.
3 *The Dark Valley* is the title of Piers Brendon's 2000 study of the decade.
4 For readings of the post-2008 European crisis in these terms, see, *inter alia*, Varoufakis 2016 and Crafts and Fearon (eds.) 2013.

reaction, but also the failure of international volunteers to recognise their manipulation by the Stalinist apparatus, and to establish a new, enduring space of commitment between intellectuals, mass culture and organised politics.

This book aims to think again about that attempt, its successes and its failures, through the lens of the British Communist novel.[5] To do so requires a certain resistance to the terms in which the literary culture of the 1930s characterised itself and diagnosed its own failures. Those terms were established before the decade had even concluded: in John Lehmann's 1940 survey of the decade's literature, *New Writing in Europe*, for instance, W.H. Auden and the group of writers who have come to be associated with him (Christopher Isherwood, Stephen Spender, Louis MacNeice and Cecil Day Lewis) are firmly identified as 'the real core of the movement of the 'thirties, its central and most active motor'.[6] There is remarkable tenacity in this impression of thirties writing as the province of young, upper-middle-class, university-educated, metropolitan (London-based) English leftists, the 'little circle of English writers', as Spender called them, whose political phase ended with the departure of Auden and Isherwood for America and which was obituarised in Auden's 'September 1, 1939'.[7] This focus is not simply demographic; it also reproduces the terms in which a particular current of writing reflected on its political engagements as a temporary deviation from a normative position of liberal neutrality. A particularly enduring expression is Auden's 'September 1, 1939', a poem that seeks to cancel the 'clever hopes' and murky compromises of the 'dishonest' decade with its concluding 'affirming flame' of renewed liberal humanism.[8] In Lehmann's *New Writing in Europe*, the best writing of Auden and his associates is redeemed by the 'pure flame of life' that it evinced in spite of the ways in which writers allowed themselves to be misled, under great historical pressures, by 'politicians'.[9] Lehmann implies that these writers' engagements were doubly dishonest: manipulated by the hidden agendas of politicians, they also betrayed their own reason; 'hoodwinked', Lehmann writes, until they again 'began to see and hear with their

---

5 In this book, the capitalised 'Communist' refers to people, ideas and institutions closely aligned with the Communist Parties of the Third International, such as the Communist Party of Great Britain.

6 Lehmann 1940, p. 47.

7 Spender 1997, p. xvi. The major study that institutionalised Lehmann's grouping was Hynes 1976; Bergonzi 1978 and Johnson 1982 adopt the same critical focus.

8 Auden 1977.

9 Lehmann 1940, p. 151.

own eyes and ears.'[10] When Stephen Spender published his contribution to Richard Crossman's 1948 collection of recantations by former Communists, *The God that Failed*, it was made explicit that the 'politician' was a Communist. There, Spender describes his experience of commitment as one of religious conversion arising from his personal apprehension of a crisis in the liberal intellectual life in which he was raised. Communist commitment is figured as an act of faith demanding the sacrifice of individual reason and agency, and the acceptance, in their stead, of an essentially mystical and anti-humanist view of history as the inexorable revelation of Marxist truth.[11] The inertia of liberal institutions drove 'men of good will' into the manipulations of single-minded ideologues so that a 'resurgent liberalism in its anti-Fascist form was exploited by the Communists.'[12] Communism on this reading was a destructive element that squandered the cultural energies and potential evoked by the threat of fascism and enforced a regime of intellectual orthodoxy which 'produced an increasingly deadening effect on all discussion of ideas, all witnessing of the complexity of events.'[13]

Such accounts as Spender's rest on the claim that the appeal of Communism was chiefly a reaction to the diminishing security of the middle-class intelligentsia. For George Orwell, writing late in 1939, Communism held an 'almost irresistible fascination' for the public school and university educated writer, whose faith in the prospects previously assured by their class had been shattered.[14] Virginia Woolf at almost the same moment saw commitment as a reaction to the leaning of the 'tower' of middle-class privilege.[15] Writers' engagements with leftist politics during the 1930s have been overshadowed by a narrative of 'going over to the workers' in which middle-class disaffection finds its form in acts of largely emotional and ultimately negative social identification with the working class and/or the Soviet Union, aided by a Communist Party whose compulsive dishonesty bred a critically blinding, 'simple, sentimental Russophilia', as Bernard Bergonzi puts it.[16] The image of commitment as a transitory response to be disavowed in the more sober environment

---

10   Lehmann 1940, p. 149.

11   Spender 1948, p. 237.

12   Spender 1948, p. 246; echoed in the same volume by Koestler 1948, p. 62.

13   Spender 1948, p. 248.

14   Orwell 1970a, pp. 561–2.

15   Woolf 1992.

16   Bergonzi 1978, p. 135. Cunningham 1988, pp. 211–41 gives a thorough account of the literal and metaphorical crossings of borders and frontiers in the decade's literature.

of the post-war decades was firmly established in the early Cold War years and, sustained by the currents of anti-Communist discourse, it shaped not just literary scholarship but also the cultural memory of 1930s in politically significant ways. As E.P. Thompson's reading of Auden's 'September 1, 1939' suggests, the terms of intellectual recoil from engagement in specific historical conditions could be generalised, in the first years of the Cold War, to legitimise a rejection of intellectual engagement under any conditions, so that what had been a 'provocation' on Auden's part could, within two decades, be taken as 'sober historical evaluation'.[17]

Other stories of the thirties are now being told: of women writers on the left, of working-class cultural producers, of the rich cultural lives of Communists and fellow travellers, all of which speak against the retrospective image of an attempted engagement that was blighted by stifling orthodoxy, anti-intellectualism and a totalitarian faith in the justice of the Soviet Union.[18] Spender's association of Communist commitment with intellectual dishonesty is increasingly pressured by nuanced critical examinations of the nature and valences of commitment.[19] This book seeks to contribute to this increasingly pluralist field by reading back beyond what E.P. Thompson called the 'cultural default' of the British intellectuals to reconstruct the relationships between the politics of Communism, anti-fascism and novelistic form, and in so doing to recover resistance to the closure Auden announced on the outbreak of war: a consignment of the cultural radicalism of the thirties to a dead end, a 'clever hope', and nothing more.[20] More particularly, this study aims to show that an understanding of the politics of the Popular Front, the anti-fascist strategy endorsed by the Third International (Comintern) in 1935, is integral to a critical reassessment of cultural activism during this period. Redirecting attention from the English poetry that has been central to so much literary scholarship, this book traces the engagements of a demographically and politically diverse range of British novelists with the populist anti-fascist politics of the years leading up to the war. In contrast to accounts such as Spender's, which suggest that Communism was a monolithic ideology to which writers had to capitulate, the chapters that follow will seek to demonstrate that the realist novel – an under-

---

17 E.P. Thompson 1978, p. 225.

18 Of particular significance are: on women writers, Ewins 2015, Montefiore 1996, Joannou (ed.) 1999; on working-class cultures, Croft 1990, Hilliard 2006a and 2006b; on British Communist culture, Croft (ed.) 1998, Wallis 1995 and 1998, Harker 2009, 2011a and 2013.

19 Recent interventions on the question of commitment include Kohlmann 2013 and 2014, and Taunton 2012.

20 E.P. Thompson 1978, p. 214.

explored aspect of the cultural landscape – functioned as a site of negotiation for the imaginative making of a politics. To recover these constitutive tensions is not to defend the politics – deeply ambiguous in its own right – but rather to attempt to see the dynamic fluidity of an interaction between a politics and a cultural form, a fluidity written out in retrospect in accounts that perceive failure not as history but as fate.

The central novelists in this book are John Sommerfield, Arthur Calder-Marshall, James Barke, Lewis Jones and Jack Lindsay. These writers were all active participants in the cultural life of the left, and were all self-identified Communists during this period. Not all were card-carrying members of the Communist Party of Great Britain, and they occupied different positions of tension in relation to the 'official' line of the Party. They represent something of a cross-section of the literary left: from the almost archetypal fellow-traveller Calder-Marshall, educated at public school and Oxford, to the thoroughly proletarian Lewis Jones, educated in the Labour Colleges and with a background in grassroots industrial organisation.[21] The largely self-educated Scottish novelist James Barke is a figure in whom we find a focal point for the tense entanglement of concepts of class, nation and people, engaging in sustained exploration – within and beyond his novels – of the relevance of Scottish national history and identity to the ideal of a broad, popular alliance against fascism.[22] Although his thirties novels are neglected, Barke translated his interwar engagements with popular and radical history into commercial success in the post-war period, making a lasting impression on Scottish literature with his bestselling novels about the life of Robert Burns.[23] John Somerfield, Communist organiser in working-class districts of London, volunteer in the International Brigade and author of what might be the paradigmatic Popular Front novel, *May Day* (1936), inherited and reworked the strategies of metropolitan modernism.[24] Jack Lindsay, an Australian émigré whose long career spanned seven decades, underwent a conversion from a Nietzschean modernism to Marxism during the mid-thirties, documenting his intellectual evolution in an outpouring of novels, critical works, biographies, poems and translations.[25] The length of

---

21   For Calder-Marshall's background, see his autobiography: Calder-Marshall 1991. For Jones's, see Dai Smith 1992.

22   A succinct account of James Barke's life and politics is given in Manson 2006.

23   The 'Immortal Memory' sequence: *The Wind that Shakes the Barley* (1946), *The Song in the Green Thorn Tree* (1947), *The Wonder of All the Gay World* (1949), *The Crest of the Broken Wave* (1953) and *The Well of the Silent Harp* (1954).

24   An overview of Sommerfield's life and work is provided in Croft 1983.

25   Harker 2011a, pp. 18–19.

Lindsay's career gives a unique frame in which to view his development in the thirties, especially given that he was the only writer listed here still writing as a Communist Party member after the cataclysms of Nikita Khrushchev's 'Secret Speech' and the Soviet invasion of Hungary in 1956.[26]

This grouping has its limitations, of course, especially in its all-male focus; but it does allow for the redirection of attention from the demographically and politically narrow 'Auden generation' to the work of writers of different class, regional and national backgrounds, who followed different political and literary trajectories. Seeming to iterate the 'cultural default' named by Thompson, the novelist and fellow-travelling Communist Arthur Calder-Marshall wrote early in 1941:

> I think most writers who began their careers in the 'thirties are like me in looking back on that decade with a sense not of triumph, but of shame and failure. We accomplished something, but how little it was compared to what was necessary, or compared to what we could have done if we had been wiser, braver, more provident and energetic![27]

There is, unavoidably, something of the tone of thirties recantations here; but there is, too, something important that that type of account elides, which is the deeply felt sense of responsibility to an enormous task. Calder-Marshall does not write of his delusion or accuse others of misleading him; rather he laments the inability of writers to perform a wholly unrealistic task. The note of self-ridicule seems to resonate from this realisation. It is the sense of frustrated responsibility rather than of relieved dereliction that should be kept in view. This study tries to reconstruct the literary project that Calder-Marshall was, however briefly, committed to: to think clearly about what was at stake and what success might have looked like.

The Popular Front

This book spans the period beginning in early 1934 with the formation of the British Section of the Writers' International, which inaugurated the influential journal of culture and politics *Left Review*, up until the end of the 'Popular Front'

---

26   Lewis Jones had died in 1939; Calder-Marshall had become disillusioned by 1941; Barke remained on the left but distanced himself from the Communist Party, dying after many years of ill health in 1958; Sommerfield left the Party in 1956.

27   E.P. Thompson 1978, p. 214; Calder-Marshall 1941, p. 157.

as a political strategy in the disarray that followed the Molotov-Ribbentrop Pact in 1939/1940, which brought the imperatives of the defence of the Soviet Union and opposition to fascism into direct contradiction.[28] The pact placed British Communists in an impossible situation and alienated many Communist sympathisers. The Popular Front describes a strategy endorsed by the Communist International at its Seventh Congress in August 1935, elaborated as an anti-fascist organisational technique which had as its base a 'united front' of working-class organisations and, predicated on that, a wider popular alliance of groups and individuals opposed to fascism.[29] This popular alliance extended to social democrats, socialists, liberals and some conservative elements (the 'spectacle' to which George Orwell records his revulsion in the epigraph to this chapter). The formal adoption of the Popular Front strategy marked a decisive and dramatic shift from the Comintern's earlier, ultra-sectarian 'class against class' line, which had denounced non-Communist elements as 'social fascists' and forbade Communists from seeking alliances.[30] Popular Front governments were elected in France and Spain in 1936, both of which were to fall in due course under advancing fascism, while in Britain attempts were made to construct a broad alliance to challenge the National Government's inertia and appeasement of Hitler.[31]

Behind the dramatic reorientation was the spectre of fascism sweeping Europe. The inefficacy of the 'class against class' line was brought home early in 1934 with an attempted putsch by French fascists in Paris, after which the French Communist Party entered an alliance with the social democrats.[32] The Soviet Union's entry into the League of Nations in 1934 appeared to signal its willingness to work with the capitalist countries in the interests of collective security.[33] Simultaneously, in the wake of Hitler's assumption of the chancellorship of Germany in March 1933, European intellectuals had begun exploring the possibilities for alliances. The Amsterdam-Pleyel movement, supported by

---

28   For the founding of the Writers' International, see Hobday 1989, p. 157. The period of turmoil between the Ribbentrop-Molotov Pact and Operation Barbarossa is recounted in Morgan 1989, chapters 5 and 6.

29   Morgan 1989, p. 196.

30   Worley 2002 deals in depth with the rationale and consequences of the 'class against class' line. The class against class line has been characterised as an unmitigated disaster by historians, including the Party historians Noreen Branson and Willie Thompson (Worley 2002, p. 13). Cf. Myant 1985, pp. 31–3.

31   Morgan 1989, pp. 271–2.

32   Myant 1985, p. 37.

33   Morgan 1989, p. 20.

an international body of intellectuals, was instantiated in 1932 and convened an influential congress in August of that year.[34] The congress included Henri Barbusse, Romain Rolland, Maxim Gorky, Bertrand Russell, H.G. Wells, Albert Einstein, Heinrich Mann, Upton Sinclair, Theodore Dreiser and John Dos Passos.[35] In Britain, the founding of the British Section of the Writers' International in December 1933 and the establishment of *Left Review* in 1934 provided space for a cultural discussion of the possibilities offered by the new climate of alliance and cooperation in the name of anti-fascism.[36]

The crucial articulation of the new line was the address of the General Secretary of the Comintern, Georgi Dimitrov, to the Seventh Congress. The speech encapsulates the key principles of the Popular Front: an analysis of fascism as the strategy of a section of the bourgeoisie (leaving open the possibility of alliance with other bourgeois elements), an emphasis on the need for unity, and the assertion of the importance of working, as Kevin Morgan puts it, 'with the grain of mass culture' in Communists' own countries.[37] Dimitrov, who commanded enormous personal esteem as a result of his courageous conduct on trial for the burning of the Reichstag, advanced an analysis of fascism as '*the open terrorist dictatorship of the most reactionary, most chauvinistic and most imperialist elements of finance capital*.'[38] This line of argument represented a shift from earlier analyses of fascism as the final phase of capitalist decay which could only end in proletarian revolution, a stance which implied that any effort to organise resistance was pointless and, indeed, unnecessary.[39] It also resisted a stronger equation of fascism with capitalism. Bertolt Brecht was a vocal dissenter from this equivocation, arguing in 1935 that those who opposed fascism without opposing capitalism were 'like people who wish to eat their veal without slaughtering the calf'.[40] It was this 'practical truth' of the identity of capitalism and fascism that underpinned Brecht's rejection of the Popular Front and the aesthetic controversy over realism and modernism between Brecht and Lukács.[41] Isolating fascism as a sectional attack on the masses, Dimitrov argued for broad, non-sectarian alliances. Ideological

---

34   Fisher 1988, pp. 158–9.

35   Fisher 1988, p. 160.

36   Croft 1990, p. 40.

37   Morgan 1995, p. 142.

38   Dimitrov 1935c, p. 10; emphasis in original.

39   Morgan 1989, p. 20.

40   Brecht 1966, p. 137.

41   The key texts in this exchange are Lukács 2007 and Brecht 2007.

struggle against fascism was brought to the fore; what fascism threatened, he argued, were national cultures and histories in their entirety:

> The fascists are rummaging through the entire *history* of every nation so as to be able to pose as the heirs and continuators of all that was exalted and heroic in its past, while all that was degrading or offensive to the national sentiments of the people they make use of as weapons against the enemies of fascism.[42]

The battle against fascism was a battle fought on the ground of popular and national history, a battle to defend from 'the fascist falsifiers', 'all that is valuable in the historical past of the nation'.[43] While maintaining that Communists were implacably opposed to 'bourgeois nationalism', Dimitrov nonetheless warned against '*national nihilism*': 'proletarian internationalism must, so to speak, "acclimatize itself" in each country in order to strike deep roots in its native land'.[44] This detachment of the idea of the nation from the stigma of nationalism was bound up with Joseph Stalin's turn to 'socialism in one country', which deferred the possibility of world revolution and the dissolution of 'bourgeois' nation states; likewise, the recasting of fascism as an extreme and anomalous strain of capitalism underwrote Soviet foreign policy by enabling the matter of defending the Soviet Union against fascism to be treated as a separate issue from the question of how to end capitalism worldwide.[45]

But despite its strategic service of Stalinist aims, the consequences of the speech were far-reaching in the Western democracies. As Kevin Morgan describes, such an acclimatisation of struggle meant an abandonment of 'abstract, utopian sloganising' and, as Dimitrov put it, accepting that the masses 'must be taken as they are, and not as we should like to have them'.[46] This approach encouraged Communists to cooperate with and work pragmatically within existing organisations and institutions. Shortly after the Seventh Congress, the British Communist novelist, critic and translator Ralph Fox wrote in the *Daily Worker* of the 'vast new prospects' for intellectuals promised by Dimitrov's address and the Popular Front strategy in an article pitched to simultaneously appeal to intellectuals and argue for a less dogmatic attitude towards

---

42   Dimitrov 1935c, p. 69.
43   Dimitrov 1935c, p. 70.
44   Dimitrov 1935c, pp. 70–1; emphasis in original.
45   Morgan 1989, p. 6.
46   Morgan 1989, p. 33; Dimitrov 1935c, p. 21.

them: it is 'silly', Fox felt, to criticise the 'honest intellectual' who tries and fails to fully understand Marxism.[47] While this is the first clear statement in the *Daily Worker* of the cultural implications of the Popular Front turn, it in fact reflected developments that were already happening on the left beyond the purview of the Party. Dimitrov's speech served to legitimate developments that were happening in Britain and among intellectuals in Europe at large. Six months before the Seventh Congress, the poet and dramatist Montagu Slater wrote in *Left Review*, 'Let our slogan, then, be that we are going to utilize history (and as writers let us include literature) for the purposes of the class which is going to build socialism'.[48] This rallying call to intellectuals prefigures Dimitrov's assertion that Communists should try to 'enlighten the masses on the past of their people' and to 'link up the present struggle with the people's revolutionary traditions and past'.[49] This turn towards the popular and the historical displaced a rhetoric of class and of imminent revolution; instead, the 'outlines of a better future were now to be detected in the patterns of the nation's past'.[50] These prefigurations may explain why Dimitrov's speech seemed to enter the bloodstream of the left almost immediately, and why Dimitrov himself became a crucially inspirational figure.[51] In John Cornford's 1936 poem, 'Full Moon at Tierz: Before the Storming of Huesca', the poem's agonised moment – the war in Spain in which Cornford would shortly lose his life – is constructed explicitly as the extension of Dimitrov's lone heroism:

> But now the Leipzig dragon's teeth
> Sprout strong and handsome against death
> And here an army fights where there was one.[52]

---

47   Fox 1935, p. 4.
48   Slater 1935b, p. 127.
49   Dimitrov 1935c, p. 70.
50   Callaghan and Harker 2011, p. 127.
51   Dimitrov himself offered his experiences at Leipzig as an 'invaluable stock-in-trade of revolutionary practice and thought': Dimitrov 1935a, p. 344. Ralph Fox described Dimitrov's story as 'an epic of our time which demands that the artists should give it life': Fox 1979, p. 121. Jack Lindsay's 1937 essay 'The Historical Novel' and Georg Lukács's influential work of the same title both quote the report in making comparable cases for the vital role of historical writing in the anti-fascist struggle: Lindsay 1937d, p. 16; Lukács 1976, p. 325.
52   Cornford 1964, pp. 137–9. For a reading of the tensions in the poem's attitude to 'what the Seventh Congress said', see S. Smith 2008, pp. 357–73.

Essential to the strategy advocated by the Comintern was the building of a mass movement that extended beyond the Communist Parties, which remained small in Europe (the membership of the British Communist Party never exceeded 20,000 members in the 1930s; at its wartime peak it had around 55,000).[53] The sudden Communist enthusiasm for working with groups so recently denounced in the strongest terms has led to the Popular Front being variously stigmatised as the dereliction of commitment to world revolution,[54] an 'unholy alliance between the robbers and the robbed',[55] a reconciliation with the forces of liberalism,[56] and as a counterproductive distraction from the real political needs of the moment.[57] Jim Fyrth, by contrast, argues that the years between 1934 and 1939 were 'the most fruitful period in the history of the British left and of the Communist Party in particular'.[58] Fyrth insists that a genuine mass (though always minority) social movement did arise and that it extended beyond the Communist Party: the women's movement, student radicalism, anti-imperialism as well as traditional labour movement priorities (workers' and tenants' rights, for example) were all resurgent in the mid- and late thirties; by 1938 some two million people were reading newspapers that supported the Popular Front, while the Left Book Club, formed in 1936, grew to number 57,000 members.[59] The institutional bases of the Popular Front continued to grow even as the international situation deteriorated, suggesting that the need for mass, allied action became more compelling as war approached, rather than ebbing away with the initial wave of optimism in 1936.[60]

Culture, Crisis and Democracy

In Britain, the strategy of the Popular Front was, as Andy Croft writes, 'crucially defined by cultural considerations – nationality, tradition, democracy, intellectual liberty and the arts'.[61] Democracy and constitutionalism were absorbed

---

53   The most detailed membership statistics available are given in Thorpe 2000.
54   By Leon Trotsky, most obviously, in *The Transitional* Programme (1938); see particularly section 2, 'The Proletariat and Its Leadership'.
55   Orwell 1970, p. 305.
56   Mulhern 2000, p. 46.
57   Pimlott 1977, pp. 162–3.
58   Fyrth 1985, p. 15.
59   Fyrth 1985, pp. 15–16, p. 23.
60   Fyrth 1985, p. 16.
61   Croft 1995, p. 92.

into Communist rhetoric, recast not as the apparatus of bourgeois power but as the materialisations of hard-won democratic liberties that had to be defended in the immediate term for any future advance to socialism to be possible. Leftist intellectuals advocating for a Popular Front rhetorically positioned themselves in relation to a crisis of democratic culture; in the early issues of *Left Review*, discussions supporting the establishment of the British Section of the Writers' International are premised on what the section's founding statement called a 'crisis in ideas'.[62] The critic Douglas Garman (who, like the poet and critic Edgell Rickword, moved in the course of a decade from the *Calendar of Modern Letters* to *Left Review* and the Communist Party) offered a contribution clearly positioning the Writers' International in a role of ideological leadership: 'the chief value of the Writers' International', he wrote, 'lies in its ability to make clearer the nature of the forces that are disintegrating contemporary society, and by doing so to show that the future of civilization depends on the achievement of Communism'.[63] The actual institutional role of the Writers' International was rather limited, and was eclipsed by PEN, so that the organised ideological leadership Garman seems to envision was not realised. But the idea of crisis and the possibility of a resurgent, wide-ranging intellectual response to it are clearly felt in the important 1937 essay collection *The Mind in Chains*, edited by C. Day Lewis. In his introduction, Day Lewis figures the crisis in an image appropriated from Shelley's preface to *Prometheus Unbound*: 'The cloud of mind is discharging its collected lightning, and the equilibrium between institutions and opinions is now restoring or is about to be restored'.[64] This revolutionary image of lightning, the moment in which separated powers that should by nature be in accord are unified, reverberates through the revolutionary and universalising gestures that feature in the novels discussed in this book. The sentiment is echoed, Day Lewis finds, in Rex Warner's statement that capitalism 'has no further use for culture'. However based on Warner's own premises it would be more appropriate to reverse his formulation: it is culture that has no further use for capitalism, which 'can no longer invite the support of the general ideals of culture and progress'.[65] The essays in *The Mind in Chains*, variable in quality, as Raymond Williams notes, are nonetheless unified by shared senses of estrangement – of the scientist from society at large, in J.D. Bernal's contribution, or the English people from

---

62   Writers' International, British Section 1934, p. 38.
63   Garman 1934a, p. 180.
64   Day Lewis 1937, p. 11.
65   R. Warner 1937, p. 24.

their 'real history', in Edgell Rickword's – that rely to a certain extent on theoretical improvisation; as Francis Mulhern points out, the advent of Marxism in Britain was 'remarkably belated'.[66] Rickword's contribution is illuminating in this regard. Rickword, who joined the Communist Party in 1934 and edited *Left Review* in 1936 and 1937, describes an alienated society, symptomatised by the relativism of High Modernism, pessimism, mysticism, the abandonment of 'absolute truth', and characterised by a failure of totalisation: 'the reason cannot classify the whole of experience'; the best minds fall victim to sophistry because 'they live in an atmosphere where the basic reasons of existence, food and shelter and love, are no longer realised in their origin as solely the emanation of human labour'.[67] There is a sense here, albeit intuitive, of the conceptual link between reification – 'the destruction of every image of the whole'[68] – and the totality, a position Rickword reaches through a kind of improvisation. Lacking the conceptual framework of Marx's *1844 Manuscripts*, or, for that matter, Lukács's elaboration of reification in *History and Class Consciousness*, Rickword arrives, as part of his programmatic call for alliance, at a Marxist humanist position: capitalism universally dehumanises and thus its overthrow is humanism's vocation.[69]

This socialist humanism – the term would be revived as a rallying cry for British Marxist dissidents after 1956[70] – wrought out of the anti-fascist struggle, is an important corollary to the crisis in humanism that Jed Esty argues emerged at the point when the onset of imperial decline meant that the English experience could no longer be taken as the normative or universal human experience; at this point, metropolitan modernists performed an 'anthropological turn' as they confronted English particularism.[71] The apparent concurrence of these two developments – the Popular Front national turn and the late modernist

---

66   R. Williams 1987, p. 270; Mulhern 1974, p. 39.

67   Rickword 1937a, p. 250. For Rickword's editorship of *Left Review*, see Hobday 1989, pp. 155–7.

68   Lukács 1975, p. 103.

69   The *1844 Manuscripts* were not published in German until 1932; the first English translation was made in the late 1950s (Connor 2014, pp. 343–4). I have found no evidence that the central writers of this study were familiar with these manuscripts in the 1930s, although Jack Lindsay read them in the 1940s (Lindsay 1976, p. 433). Lukács's *History and Class Consciousness* was supressed by Stalin for its supposed voluntarism and idealism. For the circumstances of this see Rees 2000, pp. 17–24.

70   See E.P. Thompson 1978, pp. 129–32.

71   Esty 2004, pp. 5–6. See also the discussion of Jack Lindsay as a 'premature' socialist humanist in Connor 2014.

'Anglocentric revival' identified by Esty – is striking.[72] The anthropological turn performed by writers on the left is not separate from, but nor is it equivalent to that performed by canonical modernists in their 'late' phases. As Ben Harker has shown, the idea of the Popular Front provides one way of reading the politics of late modernist works such as Virginia Woolf's *Between the Acts* (1941), with its anxious appropriations of popular cultural forms.[73] The anthropology of home, as Mass Observation had it, entailed, Esty argues, an inversion of a High Modernist epistemology that ascribed intelligibility to marginal cultures while mystifying knowledge of the centre, displacing it with a newly representable vision of a 'shrinking' England.[74] Mass Observation, for example, appears to be a sociological and epistemological enterprise endeavouring to investigate the 'British Islanders' so as 'to get written down the unwritten laws and to make the invisible forces visible'.[75] If Esty's readings of the thirties are curiously silent on the role of fascism in forcing the confrontation with national particularism, and also over the significance of the Soviet Union as offering – at that moment – one kind of universalism, they might nonetheless illuminate the tremendous appeal of the socialised humanism inscribed, however hollowly, in such documents as the speeches of the first Soviet Writers' Congress.[76] But we also find important counterpoints that suggest these currents of thought were not continuous. The Marxist critic Alick West provides one such counterpoint. West argues for the perspective of humanism against the claim he finds in Oswald Spengler and T.S. Eliot that 'cultures are mutually incomprehensible to each other'.[77] It is the world market, West thinks, that makes such a proposition invalid: to make 'west Europe into a distinct social entity' is simply 'to preserve capitalism from the consequences of its own action in creating a world market', erecting 'cultural barriers against socialised humanism'.[78] Yet this internationalist vision of mutual cultural intelligibility is tempered, as so often in Popular Front texts, with an assertion of the essentiality of the nation as the locality in which capitalism's culturally destructive energies might be confronted. In his reading of Joyce's *Ulysses*, West argues that Stephen is unable to repair the damage wrought by imperialism by his failure – Joyce's failure, West

---

72   Esty 2004, p. 12.

73   Harker 2011b, pp. 16–34.

74   Esty 2004, p. 7.

75   Mass Observation 1938, p. 8.

76   Published by Martin Lawrence as *Problems in Soviet Literature* (1935) and discussed in Chapter One below.

77   West 1974, p. 103.

78   Ibid.

assumes – to move beyond a purely negative rejection of Church and State.[79] The logic of the critique emanates from a nationally mediated cultural internationalism, with no aim in sight of the dissolution of the nation state.

Popular Front cultural practices were guided by a classically populist belief in the existence of a latent popular consensus that was repressed by authorised channels of representation, be they linguistic, aesthetic or political. While Christopher Caudwell's *Illusion and Reality*, often considered the major work of criticism produced by a British Communist at this time, resounds with loathing for commercialised mass culture, 'a mass-produced "low-brow" art, whose flatness and shallowness serve to adapt [the working class] to their unfreedom,'[80] Popular Front intellectuals – including Caudwell, who himself wrote thrillers – engaged widely with popular cultural forms not obviously amenable to a radicalised politics.[81] The most striking example is the appropriation of the pageant form by Communists. Mick Wallis's ground-breaking work on these pageants offers exemplary analyses of the rhetorical strategies of the Popular Front, the process of constructing and deconstructing relationships between viewers and participants. Wallis illuminates the complex ways Popular Front cultural productions envision the nation and the people as ideas rooted in something essentially common and pointing to something essentially universal. Such works mediate nationalist and internationalist concerns through the 'folk' and the 'people'. These mediations generated 'a sense of an international, universal folk: the roots of a common democracy'.[82] A deeply felt national sensibility resounds in many texts produced on the left, but so too does a concern with the universally human; indeed, Wallis detects in the pageants a discourse of humanism consonant with the Marx of the *1844 Manuscripts* that had yet to be discovered in Britain.[83] The pageants are an illuminating example of Com-

---

79   West 1974, pp. 107–8.

80   Caudwell's status as a major figure is suggested by R. Williams 1987, pp. 277–8; and by Eagleton and Milne 1996, p. 91. Others such as E.P. Thompson have been more cautious, both about the status of Caudwell himself and about whether *Illusion and Reality* is his major work: E.P. Thompson 1977, pp. 228–76. I would suggest that *Illusion and Reality* (Caudwell 1946) is dynamised by a tautly polarised account of class society, which in the final chapter ('The Future of Poetry') is rather laboriously transformed into a more Popular Front-style argument, although the odd rhetorical structure of the chapter is in keeping with formal preoccupations with public speech found in many of the novels discussed here.

81   Caudwell 1946, pp. 107–8.

82   Wallis 1994, p. 137.

83   Wallis 1994, p. 141.

munists working within an existing formal tradition so as to transform it, turning the pageant – with its connotations of empire and English chauvinism – to
the expression of a radical alternative tradition.[84]

The 'real history' of the English people, Rickword suggested, lies in the per-
sistent ideal of popular sovereignty, the repressed truth that 'the foundation
of law lies in the people', as he quotes the Leveller Thomas Rainborough.[85]
In the literature as much as in the social and political initiatives of the late
interwar period, there is often a tension between the idea of organised Communism as represented by the Communist Party and the utopian ideal of some
much looser and more pluralistic, radical democratic politics.[86] The shape
of such a popular, national version of Communism is best discerned in the
work of Edgell Rickword and Jack Lindsay, and especially in their anthology
of radical texts, *The Handbook of Freedom*, which traced an unbroken thread
of resistance in English history from Anglo-Saxon poetry through to opposition to the First World War.[87] Significantly, this text was a formative influence
on E.P. Thompson; in it he found 'the conjunction between an international
socialist theory and a vigorous national historical practice', an emphasis on
'complex cultural actualities' that could underpin 'the struggle for vitality and
for actuality against the *déraciné* uniformity and abstracted internationalist *lin-
gua franca*' of Stalinism.[88] Indeed, the anthology did meet with suspicion from
the Communist Party, which perceived in its eclectic presentation of voices
which were 'passionate but never "correct"', as Thompson puts it, a challenge
to the authority of the Party hardliner Emile Burns's *The Handbook of Marxism*,
and thus to Burns's selections from Marx, Engels, Lenin and Stalin.[89]

For Thompson, then, this exemplary Popular Front text performed a mediation between the national and the international that was not short-circuited
by the Soviet Union. The type of national and popular Communism that began
to be imagined in the Popular Front years was soon stifled by the outbreak of
war, which brought the Party's first priority of loyalty to and defence of the

---

84   Wallis 1995, p. 20.
85   Rickword 1937a, p. 241.
86   For an account of the practicalities of negotiating alliances from the Communist Party's
     point of view, see W. Thompson 1992, chapter 2.
87   Republished in 1941 as *Spokesmen for Liberty*.
88   E.P. Thompson 1979, pp. xxvi–xxviii.
89   E.P. Thompson 1979, p. xxviii. The Party's wary response to the anthology is described
     by Hobday 1989, p. 168. If the national and local emphases of British Popular Front
     productions suggested a covert anti-Stalinism, the principle of turning to local resources
     was, in Europe, effective as an anti-fascist strategy. See Kirk and McElligott 2004, pp. 1–11.

Soviet Union back into view, but nonetheless it is possible – indeed, valuable – to reconstruct the principles of that version of radicalism. The contradictions, however, were never far from the surface; Jack Lindsay threw himself with extraordinary energy and commitment into the historicising and popularising projects of the Popular Front, and yet, as I suggest in Part Two, his trilogy of English historical novels charting the rise of capitalism continually – perhaps unintentionally – brings into question the identification of a 'progressive' bourgeoisie. The cultural energy unleashed sometimes over-ran the pragmatic political premises that supposedly underpinned and authorised it. For this reason, I concur with Michael Denning's rejection, in his seminal study of American Popular Front culture, of a 'core-periphery' model of the relationship between the cultural formation of the Popular Front and the Communist Party in so far as such a model misleadingly suggests ideas radiated from a central point within the Party, and furthermore obscures the fact that cultural practitioners even working within the Party were not simply reproducing 'orthodox' thinking on cultural and historical issues.[90]

The Popular Front Novel

This book considers how the British novel came to be not just thematically inflected but also formally shaped by Popular Front politics, and the ways in which it performed an active role in the production of that politics. For all the official Communist talk of taking the masses as they were, of learning to speak the language of the English people, the cultural productions of the left, and especially the novel, recognised that such ideas as 'the masses' and the 'English people' could not be taken as they were, but rather required construction and elaboration if they were to perform the imaginative function of unifying an anti-fascist movement.[91] While, as Ben Harker argues, poetry occupied a special position in the cultural criticism of the Popular Front, 'a particularly striking test-case of cultural alienation', perceived as it was to originate in communal experience from which it had since been severed, I make a case here for the novel, which had less obviously communal sources, as a domain in which we see British Marxist thought developing, experimenting and confronting contra-

---

90   Denning 1997, p. xviii.
91   The 'masses must be taken as they are, and not as we should like to have them'; Dimitrov
      1935c, p. 21. 'The Communist Party is learning to speak to the English workers in a language
      they understand' – Communist Party organiser Ted Bramley in 1936: Bramley 2011, p. 134.

dictions.[92] The realist novel is informed by two dynamics at once: on the one hand, identifying real resistant structures of feeling and modes of opposition generated by the historical experience of 'the people', and on the other, searching for some more definite, politically coherent popular subject. This generates an equivocation between materialism and a more utopian sensibility that can be clearly felt in Sommerfield's 1936 novel *May Day*, which oscillates between the citation of real historical events (particularly the 1926 General Strike) and a sense of a larger, idealised history of which those events may be part.[93] I suggest that Georg Lukács's work – especially his work on realism in the thirties, but also his earlier work on the epic ancestry of the novel in *The Theory of the Novel* (1914/15) and his elaboration of capitalist subjectivity in *History and Class Consciousness* (1922) – provides the most adequate conceptual frame for reading this attempt in the thirties novel. This is not to suggest the direct influence of Lukács on British writers during this period. The (limited) engagements of the writers I focus on with his work are considered in the relevant chapters that follow, but for the most part I am suggesting only that Lukács's terms best clarify the conceptual underpinnings of their novels in ways that these writers themselves could not formulate at the time. By these means we might make sense of their preoccupations with isolation and estrangement, their epic resonances, their investment in questions of nationality and the nation-state, and their multivalent involvement in problems of collective forms and subjects.

All the novels I focus on are concerned, in different ways, with problems of alienation: in Sommerfield, the de-reifying potential of the montage form is explored; in Calder-Marshall, we find an insistent concern with class-generated self-division and disarticulation; in Barke's novels, with dispossession and the alienation of labour; in Jones's, with reification and the alienation of subjectivity under capitalism; in Lindsay's, with the long history of capitalism's severance of the people from the means of production, and of the institutions of the state from popular consensus. More generally, and with a less definite political accent, these novels are all invested in the idea of an ethics of active life, social engagement and responsibility. British novelists on the left were more concerned with capitalism's totalising effects – its universalising process of estrangement and alienation – than with the specifics of class struggle, which

---

92   Harker 2011a, p. 22.

93   The novel recasts the strike as a 'rehearsal', subordinating it to the reality of the imagined mass strike in the text: Sommerfield 2010, p. 204. A comparable tension in the leftist pageant is insightfully tracked by Wallis 1994.

led at points to little more than a rephrased liberalism, but at others towards a humanist, pluralist Marxism.[94] In suggesting the consonance of British writers' approaches to capitalism with Lukács's philosophy and aesthetics, I suggest that the theoretical and philosophical poverty of Marxism in Britain in the thirties has perhaps been overstated. Perry Anderson argues that British Marxism in the thirties,

> was the passing product of a political conjuncture, and developed no serious intellectual dimension to it at the time. Marx's own work, and the development of his theory after his death, remained virtually unstudied.[95]

Anderson explains that Marxists' 'inherited liberalism often subsisted quite unaltered, beneath their new political allegiance'.[96] The novel, with its investment in philosophical categories and its historical association with 'liberalism' as a way of mediating the relationships between individuals and society, might prove a useful testing ground for such a claim.[97] Anderson's larger argument is his well-known assertion that British Marxism lacks a conceptual centre. As to the category of totality, Anderson is emphatic: *'Britain has for more than fifty years lacked any form whatever of such thought'.*[98] To Anderson this is the 'absent centre' in British thought. I am not suggesting that a theory of totality, or of reification or mediation, can be systematically reconstructed out of a handful of leftist novels. However, I do want to suggest that their thinking tended in this direction: circumstances in which they found themselves both created a space for and actively demanded such an elaboration.

To focus on the realist novel – aesthetically complacent at best, authoritarian and monologic at worst – might seem obtuse, given the widespread engagements both with more innovative forms – documentary film, for example – and

---

94   In one of the few monographs dedicated to the British Popular Front, John Coombes situates the British Popular Front primarily in the political developments of Bloomsbury figures such as Leonard Woolf and John Middleton Murry, and in the Stalinist turn of Fabians like Beatrice and Sidney Webb (Coombes 1989). Coombes's central argument is that the Popular Front was essentially liberal in its political coordinates, a challenge I will return to in Chapter Four.

95   P. Anderson 1968, p. 11.

96   Ibid.

97   For a discussion of the relationships between the politics of the liberal state and the canonical realist novel, see P. Lewis 2004, pp. 8–10.

98   P. Anderson 1968, p. 12; emphasis in original.

with more obviously popular forms and genres (science fiction, the thriller).[99] In the genres of speculative fiction and allegory we find diagnoses of fascism and explorations of the national past. Futuristic fictions proliferated to such an extent that the *TLS* complained about the sheer number of books 'forecasting the destruction of the next war'.[100] Speculative fictions – a field in which women writers made a particularly important contribution – including Katharine Burdekin's *Swastika Night* (1937) and Storm Jameson's *In The Second Year* (1937) – envisage a fascist future for England, while Rex Warner's allegorical novels, *The Wild Goose Chase* (1938), *The Professor* (1938) and *The Aerodrome* (1940), influenced by the first English translations of Kafka, explore crises of authority and the roots of authoritarianism. This current of writing has been the subject of ground-breaking scholarship in recent decades.[101] However, in contrast to the monitory and diagnostic functions that these texts perform, the realist novel offers itself as above all a site of historical uncertainty. As against Stephen Spender's claim that Communism entailed a denial of human agency under the sign of a vast, mechanistic vision of history, the novels examined here are presented as sites of profound instability and equivocation: over nationalism and internationalism; the 'people' and the proletariat as the subject of politics; libertarian communism and Soviet orthodoxy; human agency and historical determination.

The first part of *The Popular Front Novel in Britain* takes up what might be the defining literary controversy of the 1930s: the relationships between realism and modernism. While leftist fiction is often considered simply anti-modernist, wedded to an aridly mimetic conception of realist representation, I suggest in Chapter One that writers on the left in fact theorised realism as a remedial strategy to counter the disconnection between the intellectuals and the people within a nexus of influences including British modernism, European antifascism and Soviet literary theory. Chapters Two and Three consider how these influences interplay to produce formally experimental texts deeply concerned with problems of language and representation, focusing on John Sommerfield's *May Day* (1936) and Arthur Calder-Marshall's *Pie in the Sky* (1937) respectively. In both cases, the utopian prospect of Communism is held in tension with anxieties about the nature and power of communication. In spite of their often

---

99   The classic poststructuralist statement of the realist novel's authoritarian dynamics is
      Belsey 1980.

100   Qtd. Croft 1990, p. 7.

101   For studies of leftist genre fiction, see particularly Croft 1990, pp. 220–42, C. Hopkins 2006,
      pp. 138–57, Joannou 1999, Vance 1999 and K. Williams 1999.

divergent political messages, both novels propose a solution to the isolation of the modern subject that inheres in a socialist vision projected through an oscillation between realist representation and modernist expression.

In the second part, English history is to the fore. If, as Neil Redfern argues, Popular Front politics exhibited a 'tendency to treat fascism as a threat to democracy, rather than as a response to the revolutionary strivings of the working class', Popular Front cultural productions seek to mediate this problem by asserting the significance of radical popular struggles for democracy.[102] While Spender argued that Communists were wedded to an essentially religious belief in history's inexorable progress and a mystical belief in 'the workers' as historical agent, the texts examined here are deeply engaged with questions of the role of human agency in historical change.[103] Chapter Four first discusses how British Communists constructed a radical and popular account of English history through key interventions by A.L. Morton, Rickword and Lindsay, while also acknowledging the contradictions and tensions inherent in that project. The chapter pursues these themes through a reading of Jack Lindsay's trilogy of English historical novels, focusing especially on the way Lindsay posits the loss of the common lands as a foundational experience in English history, an experience that is expressed in different forms across time. I pay particular attention to Lindsay's handling of the cataclysm of 1848 (which is also a key moment in the conditioning of the novel form, as per Lukács's account) in his *Men of Forty-Eight*. The chapter argues that the Popular Front historical novel, as represented by the texts chosen, was a space in which to think about moments of possibility when and where legality and legitimacy might converge, promising the overturning of that original injustice, while also reflecting on the cultural form of the novel in history.

In the third part, 'Class, Nation, People', I first consider, in Chapter Five, the 'national' turn in Communist politics, which seemed to be assimilated relatively unproblematically by Rickword and Lindsay, and yet which presented contradictions for novelists who wrote from within class and national communities in subaltern positions. The chapter charts the trajectory of James Barke's writing in the later thirties from the subaltern modernism of *Major Operation* (1936), in which class precedes nation, and the immediacy of crisis predominates over history, towards the popular, socialist realist epic, *The Land of the Leal* (1939). The 'national turn' performed by Barke inheres in the shift in definitions of identity from the civic, class-based identities of *Major Operation*

---

102   Redfern 2005, p. 84.
103   Spender 1948, p. 237.

to the national-popular alignments of *The Land of the Leal*. Finally, Chapter Six discusses the Welsh proletarian novelist Lewis Jones through readings of his *Cwmardy* (1937) and *We Live* (1939), in which a specific national class fraction merges with a concept of 'the people' as progressive force in history, generated by the shared experience of active and creative resistance to the violence of external authority. In both *We Live* and *The Land of the Leal*, the Spanish Civil War plays a key role in mediating the relationship between working-class historical experience and the demands of internationalist anti-fascism.

∴

Readings of leftist literature in terms of its 'failure' turn on questions of the relationship between art and commitment; in a footnote to her anti-fascist polemic, *Three Guineas*, Virginia Woolf warns – via Sophocles – that to 'use art to propagate political opinions' leads only to travesty: 'Literature will suffer the same mutilation that the mule has suffered: and there will be no more horses'.[104] For Woolf, freedom, conceived as opposed to commitment, was essential to cultural resistance to a fascism set on destroying it. In his appraisal of the problem of value in relation to thirties writing, Frank Kermode suggested that it is the attempt to 'unify bourgeois intellect and proletarian culture' that has come to seem 'embarrassing', and best forgotten, as much as its proposed failure.[105] However, in his collection of essays on literary modernism, Fredric Jameson remarks that what is needed if we are to 'de-reify' modernism's canonical texts, is an 'aesthetics of failure' that might undo the alienating power that emanates from the 'success' of institutionalised modernist works.[106] In one sense what I propose here is an inversion of Jameson's suggestion in respect of leftist novels: I suggest that the a priori assumptions of 'failure' that dominate the literary memory of the thirties alienate us from experiments made in literary form, in cultural theory and in the political imagination no less than the entrenched terms of success do for modernist works.

In the criticism of the Cold War period, the most pressing questions were of orthodoxy and dissidence, and the most pressing of all were those addressed to writers' positions in relation to the ideological lodestar of Stalinism. Here, I position these authors in relation to a Communism that was still felt to be dynamic and mutable, rather than in relation to the ideological polarities of

---

104   Woolf 2006, p. 202.
105   Kermode 1988, p. 96.
106   F. Jameson 2007b, p. 3.

the Cold War era. Such a way of seeing helps read the thirties not as a historical anomaly, a 'dark valley' or 'devil's decade', but rather as part of a longer process of cultural transformation that raises unresolved contradictions between the national and the international, as well as between the working class as subject of history and a broader conception of the people as political agent.[107] As Nick Hubble has argued, the narrative of the 'short' twentieth century, 1914–89, as posited by Eric Hobsbawm, presents problems for those of us wishing to suggest that the cultural formations of the interwar years express real possibilities for social transformation that are not sealed in a now-ended epoch of a global war between liberal democracy and Communism.[108] If 'the people', as Raymond Williams points out, turned out to be a much more ambiguous and politically malleable category than the thirties left supposed, and even if, as Fredric Jameson suggests, the optimism of the Popular Front was ultimately misled by the mirage of a progressive bourgeois culture, we may nonetheless discover that cultural productions of the anti-fascist campaigns address themselves to problems that continue to articulate themselves in the era of globalisation.[109] Contradictions between an internationalist orientation and a politics rooted in the realities of class and community remain unresolved, though no less urgent. This study examines literary attempts to face these contradictions, revealing a seam of writing that has been underexplored, and yet which forms part of what Michael Denning has described as 'the forgotten, repressed history behind the contemporary globalization of the novel'.[110]

---

107   *The Devil's Decade* is the title of an account of the 1930s by Claud Cockburn, a.k.a. Frank
       Pitcairn, *Daily Worker* correspondent (1973).
108   Hubble 2006, p. 17. For the 'short' twentieth century, see Hobsbawm 1995.
109   R. Williams 1989, pp. 108–9; F. Jameson 2007a, p. 203.
110   Denning 2006, p. 725.

PART 1

Realism and Modernism

∴

CHAPTER 1

Anti-Fascist Aesthetics in International Context

The Popular Front turn coincided with the codification of socialist realism in the Soviet Union, and the attendant surge in the repression of writers, artists and intellectuals. This chapter examines the context in which socialist realism was formulated and, in particular, how debates around realism, modernism and formalism were transmitted to writers outside the Soviet Union. It has become something of a critical commonplace that aesthetic orthodoxy mandated a return to realist forms and the rejection of 'bourgeois' modernism; in this vein Valentine Cunningham claims that in Britain socialist realism 'helped to slow down literary experiment and to smash up modernism especially in the novel, thus pushing the novel back beyond Henry James into the arms of nineteenth-century bourgeois naturalism'.[1] Cunningham furthermore claims that the aesthetic orthodoxy imposed on writers took questions of language and representation off the table, committing them to a naïvely referential view of language that maintained that the 'world was antecedent to, and more important than, the word, and words had better not stand too much in the light'.[2] And yet, in so many of the novels that emerged from the left, and particularly those on which this book will focus, problems of language and representation are foregrounded – often assertively and explicitly – rather than repressed in favour of conventionally 'transparent' realism. I wish to suggest here that writers on the left were not committed to the reductive view of realist representation that Cunningham assumes. Rather than taking such formally discursive texts as John Sommerfield's *May Day* or James Barke's *Major Operation*, discussed later in this book, as rebelliously modernist exceptions to the classically realist rule, these texts might best be seen as spaces for politically committed experimentation. Cultural-political questions manifest themselves not as naïve revivals of nineteenth-century realist form, but as anxious and experimental texts in which dilemmas over language, form and articulation are rehearsed without being resolved.

---

1   Cunningham 1988, p. 299.
2   Cunningham 1988, p. 4.

Socialist Realism

The promulgation of socialist realism as an approved aesthetic coincided with the Comintern's shift in 1935 to the Popular Front strategy against fascism and the threat it posed to the Soviet Union, and coincided more generally, therefore, with the world Communist movement's process of adjustment to the failures of revolutions in Europe and the subsequent splitting of its energies into the defence of the Soviet Union, on the one hand, and the halting of fascism's advances in Europe on the other. In the Soviet Union, cultural organisation and policy was overhauled from the early 1930s as part of the entrenchment and centralisation of power; explicitly revolutionary and avant-gardist cultural groups such as the Russian Association of Proletarian Writers (RAPP) were dissolved and replaced with broader, Party-oriented organisations.[3] A 1932 decree recommended the '[i]ntegration of all writers who support the platform of the Soviet government and who aspire to participate in Socialist construction in a single union of Soviet writers with a Communist faction therein'.[4] This reconfigured cultural policy and the conception of 'socialist realism' that was elaborated in the Soviet literary press must of course be understood as bound up with the consolidation of Stalin's power through the liquidation of the left- and right-wing oppositions, and its calls for a wide alliance of artists recognised as part of a strategy of neutralising the power of factional groups. A crucial vector for the theorisation of socialist realism and its transmission to intellectuals beyond the Soviet Union was *International Literature*, the journal of the International Union of Revolutionary Writers, a Soviet body established to coordinate revolutionary literary work beyond the Soviet Union, and which was published in Russian, English, French, German and Spanish editions from 1932 to 1945.[5] The purpose of the journal was two-fold: in the first instance it published translations of Soviet literature and literary criticism, and in the second it published translated material from European Communist journals including *Die Linkskurve* and *Das Wort* as well as contributions by non-Soviet Communists. This remit encompassed the work of major European intellectuals including Georg Lukács and Louis Aragon, American contributors such as Jack Conroy and Granville Hicks, and British contributors including John Strachey, Jack Lindsay and Sylvia Townsend Warner. It can be considered the key resource for British writers wishing to engage with Russian and European

---

3   Clark, Dobrenko et al. 2007, pp. 141–2.
4   Central Committee of the All-Union Communist Party 2002, p. 400.
5   Lodder 2013, p. 1316.

literary theory during this period. Although Philip Bounds has assumed that the journal was little read among British Marxists, in fact British writers not only read but contributed to it.[6] It was also regularly advertised, reviewed and praised in the *Daily Worker*.[7]

The journal provided a means for transmitting previously unpublished texts by Marx and Engels that were being discovered by the Marx-Engels-Lenin Institute in Moscow. From 1932 to 1934, there was a concerted effort to discourage the direct application of Marxist theory to literary works, either creatively or critically; this is the expressed intention of the publication in 1934 of Engels's correspondence with Paul Ernst, in which Engels argues that 'the materialist method is turned into its opposite when used not as a guide-line in historical investigation, but as a ready template in which historical facts are stretched and recut'.[8] The first publication of Engels's letter to Margaret Harkness in 1933 – widely quoted by British writers in the years that followed – serves a similar function by suggesting that a classically realist approach was preferable to a directly tendentious one.[9] In the journal's first years, however, some contributors seemed willing to work against a reductive equation of realism with traditional technique, and to acknowledge the transformative potential of formal experiment. In 1933 a critical symposium on John Dos Passos, whose work challenged simplistic distinctions between a politically muscular realism and an apolitical or reactionary modernism, was held and the proceedings published in the journal. While some contributors argued that Dos Passos's ideological commitments excused his experimental departures from realist convention, as when A. Leites compared him favourably to the 'really insubstantial' James Joyce, other contributors sought to question the self-defeating logic of anti-formalism itself.[10] The dramatist Vsevolod Vishnevsky, for instance, warned that, 'We shouldn't just spit at form. There is no art without form'.[11]

---

6   Bounds 2012, p. 268 fn. 54. The most striking example of British writers' interventions in the journal is the discussion of Walter Scott between Lukács and the British Communists Sylvia Townsend Warner and T.A. Jackson in 1939; this exchange is discussed in Chapter Five, below.

7   For example, Morton 1934.

8   Engels 1934, p. 81.

9   Engels 1933, p. 113. Notable citations of the letter include Fox 1979, pp. 118–19 and Strachey 1935, suggesting that it was widely circulated on the European left at the time of publication.

10   Leites 1933, p. 105.

11   Vishnevsky 1933, p. 106.

Opportunities for the discussion and analysis of form would, however, rapidly diminish. The Soviet Writers' Congress of 1934, a major event that was extensively discussed on the British left, sought to oppose socialist realism to modernism and formalism. Maxim Gorky lauded nineteenth-century realist writers, 'those great writers who created critical realism and revolutionary romanticism', as the forebears of socialist realism.[12] The 'socialist' aspect of 'socialist realism', suggested the Party functionary Andrei Zhdanov, meant its orientation towards the future, towards the fully realised socialist society.[13] Thus socialist realism is a kind of augmentation of reality, rather than a naturalistic reflection of it. A well-known passage by Gorky puts it this way:

> Myth is invention. To invent means to extract from the sum of a given reality its cardinal idea and embody it in imagery – that is how we got realism. But if to the idea extracted from the given reality we add – completing the idea, by the logic of hypothesis – the desired, the possible, and thus supplement the image, we obtain that romanticism which is at the basis of myth and is highly beneficial in that it tends to provoke a revolutionary attitude to reality, an attitude that changes the world in a positive way.[14]

Realism was not the world as it immediately appeared; realism was the world seen in relation to what it was becoming. If this suggested a vague but essentially romantic approach that had few obvious formal implications, elsewhere at the Writers' Congress, a militant anti-Western cultural politics was finding its voice. Karl Radek spelled out a stark choice for writers, 'James Joyce or Socialist Realism?', with Joyce taken to exemplify the decadence of a retrograde capitalist culture from which neither truth nor innovation could issue:

> The literature of dying capitalism has become stunted in ideas. It is unable to portray those mighty forces which are shaking the world – the death agonies of the old, the birth pangs of the new. And this triviality of content is fully matched by the triviality of form displayed by bourgeois world literature. All the styles which were evolved by past bourgeois art, and in which great masterpieces were created – realism, naturalism,

---

12   Gorky 1935, p. 41.
13   Zhdanov 1935, p. 20.
14   Gorky 1935, p. 44. Raymond Williams considered this passage a definition of socialist realism: R. Williams 1987, p. 279.

romanticism – all this has suffered attrition and disintegration; all this exists only in fragments, and is powerless to produce a single convincing picture.[15]

Ulysses to Radek was little more than the symptomatic expression of a total collapse in critical selectivity and a monstrously distorted sense of perspective: 'A heap of dung, crawling with worms, photographed by a cinema apparatus through a microscope – such is Joyce's work'.[16] The socialist realist, meanwhile, does not simply transcribe:

> We do not photograph life. In the totality of phenomena we seek out the main phenomenon. Giving everything without discrimination is not realism. That would be the most vulgar kind of naturalism. We should select phenomena. Realism means that we make a selection from the point of view of what is essential, from the point of view of guiding principles.[17]

Although in Nikolai Bukharin's contribution there is an effort to resist the simple anathematisation of the concept of form by arguing that the analysis and technical development of poetic form is necessary to any literary advance, it was Radek's splenetic attack on Joyce that prefigured what was to come.[18] By 1935, in the wake of the Zinoviev trial, *International Literature* was warning that all writers should consider themselves under the obligations of the Party, as announced by the publication of a menacing editorial entitled 'No Mercy to Terrorists and Traitors: A Statement to All Writers' calling 'all foremost writers of the world, all the best minds of progressive humanity' to 'revolutionary vigilance with respect to the false friends of the socialist revolution who are in reality its fiercest enemies'.[19] Beginning in the summer of 1936, shortly before the first show trials at which Zinoviev, Kamenev and 14 other Old Bolsheviks were sentenced to death, *International Literature* ran an extensive feature on formalism, targeted especially at European modernists. In an attack on James Joyce, the novelist Yuri Olesha wrote that,

---

15   Radek 1935, p. 151.

16   Radek 1935, p. 153.

17   Radek 1935, p. 181.

18   Bukharin 1935, pp. 199–208.

19   Dinamov 1935, p. 89. A number of the journal's editorial staff and contributors themselves became victims of the purges. See Lodder 2013, p. 1316.

In order to understand what is formalism and what is naturalism, and why they are hostile to us, I will give an example from Joyce. He has written, 'Cheese is the corpse of milk.' You see, comrades, how terrible that is. The writer of the West has seen death in milk. [It is] absolutely true. But we do not want that kind of truth.[20]

'Formalism' came to be used as a generalised term of abuse and denunciation during the many persecutions of writers on the grounds of 'literary deviation', and the term lost any critical meaning as the purges intensified.[21] The same issue of *International Literature* featured in translation the infamous *Pravda* denunciation of Dmitri Shostakovich, 'Chaos Instead of Music', which attacked the lack of 'popularity' of Shostakovich's opera *Lady Macbeth of the Mtsensk District*, condemning its experimental techniques as signs of degeneracy, 'a silly game that may end very badly'.[22]

This ossification of socialist realism into simple demands for conformity to a frequently changing political line, however, was not straightforwardly translated beyond the Soviet context. For the endorsement of realism to be compelling for writers beyond the cultural regime of the Soviet Union, it was necessary for realism to be elaborated as something other than a historical phase, the dominant mode of the bourgeois novel in its golden age. The defence of realism as a politically progressive, aesthetically challenging and urgently contemporary form for European literature was undertaken most prominently by Georg Lukács, whose essays of the 1930s sought to elucidate what he called 'the intimate, varied and complex bonds which link the Popular Front, popular literature and authentic realism'.[23] As the tone of *International Literature* became increasingly repressive, Lukács's essays on realism appeared in the journal, often in some tension with the direction of travel of Soviet policy. In 'Narration vs. Description', especially, Lukács's scant regard for Soviet writers significantly refuses the notion that socialist realism has already been accomplished.[24] The important essay 'The Intellectual Physiognomy of Literary Char-

---

20   Olesha 1936, pp. 92–3.

21   The extent of the violence against writers, composers, playwrights and artists during the anti-formalist campaign of 1935–7 is detailed in Clark et al. 2007, pp. 229–48.

22   *International Literature* 1936, p. 78. In a sign of how British Communists were out of step with these developments, Lady Macbeth was praised in *Left Review* (Findlay Henderson 1936); and also in a more muted and somewhat perplexed way, in the *Daily Worker* (Short 1936).

23   Lukács 2007, p. 58.

24   Lukács 1937, pp. 96–7. This section was omitted from Arthur Kahn's translation in *Writer*

acters', published in both *Das Wort* and *International Literature* shortly after the first Moscow trial, appears to diminish the relevance of the writer's ideological position by deflecting attention almost entirely onto the mechanics of characterisation as a measure of the text's commitment to the extensive totality of social relations. This position could, of course, be traced back to Engels, but it was rapidly being overtaken by the momentum of events. Where key contributions to the Soviet Writers' Congress (such as Gorky's) took the 'socialist' aspect of socialist realism to denote the infusion of the representation of the present with a belief in the imminent socialist future, Lukács takes the power of realism to reside in its representation of the potentialities in characters and situations in order 'to reveal the forces and tendencies whose effectiveness is blurred in everyday life at work in the bright light of the highest and purest interaction of contradictions'.[25] Lukács proclaimed the ongoing existence and vitality of a 'culture' of realism, 'based upon a concrete sensibility for what is great in life, for the portrayal of human greatness as a reality'; and this proclamation was deeply rooted in European intellectual culture.[26] This Eurocentric position – that located Marx and Hegel in a tradition with Goethe and Schiller – would be echoed in the British debates.

The political implications of this account of realism were made explicit in the debates over realism and Expressionism that took place between Lukács and Ernst Bloch in the German exile journal *Das Wort* in 1937 and 1938. (Bertolt Brecht's response, 'Against Georg Lukács', was not published at the time.) In 'Realism in the Balance', Lukács advanced the important argument that realism had not been eclipsed by modernism at all, and thus the embattled coexistence of progressive and reactionary tendencies marked culture as a field of struggle, of competing traditions.[27] Modernist writing was produced, Lukács thought, by a failure in the work of mediation exemplified by realism: naturalism on the one hand merely transcribes the objective surface of things; formalism on the other expresses a dislocated and isolated subjectivity.[28] Modernist writers developed idiosyncratic styles as 'a spontaneous expression of their immediate experience', with the result that their texts are one-dimensional as that immediate experience is not related to any larger whole. Although denouncing modernism in this way, Lukács's critique was predicated on the assumption

---

and Critic, somewhat surprisingly given Lukács's defensive preface (Lukács 1970, p. 7), in which he seeks to position the essays against the dominant tendency of the time.

25 Lukács 1936b, p. 61.
26 Lukács 1936b, p. 82.
27 Lukács 2007, p. 29.
28 Lukács 2007, p. 37.

that European bourgeois culture still sustained progressive elements within it, and he thereby departed from Radek's polemical declaration of the total degeneration of that culture. Lukács' defence of the mediating power of realism joins with his endorsement of the strategy of unifying progressive forces in a Popular Front, as the realist novel performs a key role in identifying and elaborating those progressive forces, revealing the truth underlying the appearance of fragmentation, that is, the ever-closer enmeshing of capitalism and social life. A reactivation of the revolutionary potential of realism as 'the living form of humanism' would prepare the people to 'endorse the political slogans of the Popular Front and to comprehend its political humanism'.[29] But this claim depended on the essential popularity of realism, as Lukács saw it; impossible to produce in intellectual isolation, realism emerges from and speaks to the life of 'the people'.[30] By contrast, 'the broad mass of people can learn nothing from avant-garde literature', finding themselves unable to 'translate these atmospheric echoes of reality back into the language of their own experience'.[31] For Lukács, there appeared to be some deep connection between the historical experiences of 'the people', with its ambivalent class and ethnic-nationalist connotations, and the form of the classic realist novel. Brecht, in his rebuttal, attacked the notion that only realism in the nineteenth-century mode could represent popular life; what mattered, Brecht contended, was not the form itself but its relationship with reality: whether interior monologue is to be considered formalist, as Lukács thought it should, is a question of whether in a given instance it is used skilfully to represent truth.[32] Lukács's conception of popularity, which assumed that diversity of popular life and experience was merely a surface phenomenon, was for Brecht a formalism, a privileging of the classic realist form for its own sake that left writers frustratingly 'forbidden to employ skills newly acquired by contemporary man'.[33] Such a prohibition militated against Lukács's desire for a popular literature by fostering a complacent relationship between writers and popular readerships, when, in fact, the 'intelligibility of a literary work is not guaranteed merely if it is written exactly like other works which were understood in their time'.[34] The popular for Brecht furthermore depended on the artist's *conception* of the people; where Lukács

---

29   Lukács 2007, p. 56.

30   Lukács 2007, pp. 54–5.

31   Lukács 2007, p. 57.

32   Brecht 2007, p. 85.

33   Brecht 2007, p. 75.

34   Lukács 2007, p. 85.

tends to treat the 'people' as an empirical social entity, existing prior to the forms of art that might address them, for Brecht the people could be conceived of in various politically significant ways. As to his own, he wrote, 'We have in mind a fighting people and therefore an aggressive concept of what is *popular*'.[35] Realism had to be combative and not merely progressive if it was to serve.

There is a political disagreement at root here. Brecht was deeply opposed to the principle of a progressive alliance; fascism could be tackled in *class* terms only. He considered the Popular Front to be an essentially defensive strategy that offered little prospect of anything except the defence of bourgeois culture and the class relations that sustained it. In their competing contributions to the Expressionism debate, Brecht and Lukács register opposing conceptions of the nature of the 'people' that may be considered a central fault-line in anti-fascist cultural politics. For Lukács, the 'people' appeared to be given in advance, a latent, broadly progressive formation menaced by the fascism of an ultra-reactionary minority, which had only to be politically activated through the address of a revitalised literary realism. For Brecht, the 'people' was a provisional construct that might be addressed in a range of media, genres and forms whose efficacy must be related 'not to the good old days but to the bad new ones'.[36] Fascism had to be tackled as a class offensive by a class offensive, through a militant, contemporary cultural idiom. Intellectual mobilisation in the cause of anti-fascism would be continually vexed by the contradiction between these positions.

The congresses of the International Association of Writers in Defence of Culture held in Paris 1935 and in Spain in 1937 are a useful index of what the Eurocentric anti-fascist cultural movement looked like, and also of the tensions that always underlay it. The first of these took place before the Seventh Congress; as noted in the introduction, the Comintern's shift to a Popular Front codified developments that were already taking place. Paris had been the scene of a failed fascist coup followed by days of rioting the previous year. These events provoked one of the earliest attempts by intellectuals to intervene in an organised manner: an appeal for unity was issued, signed by writers including André Malraux and the Surrealists André Breton and Paul Éluard.[37] The Paris congress brought together 200 writers from 15 countries, and featured

---

35   Brecht 2007, p. 81.

36   Brecht 2007, p. 69.

37   Traverso 2004. See also Kershaw 2007, pp. 56–8.

figures as diverse as E.M. Forster, who chaired the British delegation, André Gide and Louis Aragon.[38] Aragon announced his conversion from Surrealism to realism and Communism: 'I proclaim the return to reality in the name of this reality which has arisen over a sixth of globe, in the name of the man who was the first to foresee it'.[39] Brecht, as noted above, rejected the alliances and compromises of the Popular Front and was repelled by the congress's refusal to directly confront capitalism; a few days after attending he wrote to George Grosz, 'We have just rescued culture. It took four days, and then we decided that we would sooner sacrifice all else than let culture perish. If necessary, we'll sacrifice ten to twenty million people'.[40] The second congress, held two years later in Spain in the heat of the Civil War, included Stephen Spender, Sylvia Townsend Warner and Edgell Rickword among the British delegation and was marked by a climate in which anti-fascism and Soviet-oriented Communism were in increasingly obvious contradiction. The manifesto issued by the congress made no mention of the Soviet Union, staking anti-fascism firmly on the defence of European culture;[41] but the event itself was fraught with tensions as the Soviet delegation sought to use the opportunity to attack André Gide and other intellectuals taking a stand against the show trials.[42] The strategy of the Popular Front, originating in the experience of the French workers' struggle against fascism before its endorsement by the Comintern, was increasingly incompatible with the security demands of the Soviet Union. Technical and aesthetic questions ceded to statements of defiance against fascism conceived as menacing the existence of 'culture' in the most general sense: the role of writers, wrote Edgell Rickword in his report on the Spanish congress, was to 'create books to replace those destroyed by Fascism'.[43] While exemplifying an unsectarian stance that valued literary culture for its own sake, such a position always threatened to elide European culture, and especially literary culture and the prestige arts, with human culture as a whole and to endorse an unexplored privileging of 'great' literary works. The term 'culture' will remain a central site of tension throughout this book.

---

38   Heinemann 1988, pp. 115–17.

39   Aragon 1936, p. 101.

40   Brecht 2003, p. 162.

41   International Association of Writers in Defence of Culture 1937, p. 445.

42   Hobday 1989, pp. 189–94.

43   Rickword 1937b, p. 383. Hobday notes that Rickword focused on the congress speeches by those writers opposing the Soviet delegation's attempts to enforce ideological control: Hobday 1989, p. 193.

British Developments

Turning to the British context, discussions over modernism and realism are likewise intertwined with questions of the people and the popular; and while, at some points, these discussions responded directly to the work of Soviet or European critics, more commonly they took place in a refracted, nationally specific form. The Soviet debates were partially transmitted in Britain through the published proceedings of the Writers' Congress and the periodicals *International Literature* and *Left Review*, which published its first issue in October 1934. As Peter Marks has shown, other left-leaning journals showed relatively little interest in these developing debates.[44] The Communist Party's newspaper, the *Daily Worker*, barely covered the Soviet Writers' Congress at all, nor was there any significant development of cultural policy within the Party during this time.[45] As a result, writers and critics wishing to engage with politicised aesthetics did so without a clear guiding line. Although a British delegation – Bob Ellis and Harold Heslop – attended the Second International Conference of Revolutionary and Proletarian Writers in Kharkiv, Ukraine, in 1930, and had pledged to establish a British Section, it took three years to do it.[46] The British Section of the Writers' International was established in 1934, which meant that the establishment of revolutionary cultural organisations lagged behind that of the USA, for example, where the leftist cultural journal *New Masses*, published since 1926, and the John Reed Clubs, established in 1929, provided an institutional framework for the development of a radical literary culture.[47] The *Daily Worker* acknowledged the problem in 1934, commenting that, 'The revolutionary movement in Britain has always been weak on the literary side: compared with Germany or America, British revolutionary – let alone proletarian – literature can hardly be said to have existed at all'.[48] *Left Review* was met with suspicion and at times hostility in the *Daily Worker*, which commented in 1935 that, 'We have nothing to say against people publishing experimental exercise

---

44 Marks 1997, pp. 23–4.

45 However, the American *Daily Worker*, organ of the American Communist Party (CPUSA), did cover the conference in some depth; see for example V. Smith 1934, p. 5. The CPUSA and its press were markedly more engaged with cultural issues than their British equivalents. For the development of cultural policy, see Croft 1995, pp. 86–7.

46 *Literature of the World Revolution* 1931. The journal was retitled *International Literature* later in the year, reflecting the changes in literary organisation referred to above.

47 *New Masses* is archived online at http://www.unz.org/Pub/NewMasses (accessed 01/08/ 2016).

48 *Daily Worker* 1934.

books if they wish, but to apply the term "Left" is to indicate position, direction and purpose. These the latest issue of the "Review" hardly exhibits.'[49] In March 1935, after the Writers' Congress had announced an integral role for literature in political struggle, the paper offered the apparently rather grudging note that '[novels] are an excellent means of introducing propaganda. In discussions round the dinner-hour a tale of working-class life, tactfully sold or lent, can start the flame'.[50]

The 'weakness' of British literature in this regard, the absence of institutions that fostered engagement between writers and progressive politics, influenced from the outset the shape of Popular Front literary culture, which relied on a rhetoric of integration and popularity legitimated by a largely mythical image of past cultural harmony and frequently manifested in anti-formalism and anti-modernism. The founding statement of the British Section of the Writers' International, published in the first issue of *Left Review* in October 1934, establishes a number of themes that would shape these discussions of literary form, popularity and mediation. The statement began by declaring that, 'There is a crisis of ideas in the capitalist world to-day not less considerable than the crisis in economics'.[51] That crisis was no less than 'the collapse of a culture, accompanying the collapse of an economic system', and was symptomatised by the 'decadence of the past twenty years of English literature'.[52] Foreshadowing Lukács's later argument in 'Realism in the Balance', the statement furthermore specified the 'decadence' of recent literature in terms of a sharp distinction between form and content: 'Journalism, literature, the theatre, are developing in technique while they are narrowing in content'; the experiments in relativity and perspectivism characterising literature since 1914 were, on this view, merely overdevelopments of technique seeking to compensate for the ebbing of social 'content' generally considered to be precipitant on the increasing disengagement of intellectuals from popular life.[53] While Ralph Fox in *The Novel and the People* (1937) affirmed that form 'is produced by content, is identical and one

---

49   *Daily Worker* 1935b.

50   *Daily Worker* 1935a.

51   Writers' International, British Section 1934, p. 38.

52   Ibid.

53   Cf. Lukács 2007, p. 41: 'a growing paucity of content, extended to a point where absence of content or hostility towards it is upheld on principle'. The notion of diminishing content did not go unchallenged in *Left Review*, however. Perhaps the most memorable dissenting contribution was that of Lewis Grassic Gibbon, who announced that it was nothing but 'bolshevik blah' to 'say that modern literature is narrowing in "content"': Gibbon 1935, pp. 178–9.

with it, and, though the primacy is on the side of content, form reacts on content and never remains passive', the potential for formal analysis did not really come to fruition, and the association of modernism with an absence of 'content' giving rise to aimless formalism was characteristic.[54] British Marxist critics generally found strikingly little to say about the monumental formal achievement of Joyce's *Ulysses*; for both Christopher Caudwell and Stephen Spender, Joyce's formal method was taken to be simply 'arbitrary', a response to what Spender took to be the 'formlessness of life'.[55]

Edgell Rickword, a central figure in the establishment of the Writers' International and later editor of *Left Review*, argued that modernism was a literary corollary of fascism, its authors helplessly attracted to 'those modes of thought which are hung about like fly-papers to catch the desperate – the immaterial, the spiritual, the idealistic'.[56] Such an implicit antithetical endorsement of materialism and realism was put in the service of two historical 'truths' that were for the most part taken to be inalienable: the crisis in bourgeois culture and the embodiment of the 'hopes of all mankind' in the Soviet Union.[57] Stephen Spender's appraisal of literary modernism, *The Destructive Element* (1935), in part provoked by the publication in 1934 of Max Eastman's *Artists in Uniform*, an account of the situation Soviet writers faced, exemplifies how the argument for these twin 'realities' could not only justify repression of writers in the name of the Soviet Union, but also arrive at a position that rendered literature obsolete. For there was, of course, another historical truth: the repression of intellectuals in the Soviet Union, which British writers were increasingly forced to confront. In *The Destructive Element*, Spender traced what he took to be the waning of 'belief' through the work of modern writers who were faced with the choice to either confront or obfuscate – through increasingly ingenious formal means – the reality of the morbidity of their culture, or else immerse themselves in the 'experience of an all pervading Present' in which that history, and all history, was inaccessible.[58] Henry James, whose work was to be the original focus of *The Destructive Element*, is characterised as a writer acutely aware of a morbidity in bourgeois culture who attempted to shore his work

---

54 Fox 1979, p. 40.

55 Caudwell 1970, pp. 110–11; Spender 1936, p. 835. But see also Alick West's 1937 essay on *Ulysses* that offers a more engaged, though ultimately reproachful, Marxist reading of the novel: West 1974, pp. 104–27.

56 Rickword 1978c, p. 40.

57 The characterisation of the Soviet Union as such was made by Bukharin at the Writers' Congress: Bukharin 1935, p. 185. It was repeated in *Left Review* in Slater 1935a, p. 15.

58 Spender 1935, p. 14.

against that element by 'imposing on a decadent aristocracy the greater tradition of the past'.[59] James's characters are not 'real' people at all, but figments of an authorial resistance to history. Joyce, Yeats, Pound, Eliot and James are all taken as attempting to 'fortify' their works against reality.[60] The exemplary text for Spender is *The Waste Land*, 'a poem without a subject, in the sense that it is a poem without belief': 'instead of any statement about life or the universe having been made, a kind of historic order has been achieved when the author says, "These fragments I have shored against my ruins"'.[61] Formal order has replaced meaning: the work is neither expressive of a personal viewpoint nor representative of some objective reality. Instead, it bleakly replicates the shapeless time of secular modernity, its failures of development, progress and renewal. But Spender's account seems to deprive art of any role in the historical process; historical conditions are implacably objective 'content' to be bravely absorbed or fearfully repressed. As such, it leads (or perhaps allows) Spender, like others on the British left, to justify the persecution of the Soviet poets Vladimir Mayakovsky and Sergei Yessenin on the grounds that, 'their faulty "individualism" perhaps made it ... impossible for them to adapt themselves to the revolution'.[62] History is a vast concrete reality; Spender's is more a mirror-image than a repudiation of the denials of history he finds in modernism – precisely the position that he would decry as the apotheosis of Communist anti-humanism in *The God that Failed*.[63]

Spender's reading of Eliot is thus instructive because of the lack of critical distance it obtains from Eliot's own descriptions of his literary practice. In Edgell Rickword's essay on literature and fascism, 'Straws for the Weary', Rickword at points does succeed in reading against modernists' own positions; for example, he takes the isolation of the post-war writers not as a sign of an actual disengagement from society, but of its opposite: the increasing enmeshing of aesthetic practice and commercial society.[64] But almost immediately this more dialectical reading is undercut by a more straightforward assertion of cultural decadence: these writers 'felt the death in the veins of the society they were condemned to live in', thus pushing the argument back towards a

---

59   Spender 1935, p. 11.
60   Spender 1935, p. 189.
61   Spender 1935, p. 189.
62   Spender 1935, p. 231. Comparable arguments are to be found in Wintringham 1935, Marshall 1937 and Caudwell 1946, p. 289.
63   Spender 1948, pp. 235–8.
64   Rickword 1978c, pp. 39–40.

narrative of the decline of the west.[65] Rickword's argument restates the notion that the First World War shook Enlightenment values and especially faith in reason, a loss whose remedy was 'belief'. This forecloses another reading of the rise of fascism not in terms of rupture but in terms of continuity, as a fruition of Enlightenment values rather than their negation. Elsewhere, indeed, Rickword's indictments of capitalism for the 'vulgarity', 'anarchy' and 'cruelty' of the values it fostered have a noticeably Eliotic ring.[66] This inhabitation of certain modernist positions left little space for a critical examination of Enlightenment cultural values themselves. This is a recurring strain in British Marxist thinking during this time, and it can be traced in part to the founding statement of the Writers' International, which addressed itself in the first instance to those who saw fascism as 'the terrorist dictatorship of dying capitalism and a menace to all the best achievements in human culture, and consider that the best in the civilization of the past can only be developed by joining in the struggle of the working class for a new socialist society'.[67] This claim as a whole reflects an equivocation between the sectional analysis of fascism that would be explicitly announced by Dimitrov the following year, and the equation of capitalism with fascism in the manner of the Third Period. To isolate fascism as a sudden, unprecedented menace to 'human achievement' is to veil the violence against and amid which those achievements have always been won. Here this threat is distanced, but not contained, by the assertion that such preservation is bound up with class struggle, the priority of which would shortly be displaced by the Popular Front turn. A dissenting voice – though one attempting to suppress its dissidence – was that of Montagu Slater, whose 'minor quarrel' with the narrative of cultural crisis in fact revealed an acute contradiction within it: the truth, Slater asserted, 'is that capitalism never found literature a comfortable ally: the bourgeoisie blunted the pen whenever it could'.[68] Here, then, Slater attempts to deflect the attack from recent history and its modernist symptoms onto capitalist modernity itself, a position that spoke explicitly against the emerging emphasis on the bourgeoisie's progressive cultural history. Slater's 'quarrel' does, however, resolve into a characteristically Popular Frontist argument posed in the terms of humanist salvation: 'Art', Slater argues, has 'lost its subject matter':

---

65   Rickword 1978c, p. 40.

66   Rickword 1937a, p. 250. The obvious echo is of Eliot 1998, p. 373.

67   Writers' International, British Section 1934, p. 38.

68   Slater 1935b, p. 125.

This subject-matter – man – can only exist in social relations: and art at last may rediscover him, not in social relations in the older civilized sense of the term, but in social battle, in class war, in the war to end the atomic capitalist regime.[69]

The 'decadent' literature post-1914 represents the abandonment of art's vocation to realise the human being as social subject. But in these terms there was no obvious rationale for a return to the cultural past, to the 'best achievements' of human culture. Discussions of modern and modernist literature in *Left Review* often pull in two directions at once: on the one hand, towards a Soviet-style denunciation of modernism framed in a narrative of general cultural decline in Europe, and on the other, in the direction of a discussion of canonical modernists as representative of only a particular tendency, leaving space for the amplification of persisting progressive traditions within Europe. Underlying both tendencies, however, was the sense of a need to identify the common cultural ground on which fascism could be confronted. Two particular responses to this problem are significant for the realist novel. One was a solution proposed through the reform of literary language, and the other was a more generalised appeal to a shared cultural heritage.

Language, Form and Popularity

The recuperation of 'content' could be envisaged as a linguistic problem that could be solved by an act of social identification. Particularly in the early issues of *Left Review*, discussions tended to assume both the priority of speech over writing and the availability of a relatively homogenous 'popular' language that was in some sense more concrete than literary discourse, felt to be infused with social, and especially working-class, experience. In turn, there was an assumption that such a popular language necessarily represented a relatively homogenous community of speakers. Allen Hutt affirmed 'the particular value in the present connection of the study of English as it was written in the dawn-days of the working-class movement here, a century and more ago'.[70] Montagu Slater argued that 'The speech of the men "at the hidden foci of production", workers and technologists, craftsmen and peasants, is the air a live

---

69   Slater 1935b, p. 126.

70   Hutt 1935, p. 130.

literature must breathe'.[71] Arthur Calder-Marshall proposed that the middle-class writer does not have 'the originality that less articulate workers strike in the labour of thought'.[72] From these premises, it seemed to follow that literature would achieve greater representativeness, greater and broader 'content', through absorbing and adapting the language of everyday social life, rejecting both the arid jargon of the Marxist theoretician and the idiosyncratic expressivity of the modernist. Discussing the Auden group, Slater wrote that the material of poetry – its language – came from 'the people', and thus the only hope for the poet was to 'appeal from the monopolists to the mass of the people – the people from whom it derived its tradition, its rhythms, its language'.[73] This sentiment is echoed by Storm Jameson in her important discussion of socialist fiction, 'Documents' (1937), in which she prescribes a writing that speaks 'for the people'.[74] In this formulation, popularity is not a matter of 'setting out to be a bestseller', but rather a question of quality, of writers 'coming into relation with their fellow-men and women'.[75] The idea of an utterance arising in the people and returning, in transformed and transformative form, to address them, uniting speaker (intellectual) and audience, narrative and experience, is a recurring fantasy in leftist imaginative texts of this period. One might read this in terms of the pastoral, as Empson saw it, and which Tyrus Miller reads as a rhetorical attempt to 'span the cultural gaps between the working-class and literary intellectuals'.[76] That popular speech was in some sense inherently resistant to capitalism is suggested in Jack Lindsay's English Civil War novel, *1649* (1938):

> And then you hear that weak and rambling voice that's singing where a few poor men meet. And you hear something different. You hear this protest against the money-mongers that buy the bread of life and hide it in a private garner; against them that make such scarce of plenty; against them that make their dice of poor men's bones.[77]

The novel's prefatory poem expresses a utopian belief in a kind of preordained relationship between speakers and listeners in a revolutionary discourse: 'We

---

71   Slater 1935b, pp. 125–8.
72   Calder-Marshall 1937a, p. 40.
73   Slater 1935a, p. 22.
74   S. Jameson 1998, p. 556.
75   S. Jameson 1998, p. 559.
76   Miller 2010, p. 51.
77   Lindsay 1938a, p. 135.

go down/ but hear the shout of young men coming after ... For they will rise to hear this tale, they are part of it'.[78] The figure of the speaker works to symbolically resolve a problem that preoccupies Popular Front cultural politics: the rift between the lone intellectual and the reality of a class-divided and alienated culture, between literature and the people. The recovery of 'content' that would attend the dissolution of the rift between the intellectual and popular life was freighted with utopian potential. For Rickword, the prospect of text restored to active engagement in the world underwrote a vision of a socialist society in which 'the long antagonism between literature and life, practical, social life, can be healed'.[79]

Such imaginings of popular speech were commonly defined in opposition to the 'unpopular' discourse of the BBC. The BBC voice, constructed as authoritarian, synthetic and duplicitous, falsely homogenous and representing no genuine popular constituency, is a regular target of satire: in James Barke's *Major Operation*, for example, 'broadcasting the Geneva Lullaby', the fantasy of world peace represented by the League of Nations, in its synthetic language: 'Just a nice voice, you know: wethah fawcaust'.[80] Reviewing the proceedings of the Soviet Writers' Congress, Montagu Slater warned that the artificiality of the 'official' national discourse of the BBC threatened the language as a whole: unless BBC announcers can be got rid of and replaced with regional and class accents, 'then the living elements of such speech will wither under the sweet breath of the mannikins incubated by the public-schools and Professor Lloyd James'.[81] Growing awareness of the role of mass media in calling fascism to power in Europe engendered a suspicion of the ways that such media as radio might manipulate popular sentiment. Charles Madge noted that the BBC's broadcasting monopoly meant 'the voice of authority can actually be heard in every home by turning a switch'.[82] Edgell Rickword meanwhile warned of the spectre of creeping fascism in the standardisation of culture; a country could be 'subtly *gleichgeschaltet*' by anti-intellectualism and mass-produced culture.[83]

---

78   Lindsay 1938a, p. v.

79   Rickword 1978a, p. 122.

80   Barke 1955, p. 441, p. 375.

81   Slater 1935a, p. 22. As Keith Williams argues, 'The pastoral myth that the essential identity of a highly industrialised, largely urban/suburban, multi-cultural society like Britain consisted in Southern English rurality was reinvented by the interwar media, but especially by broadcasting': K. Williams 1996, p. 31.

82   Madge 1937, p. 148. Communist distrust of the BBC was, however, attended by an interest in the possibilities of radio in the thirties; see Harker 2013.

83   Rickword 1978c, p. 24.

A popular language was thus envisioned as a *national* language, albeit an alternative language to the official national discourse of the state broadcaster. Plebeian discourses of the people inevitably threatened to blur with discourses of nationality and nationalism. In Jack Lindsay's work, the audience with whom the poet must join are definitely a *classed* audience, though not one necessarily recognisable as proletarian. In class struggle Lindsay thought that an epic unity of audience, speaker and text could be achieved:

> The poet, while he feels that he is serving such a class, feels that he has an homogeneous audience. The unity *of* his audience and his unity *with* the audience, are necessary reflections of the inner unity of form and content in his art.[84]

But this audience was also typically imagined as a national audience. Lindsay's desire to rhetorically address a nationally located, plebeian formation that was not simply identical with the nation itself (with its potential to repress class difference within and foster hostility beyond) is at its strongest, most redemptive and utopian, in his 'not english?' (1936), a poem for mass declamation (arranged recitation by a group), in which the speaker addresses those individuals and movements who have resisted oppression and been excluded from authorised accounts of English history, 'those who are not the english/ according to the definition of the ruling class'.[85] The poem gathers these moments of resistance, but also repeats them into a new narrative and a new utterance, 'the augural moment declared by frenetic guesses,/ come clear at last' in a simultaneous articulation of nationhood and internationalism: 'England, my England – / the words are clear/ *Workers of the World, unite!*'[86] Suggesting an aspiration towards what Dimitrov called a 'truly national culture', it is nonetheless the case that this poem goes well beyond simply acknowledging the nation as the cultural reality of everyday life.[87] The discourse it aspires to is not simply 'popular', but is in some sense the repressed language of the national unconscious.

In any case, as Lindsay's own novels bear out, the tradition of the English dispossessed could not so easily be excavated and distinguished from the history of capitalist and imperialist triumph as this poem's subversive rendition of Englishness suggests. Here it is necessary to address Britain's status in the wider interwar conjuncture. British writers on the left faced several national

---

84   Lindsay 1937a, p. 514; emphasis in original.
85   Lindsay 1936, p. 356.
86   Lindsay 1936, p. 357.
87   Dimitrov 1935c, p. 76.

peculiarities in attempting to formulate a nationally located Popular Front aesthetics, which included the absence of a tradition of proletarian fiction, the specific forms and course of development that modernist writing took in Britain, and national political and developmental particularities. Where in the USA, for example, the Depression was met by the New Deal, a ruthlessly modernising programme of capitalist development, Britain, as Piers Brendon notes, 'plumped for a conservative consensus'.[88] Consumerism was stimulated and middle-class incomes rose, but the limited reach of the remedies proposed by the National Government elected on a 'doctor's mandate' in 1931 made little impact on the devastating scale of mass unemployment.[89] Although after 1918, piecemeal and belated efforts were made at standardising and stimulating technological and scientific advances, Britain continued to lag behind the USA and Germany as a competitive economy,[90] leading to what Francis Mulhern describes as a 'combination of unplanned growth and unchecked decline'.[91] The effect of such a combination of capitalist expansion without modernisation in economic and civil society could support a thesis that capitalism was entering a terminal crisis; localised effects of Britain's unevenly developed modernity could be taken as signs of the generally deleterious effects of capitalism on culture and human development.

Intertwined with British Marxists' preoccupations with language, form and popularity were a set of anxieties about modern British identity and Britain's uncertain place on the twentieth-century world stage. In the era of Soviet ascendancy, noted Montagu Slater in a review of the proceedings of the Soviet Writers' Congress, the English were now 'provincials for socialism'.[92] American cultural power was a particular source of anxiety: America was at once the fulcrum of the standardising culture industries and the location of a productive relationship between radical intellectuals and the public that British Marxists aspired to themselves. The New Deal stimulated a radical, popular modernism in the USA, so that, as Michael Denning argues, John Dos Passos's formally radical *U.S.A.* trilogy 'served as a charter for the Popular Front; its starting point, its founding mythology'.[93] For Arthur Calder-Marshall, there was an anxiety over American writers' apparently superior ability to produce 'realistic' literature; English writers were by contrast only able to achieve superiority

---

88   Brendon 2000, p. 164.
89   Brendon 2000, pp. 164–5.
90   Hobsbawm 1995, pp. 151–4.
91   Mulhern 1979, p. 6.
92   Slater 1935a, p. 16.
93   Denning 1997, p. 167.

in the 'reflective' novel.[94] Reiterating the thesis that English literary language had been drained of popular and social content, Calder-Marshall blamed the 'abstract and Latinised substitutes for plain speech', governed by 'the desire for euphemism, false social dignity and class conformity', that characterise middle-class language use for the failure of English writing to match up to American realism.[95] However, British Marxists' responses to American literature, even American leftist literature, are revealingly ungenerous. Reviewing the proceedings of the American Writers' Congress in *Left Review* in May 1936, the poet and Mass Observation founder Charles Madge used the opportunity to assert that, though American capitalism might be advanced, it was nonetheless the Soviet Union, 'a civilization which is modern in a sense in which the rest of the world has ceased to be modern', whose modernity was in the ascendant.[96] In a striking display of insecurity, Madge dismissed American writing as plagued by 'backwardness', not merely because the centre of modernity had shifted to the Soviet Union, but also because American writers lacked European cultural traditions, and were therefore accused of putting on 'the airs of a literature which belongs to another world'.[97] This dual attempt to defend both the Soviet Union (as the motor of modernity) and the privileged status of European culture (as the locus of tradition) reflects a particular set of anxieties about a modernity destined, as Madge surely realised, to be characterised by the competing formations of modernity realised in the USA and the USSR. Remarkably, Madge suggested that the material of American modernity could not produce a national literature since its markers of the modern pointed, irresistibly, to the authentic modernity of Soviet society:

> America is the country of the oil derrick, the grain elevator, the radio. But that is not to say that by introducing these positive images into literature you will have an American literature. As soon as they are introduced into literature they become images with only a shadow of their original positive force. In the USSR these images are also characteristic. Even the American engineer finds his place there. But the collective farm, the soviet, the huge banners of Lenin, are characteristic too. They are a projection of America beyond itself. They are more modern, more American, than America.[98]

---

94   Calder-Marshall 1937a, p. 39.

95   Calder-Marshall 1937a, p. 40.

96   Madge 1936, p. 405.

97   Madge 1936, p. 407.

98   Madge 1936, p. 404.

America was thus neither a model for culture nor for modernity. Madge's implication that true modernity was embodied in the Soviet Union while true *culture* was embodied in Europe, is echoed in the defensive emphasis on European cultural tradition that was a major characteristic of Marxist relationships with Anglophone modernism at a particular point in its development. The critique of modernism from the left was expedited by the rightwards shift of some major modernists – a factor more pronounced in Britain than elsewhere.[99] Chief among them was T.S. Eliot, whose *After Strange Gods*, published six months before *Left Review* was established, was reviewed by Douglas Garman in the first issue as exemplifying a writer whose 'graph of development is closely parallel with that of Fascism'.[100] But what is striking in Garman's attack is his broad acceptance of Eliot's concerns, particularly his investment in tradition. However, it is a miscarried and dangerous effort:

> In a world which is hungry for some form of order and authority, there will be many who will grasp at the authority that is here so speciously offered them without much enquiry as to its value; and when they are ultimately forced into political alignment there is no doubt which it will be.[101]

After Strange Gods has achieved a certain notoriety as enshrining Eliot's conservatism, rechannelling his longstanding preoccupation with tradition into an ethnic conception of race and people.[102] That Garman finds himself broadly sympathetic to Eliot's investment in nation and tradition – indeed, 'his search for a system of thought which would, by again relating art to society, nourish the former and be of service to the latter' is read as potentially Marxist – indicates a critique of major modernists that was not an outright attack, but rather a resistance to a certain turn in their development. Garman expressed suspicion of Eliot's identification with English culture: 'Not, of course, that Eliot is without tradition: but the one into which he was born – that of New England, and presumably of Protestant-agnostic New England – is not the one under whose banner he fights'; and indeed his claim to a tradition that Garman considered barred to him leaves Eliot 'susceptible to the vices of the parvenu'.[103] Taken together, Madge and Garman imply that Eliot had no culture to defend:

---

99   See R. Williams 2007, p. 61.
100   Garman 1934b, p. 36.
101   Ibid.
102   Esty 2004, pp. 109–10.
103   Garman 1934b, pp. 35–6.

his elective tradition was forbidden to him, while the culture of his birth was merely the pale reflection of a modernity it could not realise.

Ralph Fox's Realism

In approving of Eliot's emphasis on tradition and his desire to recover a relationship between art and society within a defined cultural (European) or national (British) context, Garman identifies priorities that were not just central to Marxist critical discussions of the realist novel, but were also explicitly thematised in many leftist novels themselves. In the critical sphere, the major statement is Ralph Fox's *The Novel and the People* (1937), which Fox makes clear is an attempt to prove that the 'solution to the problems that vex the English novelist lies precisely in Marxism with its artistic formula of a "socialist realism" which shall unite and re-vitalize the forces of the left in literature'.[104] Among British Marxist writers, Fox was perhaps best placed to absorb and mediate Soviet influences; a long-standing Communist Party member, he had spent two years (1930–2) in Moscow as the English librarian of the Marx-Engels-Lenin Institute, translated works including Nikolai Bukharin's *Marxism and Modern Thought* (1935), and was a founding committee member of the British Section of the Writers' International.[105] At this time the Institute was engaged in preparing previously unpublished correspondence and manuscripts, including Engels's 1888 letter to Margaret Harkness which was given a prominent place in *International Literature*'s documentation of the origins of Marxist criticism, with the Institute providing an extensive commentary.[106] However, *The Novel and the People* largely bypasses Soviet criticism. Indeed, Fox's account of the history of the novel is also unmistakably an account of European modernity, and of the duty of the writer to defend the 'best achievements in human culture' of the past taken, for the most part, to be synonymous with European culture.[107] For Fox, the European writer was heir to a 'unified outlook' that

---

104 Fox 1979, p. 26.
105 Hawthorn 1979, p. 6.
106 Engels 1933.
107 Writers' International, British Section 1934, p. 38. This focus on European culture should not be taken as simply short-sightedness on Fox's part; one of the most widely travelled and internationally culturally literate of British Marxists at this time, he nonetheless took European development as the normative course that the rest of the world would follow (Fox 1979, p. 52).

held sway 'from the Renaissance to Kant'.[108] That unified outlook had nourished and found expression in the classic realist novel, which could condense
epic and popular qualities in an inherently modern form. This account of the
novel's popular and modern qualities relied on a narrative of literary history
that claimed that the canonical realist novel of the nineteenth century had
an especially strong relation with its historical context, a special plenitude of
social 'content', and the designation of that form as an authentically popular art. Popularity here implies that the novelist was integrated into society,
sharing in a unified outlook with the people, and this situation enabled the novelist to mediate between the subjective and the objective: 'The novelist cannot
write his story of the individual fate unless he also has this steady vision of the
whole'.[109]

That unity placed the realist novelist in the lineage of the epic, so that their
characters might be modern heirs of 'epic man', 'man in whom no division any
longer occurs between himself and his sphere of practical activity'.[110] The disintegration of that unity is traced to 1848, when the French bourgeoisie crushed
the workers' uprising of the June Days and with it the prospect of a vision
of the whole: after 1848, Fox suggested, 'you could not observe and express
life in its development because that development was too painful, the contradictions were too glaring'.[111] As the bourgeoisie broke with its revolutionary
past, so the novel broke from its epic roots in the 'complete harmony between
the rhapsodist and his audience'.[112] The novel then began a long retreat into
the self that records the bourgeoisie's fear of reality and fear of showing the
'whole man'.[113] This anti-humanism, as Fox saw it, was instanced in *Ulysses* in
particular; Joyce's treatment of Bloom is condemned as a 'denial of humanism, of the whole Western tradition in literature', a tradition bound up with
the presentation of the 'heroic personality'.[114] Where debates discussed above
focus on language as the marker of the popular, Fox argues for a turn towards
the socially normal and proportionate, as against what he considered to be
Joyce's morbid fixation with naturalistic detail. The fetishisation of the 'mad
and the sick' that represented no general social tendency was a mark of modern literature's inability to face its society, and hence the failure of modern

108   Fox 1979, pp. 96–7.
109   Fox 1979, p. 34.
110   Fox 1979, p. 105.
111   Fox 1979, p. 81. Cf. Lukács 1976, p. 202.
112   Fox 1979, p. 70.
113   Fox 1979, p. 101.
114   Fox 1979, p. 90.

writers to countenance the whole of their society after the manner of their nineteenth-century forebears.[115] Fox's arguments regularly draw on the idiom of disease and degeneration that was at best politically ambiguous: the aloof author suffers 'anaemia'; 'the living body of tradition' is somatically compromised.[116] Fox was far from alone in this tendency; there is clearly a comparable potential for chauvinistic normativity in Arthur Calder-Marshall's assertion that 'bourgeois novelists' pursue 'the abnormal, the perverted or the minute, in order to find fresh material.'[117] But an emphasis on the socially 'normal', even as it threatened to connive in social oppression, is central to Fox's Lukácsian endorsement of a version of realism in which transformative possibilities were written into everyday reality. The model he offers for a hypothetical socialist realist novel is the Dimitrov trial. Fox is anxious to argue against the 'mass-produced intellectual life of our age' as the corollary of Fordist production, forms which together perform complementary fascistic roles in dehumanising and de-individualising the workers.[118] Dimitrov is the exemplar of what Fox considers the continuity between resistance to capitalism at the level of everyday work and resistance to fascism on the world stage, developing from trade unionist to Communist and anti-fascist, finally becoming 'defender of all humanity and its culture against fascism barbarism' in Leipzig.[119] The intention is to typify Dimitrov; to show his conduct as emerging organically from his development in concrete political struggles, echoing Lukács's insistence that popular revolts should be portrayed not as acts of extraordinary heroism but as 'necessary continuations and intensifications of normal popular life'.[120] But more strongly than Lukács, and more strongly than the Soviet critics, Fox pictures the novelist as struggling against reality: the really great writer must be 'engaged in terrible and revolutionary battle with reality, revolutionary because he must seek to change reality'.[121] Fox therefore moves well beyond Spender's account of writers' heroic or tragic encounters with an implacably objective history, and instead towards a sense of the text's transformative possibilities, generated through the realist writer's mediation of the subjective and objective. The proper subject of literature was neither the romantic individual freed from

---

115 Fox 1979, p. 149.

116 Fox 1979, p. 156, p. 141.

117 Calder-Marshall 1937c, p. 116. As I suggest in Chapter Three, however, Calder-Marshall's own novelistic practice suggests he was less than convinced by this argument.

118 Fox 1979, p. 121.

119 Fox 1979, p. 121.

120 Lukács 1976, p. 360.

121 Fox 1979, p. 38. Cf. Lukács's account of the 'labour of the realist' in Lukács 2007, pp. 38–40.

social convention nor the naturalistic transcription of reality as it appeared; instead, the work of art is the realisation of the human being as social subject.

For Fox, then, the political crises of the 1930s presented writers with the prospect of a new, unified outlook that would enable the recovery of the 'heroic personality' through restoring 'the historical view which was the basis of the classical English novel'.[122] Such a realism would be reparative, unlike the modernism that merely symptomatised the fractured, relativised spaces of imperial modernity. The task was intertwined with the fate of the nation: the novelist 'has a special responsibility both to the present and the past of his country' since 'the fate of our language and the struggles to develop it, have in the past always been most closely bound up with the struggles of our country for national salvation'.[123] The silence of *The Novel and the People* over the violence of 'national salvation' committed under the sign of the unified outlook of the Enlightenment, the absence of critical discussion of that totalising outlook, and any challenge to its appearance of wholeness, its role in the production of unevenly developed modernity, reflects the limits of conventional Marxist analyses of imperialism between the wars.[124] Fox saw the project of empire as 'progressive' in so far as it established the conditions for capitalist modernity throughout the world as a necessary precondition for socialism. In the future he envisioned, after Marx, a 'world literature': 'But that world literature is a weakling child, prevented from natural growth by the very conditions of capitalist production which gave it birth'.[125] The assumption that capitalism would modernise – and thus ultimately liberate – all corners of the world in a relatively even and comparable way could enable Communists to take European modernity not as a historically specific formation available for critical analysis, but as a necessary phase of human development to which all other societies would eventually accede.

---

122   Fox 1979, p. 105.
123   Fox 1979, p. 138.
124   As Fredric Jameson suggests, most Marxists between the world wars took the primary relationship of imperialism to be that between rival imperial powers, rather than between imperial metropolis and colony, and assumed – as Fox does – that 'capitalist penetration would lead directly to positive economic development in what are now known as Third World countries': F. Jameson 1990, pp. 46–8.
125   Fox 1979, p. 52.

Conclusion

Ralph Fox died fighting for the Spanish Republic in December 1936, several months before *The Novel and the People* was published.[126] Montagu Slater's review of the proceedings of the Soviet Writers' Congress, published in early 1935, greeted the 'turning point' announced by Nikolai Bukharin (soon to become one of the most high-profile victims of the terror) as 'a turning point in world politics at a moment when all men are holding their breath seeing mankind plunged into the latter phase of the crisis, the world tremors of the end of a system'.[127] But the 'turning point' did not mark a surge in the advance to a new world, and the tremors felt throughout Europe were not those of capitalism's death throes. The war in Spain galvanised a mass, anti-fascist movement, but for Communists it also curtailed a discussion of the relationship between capitalism, fascism, and the 'culture' that was rhetorically positioned to be at stake. It is a striking irony that it was in the cause of Spain that this antinomy was most emphatically articulated, for Spain was in some senses the hinterland of European modernity; it embodied fractures and contradictions of modernity that had to be repressed in order for it to function as a stage on which 'culture' confronted fascism.[128] Fox's work is conflicted in its endorsement of the realist novel as a revolutionary form which could speak both from and for popular experiences of struggle while aligning itself with a cultural tradition of dominance. These conflicts, as we shall see, are rehearsed within the Popular Front novel itself. The following two chapters discuss two novels in which realist and modernist impulses interplay. The incompleteness of the British Marxist reckoning with modernism contributes to an unsettling failure to examine with clarity the tradition they sought to defend. But this very incompleteness also, I would argue, mitigated an attack on modernist technique, leaving a space open for an assimilation and reorientation of certain modernist techniques that enabled the production of leftist texts that addressed themselves to the agenda Fox proposes in innovative ways.

---

126   Fox and John Cornford died on or around the same day in late December or early January, the first high-profile British fatalities in the war. See Hawthorn 1979, pp. 9–10.

127   Slater 1935a, p. 23.

128   Rogers 2012 examines the interrelationships between Spain, modernism and modernity.

John Sommerfield, *May Day* (1936)

John Sommerfield's *May Day*, published just after its author had left for Spain to join the International Brigades, is perhaps the exemplary Popular Front novel in terms of political theme. In its enactment of class alliance, bourgeois dissidence and mass solidarity, it is deeply infused with the political mood of its conjuncture. But it is also a formally experimental novel that appropriates a number of techniques and themes closely associated with the literary modernism of the 1920s. While George Orwell could declare that the 1930s were rendered uniquely 'barren of imaginative prose' by an atmosphere in which writers were 'conscience-stricken about their own unorthodoxy', it is hard to see how such a milieu could produce a novel so openly reflexive about form and technique and so overtly committed to Communist politics.[1] Nick Hubble argues that *May Day*'s 'overt usage of modernist techniques has to be seen as a deliberate act of defiance'.[2] But like Arthur Calder-Marshall's *Pie in the Sky*, discussed in Chapter Three, this is a novel preoccupied with questions of language and articulation, forms of activism and tradition; concerns that were, as I suggested in the previous chapter, at the heart of leftist discussions of realism. Sommerfield's appropriations of modernist techniques in the service of a politically active, modern realism intended to envisage solutions to the problems of alienation are the subject of my discussions here.

John Sommerfield: Literature and Activism

After several directionless years as a sailor and theatre carpenter, John Sommerfield came to Marxism in the early 1930s through the influence of his friend, the philosopher Maurice Cornforth, who, Andy Croft reports, lent him Lenin's *Materialism and Empirio-Criticism*.[3] This led him to join the Communist Party of Great Britain, at the time less welcoming to writers than it was in the Popular Front period, and he turned his literary attentions to the depiction of class struggle, becoming in the mid-thirties a key figure in Popular Front intellec-

---

1 Orwell 1970a, p. 519.
2 Hubble 2012, p. 140.
3 Croft 1983, pp. 62–3.

tual life. As well as writing for the *Daily Worker*, Sommerfield fought with the Marty Battalion of the International Brigade in Spain, and was twice reported killed.[4] He wrote a critically maligned memoir of the conflict, *Volunteer in Spain*, among the earliest accounts by a combatant and dedicated to John Cornford, summarily dismissed by George Orwell as 'sentimental tripe'.[5] In 1938, he wrote a novella, *Trouble in Porter Street*, at the behest of the Party, fictionalising a successful strike along the lines of similar actions taken by tenants in Bethnal Green and Stepney in the summer of that year.[6] He was a key participant in Mass-Observation, doing most of the writing for its wartime publication, *The Pub and The People*.[7] Sommerfield, however, was by no means a straightforwardly 'Party' writer, and he publicly complained about the dogmatic and simplistic criticism that appeared in the *Daily Worker*, which he felt exhibited the 'tendency in Left-wing literary criticism that if carried to its logical conclusion leads to the worth of a book being estimated on the grounds of its author's political life'.[8] In *Left Review*, he objected to the assumption that only literature written from a 'Party-Orthodox' position was valuable, asserting that 'literature that deals with the struggle to free the mind from bourgeois standards without gravitating immediately to Marxism' should also be welcomed.[9] His earlier literary endeavours also brought him into contact with a wide social circle beyond the Party. Malcolm Lowry admired his first novel, published in 1930, so much that he tracked Sommerfield down to the carpenter's shop where he was working, and Sommerfield became part of Lowry's bohemian circle that included Nina Hamnett, Elsa Lanchester and Dylan Thomas. Despite Lowry's lack of interest in politics, he regarded Sommerfield as 'approximately the best man I've ever met'.[10]

His early, pre-Communist novel, *The Death of Christopher* (1930) is a curious and decidedly experimental text.[11] *Granta* found it too self-conscious; 'essentially Georgian in feeling' but sprinkled with modern phrases and typographical tricks; a text hoping to 'attract the modernist hangers-on as well as the

---

4   Ibid.

5   Sommerfield 1937b; Orwell cited in Cunningham 1988, p. 54.

6   Sommerfield 1938. For East End rent strikes, see Stevenson 1990, p. 230.

7   Mass-Observation 1943. Tom Harrisson confirms in his 'Preface' that the project was mostly Sommerfield's work, p. 11. For an insightful account of Sommerfield's activities in Mass Observation, see Hubble 2012.

8   Sommerfield 1937a, p. 7.

9   Sommerfield 1935, p. 367.

10   Bowker 1993, p. 141.

11   Published in Britain as *They Die Young*.

conservative public'.[12] The novel plays liberally with its own fictionality, as exemplified in the wandering protagonist Christopher's chance encounter with a character called John Sommerfield, whose conversation is oddly 'literary' and whose name is uncannily familiar.[13] This self-referentiality, which it is tempting to read as prematurely postmodernist, is perhaps more usefully traced to a modernist problematic of subjective isolation that was in a certain way inherited by leftist thinkers after 1933. The problem was transposed, however, into the social split between intellectuals and the 'people' that is the characteristic ground of Popular Front literary debate. In *May Day*, a modernist attentiveness to form is channelled not into sceptical introversion but into a politicised literary practice that crucially includes rewriting elements of the earlier novel. This intertexuality indexes both Sommerfield's development and Popular Front thinking on modernism.

Near the novel's conclusion, Christopher finds himself returning to the country he left behind:

> Now each turn of the screw that pushed so many feet of the ocean behind the *Halcyon* brought him so many feet nearer home. This long-cherished return of his, for which he had so much hoped and despaired, was actually going to happen: the remote and unbelievable would soon be near and actual.[14]

This hope for a felicitous coincidence of space and time is, however, thwarted from the outset as the novel begins with a description of Christopher's death in a car crash, to which he is propelled by an irresistible need for time and space to coalesce in motion: driving towards death he feels that 'Swifter than light and thought he had freed himself from dimension and overtaken the trampling feet of time, so that the past yet lay in the future and he was once again the Christopher of two years ago'.[15] In this early novel, the forces of time and history can only be managed by fantasy and escaped from in death. *May Day*, however, written six years later and after Sommerfield's political conversion, proposes a different solution. In a passage that recalls the one quoted above, the returning sailor in this novel feel that 'scenes, half-remembered, half-anticipated moved in his mind, of London in spring ... memories and dreams that were about

---

12   Bowker 1993, p. 141.

13   Sommerfield 1930, p. 291.

14   Sommerfield 1930, p. 345.

15   Sommerfield 1930, p. 12.

to become realities again for him'.[16] Return has become a material possibility, and in this fusion of past and present is the prospect of redemption. In the earlier text, the mixing of past and present is a sign of Christopher's delusions, already rendered ironic by the revelation of his death at outset. Both novels address themselves to the same subjective quandary: the physical and psychological dislocation of individuals from their own histories and world-historical realities. In *The Death of Christopher*, this is narrated through the futile and ultimately self-destructive pursuit of a sense of belonging, an attempt to find a way of re-integrating 'that most ungetatable thing – his real self'.[17] In *May Day*, a comparable plot is ambitiously constructed both in terms of individual dislocation and return, and through the socially redeeming possibility of collective action. *May Day*'s key statement is its implication that these two plots are interdependent: that the divided self of the sailor James Seton, around whom the psychological concerns of the novel converge, can only be remade through the participation in the mass action of the May Day demonstration. In so doing, Sommerfield attempts to offer a socialist solution to a modernist problem.[18]

Vox Populi and Bird's Eye

But how does a Communist write the modernist city? City spaces inspired a number of expansive, panoramic leftist texts in the 1930s, an inventory of which would include *May Day*, Arthur Calder-Marshall's *Pie in the Sky* (1937) and Ashley Smith's *A City Stirs* (1939). Absorbing the influence of Soviet cinema and documentary film, these texts are characterised by a particular use of aerial perspectives, detached from individual observers, utilised to make visible the connections immanent in urban life. Smith's *A City Stirs*, for example, is an ambitious text describing one London day, but which seeks to represent history on a large, supra-individual scale: 'You are an individual but here is the long sleep of centuries which you daily disturb. Mighty forces now are turning to greet the day. Ancient towers, buttressed monuments by the score,

---

16   Sommerfield 2010, p. 30. Subsequent references to this novel are given in parentheses in the text.

17   Sommerfield 1930, p. 30.

18   These fundamental concerns are visible too in Sommerfield's much later work: his 1977 novel-memoir *The Imprinted* (1977) is a text involved with the relationship between personal history and political history; with the question of whose narratives survive and whose are erased.

are emerging from the darkness'.[19] This combination of depersonalised voice and epic spatial and temporal perspective registers one effort to resolve the anxieties about form set out in the previous chapter: the personalisation and potential relativism of individual speech and the absence of shared historical and cultural perspectives. *May Day*'s opening pages exude confidence in its theoretical insight expressed through the device of the bird's-eye view. In spite of the Soviet critics' warnings against the direct application of Marxist theory to literary writing, *May Day* begins with a firm articulation of its theoretical premise: its epigraph is 'Men Make History, But Not As They Please'.[20] The early pages feature a cinematic passage that zooms in, from the bird's eye to the worm's eye perspective: *'Let us take factory chimneys, cannons trained at dingy skies, pointing at the sun and stars'*, the camera-eye moves through an emerging human perspective, *'It's rather hard to see where they come in, these quivering shreds of flesh amidst so much concrete and steel'*, through to the assertion that, *'These fragile shreds of flesh are protagonists of a battle, a battle where lives are wasted, territories destroyed and populations enslaved'* (25, emphasis in original). The voicing and perspective are, importantly, synthetic, drawn from the repertoire of technologised media.

But these aloof voices, articulating totalising perspectives from privileged and synthetic positions, are balanced in the novel by a concern with more organic, and less absolute, modes of articulation. Of the young girls who work at Langfier's, the factory at the centre of the novel's strike-plot, Sommerfield writes that '[w]hen their moment of deep discontent comes to them in a mass, taking form in the words of their class leaders, then there are revolutions' (50). 'Form' here signifies the role of the intellectual in formalising existing (and authentic) popular feeling. As suggested in the previous chapter, there was a recurring fascination with the image of a voice speaking for the people, and a faith that such a mode of articulation would be transformative and redemptive. In *May Day*, this fantasy is enacted through the work of the Communist slogans: they help give definition to undefined and unrecognised discontent. In one way, Sommerfield is simply offering an idealised image of the role of the Leninist party in supplementing working-class consciousness; but Sommerfield's figuration of organic leadership as a receiver and transmitter of popular feeling is also part of the novel's wider engagement with an emerging awareness of the role of different discourses in shaping perception and social reality,

---

19   Ashley Smith 1939, p. 31.

20   Such a warning was included in the commentary by the Marx-Engels-Lenin Institute published as a foreword to Engels 1934.

and the consequent impetus for Communists to construct a persuasive discourse of their own. The Communists' slogans in the novel are presented as
providing a counter-discourse to the channels of capitalist media. The recurring variations on 'Forward for a Soviet Britain' evoke the Communist Party's
1935 programme, *For Soviet Britain*, which in fact reflected the sectarian politics
of the earlier Third Period, but in the novel Sommerfield uses these phrases to
suggest the ways that heterogeneous existing grievances and sentiments might
be connected and hence transformed.[21] Stuart Laing has noted that both the
Communist slogans and the newspaper headlines 'are illustrating the fact that
a situation common to all exists, but also they are the agency that effectively
generates that situation by making knowledge of it commonly available'.[22] Such
acts are represented as capable of changing perceptions of social reality, as the
Communists' disruption of the channels of official culture shows: the inter-
jection into the broadcast of a Mozart sonata, 'Workers, all out on May Day.
Demonstrate for a free Soviet Britain', has the effect that '[e]yes remembered
the chalked slogans on walls and pavements' (67). The Communist journalist, Pat Morgan, imagines this as the Communists 'hammering home the May
Day slogans until their clangour sounded everywhere, until even the radio and
the newspapers, the loudest instruments in the orchestra of suppression were
forced to echo the undertone of a working-class motif' (67). Charles Madge's
essay on the mass media, published a year after *May Day*, provides a real-life
example of such an intervention: 'The man who interrupted a variety broadcast with a cry of "Mrs Simpson" was voicing the desire of millions of listeners
to break down official reticence'.[23] This action made public what was at one
level publicly known but officially repressed. Radicalisation in *May Day* tends
to be catalysed by these types of articulation and clarification, as when one
dockworker tells another 'There's a big change needed', realising immediately
that '[h]e had never spoken to the mate like that before' (159). Such interventions were central to the political imagination of Popular Front writers, and
reflect a belief that a broad, progressive formation, alienated and ignored by
mainstream representational forms, already existed in latent form, awaiting
activation: in Jack Lindsay's *1649*, the radical Levellers pursue a popular consensus felt to be immanent: 'The voice was there, speaking, desired, awaited.
But could it speak loud enough and soon enough?'[24]

---

21   Communist Party of Great Britain 1935; see especially section v, 'The Communist Party',
      which emphasises the superior insight and vanguard role of the Party.
22   Laing 1980, p. 147.
23   Madge 1937, p. 159.
24   Lindsay 1938a, p. 240.

The novel is committed to the transformative potential of articulation: the notion that popular feelings, incoherently or indistinctly felt, could be clarified by Communist discourse. The naivety of such a faith in the possibilities of public utterance is obvious, and echoes the ideal of a popular speech that was somehow considered a vehicle for social 'content' in the early *Left Review*. But notably *May Day* also reflects on the limits of linguistic representation and public articulation. This is exemplified by a page featuring a paragraph of decontextualised phrases from documents, followed by the comment that 'one half of contemporary life can be deduced and a material history and philosophy of the organization of society.' The other half, the novel tells us, is composed of the 'lonely and incommunicable private lives and thoughts' (135). The text gestures to what it can neither express nor represent: the residue of lived experience that is not 'absorbed' in the manner that some of the *Left Review* discussions supposed.

Montage and Memory

The possibility that a latent popular formation might be called to conscious-ness is explored through the montage form of the novel, which tracks a range of characters in the run-up to the May Day demonstration. Thematically, the novel treats exile and estrangement as conditions operating at different social levels. The possibility of return from exile is also a return both to society and to a socially integrated sense of self. The tone is set by the opening scene in which James Seton, a working-class Communist sailor returned to London from sea, awakens as his ship docks. This moment of return is figured as a fulfilment of something anticipated in a dream: 'An image floated in his drowsing mind, an image that had accompanied him to sleep, of a drifting constellation of lights seen across dark waters' (27). James's exile from London has produced a tem-poral and spatial dislocation: 'They had been away too long; they had been too far' (27), and he contemplates the 'coming break as if it were a new, strange thing'; a rupture in which his workmates will find their hopes and fears 'no longer bound together' (28). This estrangement is mirrored in his brother John's state of displacement. He is re-entering work after a spell of unemployment, a change that he experiences as a decisive temporal break separating 'now' from 'then' (32). The security proffered by work fortifies his sense of identity against the alienation of unemployment, the 'shut faces' of the authorities to his plight. For James, the reverse is true: returning from sea he is now work-less and placeless. Life on land is alienating: 'All these faces had been and were shut from him: he was a stranger who did not exist for them' (53). The echoing of 'shut' confirms the connection between the brothers and the analogy of their experiences. This return from exile is figured, though the novel's intertwining of personal and political memory, as offering James redemption: 'it seemed to James as if that kind, honest solidity of his brother was a thing of which he had long been in need, a balm for the disquietude which he had suffered since he had left Spain, a fugitive from a revolt drowned in blood' (29). The interdependence of personal and political exile is expressed in humanist terms as an image of alienation from human fulfilment: 'Beauty, the token of his exile, flowered from bricks and pavements' (74). The novel takes up several modernist themes – exile, sympathetic connections between characters, and the work of time and memory – but recalibrates them in materialist terms, as symptoms of the dislocations and displacements wrought by capitalism.

Sommerfield develops his earlier subjective preoccupations into a sustained exploration of alienation, and the politics of alienation are central to the novel's experimental form. Readings of the novel have tended to argue that its structure privileges the reader, giving them a totalising perspective to which the characters do not have access within what Brian McKenna calls their own 'micro-stories'.[25] But Sommerfield's uses of memory infuse characters' perceptions with a plenitude that extends towards what Walter Benjamin describes as the 'epic and rhapsodic' qualities of 'genuine memory', which must 'yield an image of the person who remembers'.[26] James Seton returns to a city layered with memory: he must 'live again the memory-changed scenes of childhood, from whose actuality his memory had travelled so long a journey that he recollected them half-uncomprehendingly, half with an adult stranger's sight' (71). The images that memory yields suggest a utopian function:

> And his mother gave him an orange. 'Share it with John', she said, and he did, amicably for once. Her worn face creased peacefully. This was the scene he now remembered, sweet with the overtones of remoteness, loaded with the rich harmonics of past time. The heavy blossom-scent and the evening's islanded quiet affected him now, not as if it was an image of a scene through which he had lived but the memory of some picture seen long ago.
>
> p. 72

---

25   McKenna 1996, p. 376.
26   Benjamin 2005a, p. 576.

Sommerfield is adapting a modernist emphasis on time and memory, an emphasis in which memory indexes the fractures and otherness of the self (as in Woolf's *Mrs Dalloway*, for instance), but in a certain way inverting it, so that memory is now the connection-making process that might transform the fragments, and not the dislocated images themselves. The Communist poet, historian and novelist Jack Lindsay described this narrative tendency, in a survey of socialist novels in *Left Review*, in terms of 'recognition'. In classical drama, Lindsay argued, recognition

> lay in the sense of getting back to a contact with the fullness of life, of entering into a larger life, a more conscious relationship. *Now* Recognition appears as the point where the shell of the old self cracks and the new self is born, breaking into new spaces of activity and achieving fullness of social contact.[27]

The 'new self' in *May Day* is expressed in the self-recognition that James finds in the mass demonstration: 'the dear familiarity of these surroundings and the deep meaning of my own life for this scene' (213). Integration of past and future selves is continuous with social integration – that is, the realisation of the individual as social being.

May Day's narrative technique moves between different individuals, but also between different styles and genres: it includes 'factual' and statistical sections that anticipate Sommerfield's extensive work with Mass-Observation; a section called 'The Movements of People in London on April 30th' emulates documentary-style voice-over (175); another short section simulates the sound of typewriters and printing presses, 'Dear Sir Madam Sir Dear Comrade Yours faithfully truly fraternally Thanking you in anticipation' (135), in one of several echoes of Walter Ruttmann's 'city-symphony' of Berlin.[28] In an essay in the leftist journal *Fact*, the novelist Arthur Calder-Marshall wrote in 1937 of the prospects for a new type of 'social' novel written through a 'composite method'.[29] Sommerfield's novel adopts such a 'composite' structure, and this montage principle is the means by which Sommerfield attempts an expression of the social totality. In its expansive, multifaceted form and totalising ambitions, we may consider *May Day* as an experiment in the epic. Walter Benjamin made the connection between epic and the montage form in his review of Döblin's

---

27   Lindsay 1937b, p. 840; emphasis in original.
28   In Ruttmann's *Berlin: Symphony of a Great City*, the second 'akt' features a scene of office workers typing furiously which resolves into a swirling shot of typewriter keys.
29   Calder-Marshall 1937a, p. 42.

Berlin Alexanderplatz, a text in which documents, incidents, songs and advert-isements 'rain down' in such a way that the montage technique 'explodes the framework of the novel, bursts its limits both stylistically and structurally, and clears the way for new, epic possibilities'.[30] The formal plurality of Sommer-field's parodies however coalesce – as quantity turning into quality – into a new, more complex meaning; for John, the sight of a Communist leaflet serves to temporarily focalise his entire situation: 'He saw it with a sense of recogni-tion, he knew it was connected with a whole group of feelings, associations and events' (180).

Sommerfield's decision to compress the action of the novel into a short time frame enables the use of a montage method composed of short scenes taking place almost simultaneously. Recurring images and phrases provide much of the connecting framework between these scenes, rather than a direct narrative method.[31] In his deployment of montage, however, Sommerfield is at important variance with Georg Lukács, a major theorist of the epic and its relationship with realism. Lukács developed Hegel's central category of totality into a vision of the social totality marked by 'the all-pervasive supremacy of the whole over the parts'.[32] In such a structure, all parts are 'objectively interrelated'.[33] This objective interdependence, however, may be experienced as its opposite – as the apparent autonomy of the parts. Lukács rejected the technique of montage and other modernist forms on the grounds that they merely reproduced this superficial fragmentation. Remaining 'frozen in their own immediacy', they 'fail to pierce the surface to discover the underlying essence, i.e. the real factors that relate their experience to the hidden social forces that produce them'.[34] The apparent incompatibility of Sommerfield's form with Lukács's version of realism has been noted by Gustav Klaus, but to argue as Klaus does that 'Sommerfield simply starts from different premises', so that Lukács's criticisms are 'irrelevant', is to overlook important points of correspondence.[35] In spite of Lukács's rejection of montage as fragmentary and incoherent formalism, Sommerfield's montage articulates a model of the relations between the parts and the whole that is essentially congruent with Lukács's version of totality. Sommerfield attempts to show both the appearance of reification and the actual 'objective' relations.

---

30   Benjamin 2005b, p. 301.
31   Laing 1980, p. 149.
32   Lukács 1975, p. 27.
33   Lukács 2007, p. 32.
34   Lukács 2007, pp. 36–7.
35   Klaus 1985, p. 117.

In the reified world of the bourgeois characters in the novel, power is a mystery: doors are opened 'by men who moved as if they were trying to be invisible' (63). The façade is such that it can absorb inconvenient realities: had 'an elephant' appeared 'they would have managed to make him seemly and unobtrusive' (63). This is a world of illusion in which labour is thoroughly disguised, in which phenomena do appear as independent. Indeed, through the upper-class characters Peter Langfier and Pamela Allin, Sommerfield seems to echo Lukács's account of the antinomies of reified bourgeois consciousness elaborated in *History and Class Consciousness* (1922): Pamela's minutely descriptive perceptions make her a 'completely passive observer moving in obedience to laws which [her consciousness] can never control'; Peter, meanwhile, is paralysed by his freedom of choice and is thus unable to distinguish real life from fantasy, revealing a consciousness that 'regards itself as a power which is able of its own – subjective – volition to master the essentially meaningless motion of objects'.[36] But Sommerfield is anxious to acknowledge the progressive potential of bourgeois dissidence as part of the alliance-making ethos of the Popular Front. Peter's flights of fancy, his romantic attachment to 'the heroics of technology' (55), are abruptly terminated when, visiting his father's factory after an accident in which a factory girl is scalped by a machine, he sees the grotesque evidence of the realities of exploitation: a 'tangle of blood and hair ... wedged between the belt and the pulley wheel' (228). This encounter with the reality of technologised production deflates his earlier heroic fantasies, but his romantic temperament is shown to have its positive effect, enabling him to recognise the victim as 'a young girl who may have been looking forward to seeing a lover that evening' (229). While typifying Peter as bearing the modernist sensibility characteristic, for Lukács, of polarised bourgeois consciousness, Sommerfield is also anxious to identify recuperable tendencies and incorporate them as moments of dissidence. This is a dissidence that occurs, however, at the level of individual ethical action, rather than the revolutionary transformation of consciousness projected by Lukács in 1922. I will return to the question of the limits and possibilities of bourgeois dissidence in relation to Jack Lindsay's fiction in Chapter Four.

While this transformation is limited to an individual change of heart, Sommerfield's use of the commodity as a narrative device suggests the way that montage might effect a more fundamental change of perspective. Through the recurring references to a single commodity, the artificial leather product produced by Langfier's factory, Sommerfield links together the moments of the

---

36   Lukács 1975, p. 77.

productive process, and thereby de-reifies the commodity, stripping it of its appearance of objective independence. If, in Adorno and Horkheimer's well-known formulation, 'all reification is a forgetting', Sommerfield's use of montage and juxtaposition engages the reader's memory to continually resituate the commodity in context, referring the product back to the productive process.[37] The commodity in circulation is seen from a range of perspectives: the artificial leather features in John's wife Martine's dreams of a better domestic life (128), on the seats of taxis, and in the study of the reactionary union leader Raggett (141). Each scene bears the legible trace of the economic mode. In one short, isolated scene, a destitute old woman is seen 'grubbing in Soho dustbins for scraps of food', carrying 'a shabby bag made of squares of artificial leather' (192). The detail gives the commodity concrete social significance that serves to emphasise the isolation of the character, who does not reappear in the novel. The montage therefore restores the link between commodity and labour that Lukács assumed could only be lost by the fragmentation of aesthetic form. Yet such de-reification was essential to Lukács's sense of epic in the thirties.[38] Once again, Sommerfield appears to be working towards the epic and totalising ambitions that define Lukács's programme – suggesting that those ambitions resonated for British novelists even if they were not fully theorised – but doing so without being committed to a traditionally realist form.

Sommerfield indeed appears at one point to deploy montage juxtapositions to dramatise thirties aesthetic debates over modernism and realism, and over the position of intellectuals in relation to mass culture. Sommerfield narrates a scene set in a music hall, where a strike threatens to disrupt the opening of the appositely titled *Backwards and Forwards*, 'the musical comedy that is going to be DIFFERENT', and follows it immediately with an antithetical scene featuring a lone man who 'looked like an intellectual' (146–9). In the theatre, a bustling scene featuring a vast list of characters involved in the production of the musical resolves into a demand for a strike. This suggests that this collective – though commercial – form of art has affinity with collective forms of action (even if the musical's title suggests that such action will not necessarily mean an advance). The succeeding scene concerns a lone intellectual who seems to stand for the inadequate response of many of the intelligentsia to the demands of anti-fascism. Reluctantly and bitterly politicised, he regards the masses as to be 'alternately pitied and despised' (150). He loathes both mass culture, 'people sitting in the warm darkness of the picture houses, lapped

37   Horkheimer and Adorno 2002, p. 191.
38   The connection is most explicit in Lukács 1936a, p. 74.

with the sickly disgusting tide of drugging, lying thought', and a high culture in decay (151). His inability to meaningfully discriminate is encapsulated in a passage that presents images, theories and commodities as a jumbled, undifferentiated mass in a bookshop window: 'Cover designs abounded with romantic photomontage and abstract representations of the Workers, red flags, hammers and sickles, fasces, swastikas, a chaotic jumble of baggage dropped in the great retreat of bourgeois thought' (151). This is precisely the decadence Lukács identified in the bourgeoisie, an abdication of critical thought and discrimination, a 'sticking together of disconnected facts'.[39] What this character is unable to see is the strike being orchestrated behind the scenes in the music hall. He mistakes the product for the labour process that creates it, and thus is blind to the radical potential of popular culture. Sommerfield's use of juxtaposition here reflects a Lukácsian critique of bourgeois intellectual culture while asserting the revolutionary potential of the collective aesthetic labour that produces the mass cultural form.

Myth and Tradition

As I suggested in the previous chapter, the terrain of tradition was an important intersection between British Marxists and Anglophone modernists. While the montage method described above aims to solve problems of alienation through connection making, Sommerfield's novel also makes use of the collective psychological power of myth and the socialising force of tradition. The central myth in *May Day* is the General Strike, encompassing both the historical strike of 1926 and an ideal form of it. Tradition – the May Day tradition that is both a festival of springtime and a monument of the labour movement – mediates between individual memory and the totality of history. The practices of tradition give graspable and intelligible form to historical processes, both informing events in the present and suggesting the shape of those in the future: 'A revolution is not a fight between those on one side of the line and those on the other. But today things are artificially simplified' (203). Tradition was central to the Popular Front's most defining ambition of activating a progressive, popular consensus, drawing from the past the images of popular resistance from the Peasants' Revolt through to the anti-fascist struggle. 'Things aren't the same in England', the narrator of *May Day* tells us, identifying in the English May Day traditions a possible way of staging resistance to the increasingly

---

39   Lukács 1976, p. 302.

invisible, decentred and denationalised forces of capitalism (204). The temporary massing of the workers overcomes that dislocation, just as, more widely, the labour movement is figured as the 'home' of the alienated sailor James Seton.

May Day on the one hand stands for the modern, working-class, internationalist movement, and on the other as a folk festivity in which communities would celebrate the coming of summer. As in the work of Jack Lindsay, there is an attempt to align these two cultural practices in the cause of defining a resistant, alternative tradition in which all those opposed to capitalism could position themselves.[40] Sommerfield exploits the ambiguities of May Day traditions in a way that corresponds to one of the emphases of socialist realism as defined by both Maxim Gorky and Nikolai Bukharin. Both these writers envisage socialist realism as aiming for the quality of myth, for, in Bukharin's phrase, 'extreme generality'.[41] May Day opens with a statement of its generalising and typifying strategy: it claims to be set 'in an average year between 1930–40', both distancing it from real events and claiming for itself the status of a document of general social forces and tendencies.[42] Tradition is a key organising principle by which those tendencies are given shape in the novel. The May Day celebrations of 1935 and 1936 in particular gave Communists and socialists the occasion to attempt to define a unifying tradition. In 1935, the celebrations coincided with the Silver Jubilee of George v, and the programme for the London May Day march presents it as the means of 'extending and spreading working-class internationalism as a reply to the poisonous and false patriotic propaganda that will be spread during the Jubilee'.[43]

Part Three, covering the May Day demonstration itself, is organised by a sustained performative metaphor that attempts to deal with the traumatic memory of the 1926 General Strike. May 1936, the month that Sommerfield's May Day was published, also saw the tenth anniversary of the strike, and recollections and discussions of its relevance appeared in the left-wing press; the Daily Worker ran the headline '1926 Inspires 1936', while in Left Review, Eva C. Reckitt recalled that, 'The mosaic of the working-class movement, split up into a thousand fragments, was for those nine days welded into a real class unity, a spontaneous rallying of all working-class forces in a way which

---

40   Lindsay's key statement of alternative traditionalism was his poem 'not english?' which
      appeared in Left Review the same month May Day was published: Lindsay 1936.
41   Bukharin 1935, p. 256; Gorky 1935, p. 44.
42   Sommerfield 2010, p. 20.
43   All-London First of May Demonstration Committee 1935.

transcended all the barriers of divided industrial and political organisation'.[44] Perhaps most significantly, however, the souvenir programme of the London rally contained a piece in which Ben Lennard declared that, 'Not yet, but certainly one day, we shall be able to look back to 1926 and say that it was our 1905 – the defeat that made possible and certain our final triumph'.[45] The General Strike that is imagined in *May Day* operates at two levels: at one level the actual historical legacy of the 1926 strike presents itself as a problematic legacy from which lessons can be learned, but which haunts the text as a failure (223). At a second level however one finds the General Strike presented in a manner consonant with Georges Sorel's analysis of it in terms of myth. The prospect of a mass strike presents itself as an outpouring of possibility: 'Everywhere the accumulated bitterness of weeks and months and years' is 'bursting forth' (160). These levels of history and myth, inglorious past and radical possibility, conflict in the characters' minds in order to recast the events of 1926 as a 'rehearsal', subsuming them to a greater, as yet unrealised event (204). The demonstration is therefore both production and reproduction: the reproduction of tradition and the production of a new situation, the 'new thoughts' in people's minds (211). James feels himself no longer a 'spectator', alienated from historical reality, but instead a participant and actor in a mass drama; the move from contemplation to activism, as prescribed by Fox as a necessary measure for the recovery of the 'lost art of prose', is clearly marked.[46]

The power of the 'myth' of the General Strike is to augment the consciousness of a scheduled interruption of the labour process – the May Day holiday – with radical future possibilities. The strike, for Sorel, is a way of imaging to the proletariat its own history: 'appealing to their painful memories of particular conflicts, it colours with an intense life all the details of the composition presented to consciousness'.[47] Political consciousness arises *in* the strike, and the acquisition of such consciousness is described in epiphanic terms: 'We thus obtain that intuition of socialism which language cannot give us with perfect clearness – and we obtain it as a whole, perceived instantaneously'.[48] In Sommerfield's novel, both these aspects are suggested in James Seton's sense of unity with the crowd. He finds in the demonstration the solution to his 'painful memories' of the failed revolt in Spain: 'I sink my identity into the calm

---

44   *Daily Worker*, 25 April 1936, p. 1. Reckitt 1936, p. 352. The strike is also an important narrative point in another novel of 1936, James Barke's *Major Operation*, discussed in Chapter Six.

45   Lennard 1936, p. 3.

46   Fox 1979, p. 136.

47   Sorel 1999, p. 118.

48   Ibid.

quietness of this waiting crowd, I am part of it, sharer in its strength ... and the solution of my conflicts is bound up with the fate of this mass' (213). Although the violent conclusion of the novel is suggestive of the limits of this possibility, Arthur Calder-Marshall made the case that this narrative tendency in socialist fiction was in fact a way of managing and transforming the reality of political violence: 'Taken in its wider context, it becomes an incident in the political education of the group, not the end of protest, but the beginning of militancy'.[49]

If this politicised commemoration is the expression of one of the two poles of the May Day tradition, that of political, rather than social, revolution, then Pat's feeling that there are 'new thoughts in people's minds' evokes the second possible meaning of the tradition: as a spontaneous community celebration of rebirth and renewal. This is a reading of the May Day tradition articulated in a *Left Review* editorial produced the following year by the poet Randall Swingler, which asked, 'What is the deepest concept in all art, the form on which our dramas and lyrics depend? It is the concept of struggle forged by men at work, by men and women joined in harmony in the struggle against Nature. It is the story of the death and re-birth of the Year'.[50] In *Left Review* in May 1938, Jack Lindsay argued that the May Day tradition was part of the deep structure of culture itself: it symbolises 'all that is joyous, vital, constructive in the tradition of human activity, cultural as well as productive'.[51] Lindsay stressed the unifying potential of this tradition, which he saw as a cultural expression of the fundamental relationship between man and nature, of 'his courageous attempts to merge dialectically with nature through work'.[52] The redemptive and revitalising qualities of the tradition give a kind of mythic underpinning to the novel's political plot, but it is a myth that is both available and useful to the characters. In James Seton, the frustrated desire for rebirth and renewal, reminiscent, especially, of *The Waste Land*, is explicitly redirected to a political goal: '[t]he trees had hung out flags of a foreign country to him, and he had got himself a new flag, the banner of a different spring, whose harvest would be plentiful – the spring of revolution' (74–5).

The unifying potential of May Day comes, therefore, from its popular utopianism, from its augmentation of reality by 'the desired, the possible' that Maxim Gorky identified as the essential structure of socialist realism, with which Sommerfield underwrites the novel's plot.[53] Lukács suggested that the

49   Calder-Marshall 1937a, p. 43.
50   Swingler 1937, p. 130.
51   Lindsay 1938c, p. 963.
52   Lindsay 1938c, p. 966.
53   Gorky 1935, p. 44.

representation of popular and revolutionary movements presented one of the greatest technical challenges for the novelist; characteristically, the relationship between the individual and the social collective is distorted so that 'the problems of popular life take on an abstract sociological, merely descriptive, lifeless and falsely objective character' and 'the popular movement appears as a homogeneously chaotic mass impelled by some mystical natural force'.[54] Sommerfield, while utilising the formalising potential of myth, seems anxious to avoid employing myth as a scripted or generic reality that characters can neither acknowledge nor control. *May Day*'s synchronised narrative, moving between different individuals and groups in urban space in a narrow time frame, dispenses with linear cause-and-effect to demonstrate how specific combinations of circumstances conspire to drive individuals towards a shared point of convergence. The novel thus writes against several conventions of urban writing, and particularly the mythic and mystical renderings of urban life in Woolf, Joyce and Eliot. Sommerfield critically rewrites the city against the conventions of alienation and the unknowable mass, a humanising process that Fredric Jameson envisages as 'the practical reconquest of a sense of place and the construction or reconstruction of an articulated ensemble which can be retained in memory and which the individual subject can map and remap along the moments of mobile, alternative trajectories'.[55] Perhaps the best counterpoint to *May Day*'s vision of the political possibilities of the modern city is Graham Greene's *It's A Battlefield* (1934), another novel concerned with the London working class and Communist politics. But Greene's London is a city of missed connections, in which characters fail to experience the solidarity in action that is the heart of Sommerfield's text. The novel's densely ironic structure reveals a world of arbitrary systems of exchange and murky, but always mundane, corruption. Characters are shown to be without hope of grasping the connections between them and the networks of power surrounding them: 'Oh, the pattern. No-one can understand the pattern', one character bleakly acknowledges (referring, with typical irony, to a crochet pattern).[56] In turn, Greene is rewriting the London of the classic detective novel, and especially of Conan Doyle's Sherlock Holmes, drawing instead a city that individual reason cannot penetrate and in which justice cannot be done. Against both these traditions, of the triumph of individual reason and of the despair of urban alienation, Sommerfield narrates a comprehensible, and hence transformable, city, aligning

54   Lukács 1976, p. 360.
55   F. Jameson 1991, p. 51.
56   Greene 1980, p. 120.

elements of resistant and emergent traditions, in Raymond Williams' terms, to suggest the beginnings of a new, popular organised politics.[57]

Conclusion

Although on its publication the *Times Literary Supplement* considered *May Day* simply 'communist propaganda in the form of fiction', I have tried to show here that the novel gives a politicised, materialist orientation to modernist themes and strategies not obviously compatible with the propagandist interpretation of socialist realism.[58] By contrast, Nick Hubble has argued that, given Karl Radek's denunciation of Joyce at the Soviet Writers' Congress, *May Day*'s 'overt usage of modernist techniques has to be seen as a deliberate act of defiance', but this, too, I would suggest, misrepresents British Marxists' relationships both with literary modernism and with Soviet-oriented socialist realism.[59] Sommerfield was clearly aware of the relationship between certain modernist techniques and a problematic politics, but the novel is dynamised by a confidence in the possibility of taking over and transforming those techniques and the perspectives that underpin them. In its quite nuanced understanding of a politics of modernist form, *May Day* may be said to articulate a deeper and more sophisticated critique of modernism than can be found in the work of Ralph Fox or Alick West, effecting the kind of absorption of modernism's critical power that British Marxist critics were unable to achieve. There are certainly moments when *May Day*'s confidence in its political messages drowns out its more subtle effects, but to read this, as Frank Kermode does, as a sign that Sommerfield was uncomfortable with his 'bourgeois' literary gifts and felt compelled to use them in the production of a kind of 'anti-bourgeois bourgeois novel', is to overstate the demands placed on writers during the Popular Front period in relation to the 'bourgeois' heritage.[60] This novel, then, may be seen as a site of important formal and critical debate, not merely a statement of defiance. This is a fact necessarily occluded by studies that have focused exclusively on critical writing in their considerations of British Marxists' literary politics.[61] *May Day* is, as its

---

57   R. Williams 1977, pp. 122–4.

58   *Times Literary Supplement* review quoted in Laing 1980, p. 147.

59   Hubble 2012, p. 140.

60   Kermode 1988, p. 95.

61   Bounds 2012 is the best example of this view; while detailed in its examination of important Marxist critics (chiefly Fox, West and Caudwell), it does not extend its perspective to the wider literary culture.

author admitted much later, idealistic to the point of naivety.[62] In this sense, it aligns itself with the utopian valence of socialist realism's commitment to 'the desired, the possible'. On the other hand, on May Day the following year, unprecedented strike action did break out in London, led by Communist transport workers but spreading to a wider movement, given urgency and vitality by the symbolic force of the bombing of Guernica a few days before.[63] In this sense, the novel functions as a kind of mythic model for energies and possibilities that did in fact exist, rather than as simple wishful thinking. The next chapter, however, extends this discussion of the politics of form and of the ideal and the realistic to a novel very preoccupied with wishful thinking, Arthur Calder-Marshall's *Pie in the Sky*, a text much more marked by anxieties about Stalinism and the repressive potential of realism, and much more doubtful of the transformative powers of language.

---

62   Sommerfield 2010, p. 243.
63   For an account of these events, see Saville 1977.

CHAPTER 3

Arthur Calder-Marshall, *Pie in the Sky* (1937)

In the previous chapter, the formal experiments of John Sommerfield's *May Day* were considered in terms of critical appropriations from the modernist repertoire which sought to give materialist bearings to High Modernist tropes while also dramatising aesthetic controversies. Sommerfield's novel is a product of a moment in which Communists were encouraged to mute vanguardist accents in order to emphasise the building of a mass movement; the collective narration and circulation of Communist language in the novel attempts to bind the city into a new, popular formation. The ability of the Communists' slogans to perform this connecting work exemplifies a faith in the existence of a radical, popular consensus that had only to be activated through language. *May Day* works to assert the capacity of traditional rites and practices to provide the ground for an overcoming of social fragmentation and the bridging of gaps between popular life and organised politics. This chapter considers another novel published by a Communist, Arthur Calder-Marshall's *Pie in the Sky*, which appeared in January 1937. The novel provides a useful counterpoint to Sommerfield's in so far as it explores comparable questions – questions of articulation and of how connections can be made – as well as adopting a collective form, moving through the perspectives of a variety of characters and adopting a range of modes, tones and formal devices. However, this novel is far more sceptical and conflicted than Sommerfield's about whether and how a unifying language could speak to and for a fragmented society.

The novel plots the intertwining stories of two families, the Yorkes and the Boltons, in a fictional industrial town. Carder Yorke has risen from working-class origins to become a factory owner, while his childhood friend, Henry Bolton, has remained a worker and been made unemployed by Carder during the Depression. The connection continues in the next generation, as Yorke's son Fenner, a journalist and writer, engages in a relationship with Bolton's Communist daughter, Caroline. Yorke's other son, Bernard, is a priggish bully who despises his father's relationships with women. These central figures are used to typify class and generational positions: Carder has benefited from the Great War and become middle class, while Henry has borne the brunt of the Depression in long-term unemployment. Caroline and Fenner are representatives of the educated young people (like Calder-Marshall) who turned to Communism under the threat of fascism and the lingering effects of the Depression; while Bernard – as I discuss below – is a proto-fascist, representing the 'most reactionary, most chauvinist' elements of the bourgeoisie.[1] The key outcome of the novel is Fenner's declaration of commitment to a new kind of writing, thus renouncing his earlier individualism. It is Fenner's struggle to this point that is the core of the text's intervention in questions of political aesthetics, and should be seen within Calder-Marshall's own developmental trajectory. In the introduction to this book, Calder-Marshall was described as something of an archetype of the fellow-travelling Communist of the thirties: educated at public school and Oxford, he was drawn to Communism before publicly breaking with it at the decade's close. It is easy to assume from his subsequent recantation that his commitments were superficial; nonetheless, the considerable energy he poured into his literary-political activities should at least suggest that he himself took his political engagements seriously, for however short a time.[2] He was a regular contributor to left-wing periodicals including *Left Review* and *Fact*, contributing an essay on narrative to *Fact*'s influential 'Writing in Revolt: Theory and Examples' edition.[3] He was closely connected with organisations such as the Left Book Club Writers Group, and a key part of Communist social life in London in the mid-thirties.[4] Like Sommerfield, he was an important influence on the social and literary life of Malcolm Lowry; in a publication commemorating Lowry, he recalled an eventful visit to Lowry's home in Mexico in 1937, shortly after *Pie in the Sky*'s publication, in which he describes himself as at that time 'frightfully, boringly Communist', and that Lowry used 'all the boring bits' for his Communist character, Hugh, in *Under the Volcano*.[5]

Calder-Marshall's strongest statements on what he took to be the role of the novel in political struggle and the responsibilities of the Communist writer were published during 1937. These include his essay in *Fact* and his collection of essays on social topics, *The Changing Scene*, in which he closely echoes Ralph Fox and, to a certain extent, the programme of socialist realism more generally. These commitments were, however, relatively new for Calder-Marshall. I will suggest that *Pie in the Sky*, published in January 1937, is a text bearing out the transition of his thinking between his contribution to Geoffrey Grigson's symposium *The Arts To-Day* (published in September 1935) and his volume of essays on social and cultural subjects, *The Changing Scene* (published in July 1937). In his contribution to Grigson's collection, Calder-Marshall is chiefly concerned with two related topics: the after-effects of the First World War, and

---

1   Dimitrov 1935a, p. 10.
2   Calder-Marshall's break with Communism was announced in Calder-Marshall 1941, pp. 157–8.
3   Calder-Marshall 1937a, pp. 38–44.
4   Croft 2002, pp. 70–1.
5   Calder-Marshall 1985, p. 113.

the collapse of religious belief. The collapse of faith in God, he thought, led to 'a disbelief in the goodness of the parent', which in turn led to a 'union of the children to take over the task of self-preservation', a generational revolt he saw manifest in both Communism and fascism.[6] This generational conflict within British society was exacerbated by the stalled progress of post-war reconstruction. The 'uneventfulness' of the immediate years after the war, Calder-Marshall thought, had provided no outlet for the emotions the war had stirred; the 'problems of reconstruction, which might have provided a release of national feeling, if properly organised, were shelved'.[7] Without 'the old neurotic outlet', either in war or in the peaceful rebuilding of the country, the British people were 'faced again with their own neuroses'.[8] The crisis posed by the thirties provided an opportunity to divert those neuroses into social action: 'The war within the self can be postponed in face of objective war and the fear of it'.[9] In the same essay, he identifies two tendencies within fiction that would secure the future of the novel against the threat of what he considers vapid and commercialised 'fictioneering', in which the 'desire to amuse, soothe or terrify has supplanted the ability to feel, sympathise and judge'.[10] One tendency, represented by Joyce, Lawrence and Kafka, is towards the 'deepening of the novel'; the other, represented by Dos Passos's novels and Alfred Döblin's *Berlin Alexanderplatz*, is towards the 'broadening' of it.[11] Calder-Marshall suggests – but does not make explicit – that the novel has a role to play in the reversal of the inward turn provoked by the failure of post-war national reconstruction; literature must re-establish contact 'with the centre of English life' in order to overcome the 'split between the artist and his public', moving to an envisioned point beyond modernism.[12] The publication of this essay in 1935 coincided with the appearance of Calder-Marshall's novel *Dead Centre*, which presents something of a corollary of the essay's argument. *Dead Centre* examines the collapse of bourgeois culture through the lens of a fictional public school, Richbury; the 'dead centre' of the title refers to the school's most brilliant pupil, who was killed in the war and from whose death the school's masters are

---

6   Calder-Marshall 1935b, p. 119.

7   Calder-Marshall 1935b, p. 121.

8   Ibid.

9   Calder-Marshall 1935b, p. 122.

10   Calder-Marshall 1935b, p. 124.

11   Calder-Marshall 1935b, p. 146. Kafka's work began to be translated by the Scottish writers
      Willa and Edwin Muir in the early 1930s, beginning with *The Castle* (Martin Secker, 1930).

12   Calder-Marshall 1935b, pp. 147–8.

unable to recover in an atmosphere of emotional repression.[13] The climate is one of morbidity, expressed both in a curricular fixation with 'dead languages and dead people' (58) and the compulsive war games of the Officer Training Corps (164). The 'dead centre' is also, however, reflected in the novel's structure, composed of 70 short first-person chapters providing limited perspectives that revolve around, without ever articulating, the great silences and traumas – war, sexual and emotional repression – at the novel's core. *Dead Centre* sees no way of connecting these fragments of experience or of breaking out of the cycles of neurotic repetition.

The question of how to break out and 'reconnect' in his own work would be the central problem in Calder-Marshall's work for the remainder of the decade. The problem of the relationship between individual neuroses and political action would be a particular preoccupation in *Pie in the Sky*. In his 1935 essay, Calder-Marshall privileges psychoanalysis as the means of traversing the impasse, arguing that there is 'no part of life on which psycho-analysis ... cannot throw light' and that it provides superior insights to both Marxism and fascism, encompassing 'the whole mental life of man'.[14] Furthermore, he seems in passing to express scepticism about Marxist criticism, noting in relation to Granville Hicks's pioneering study of American fiction, *The Great Tradition*, that 'it must be remembered that his measure is not literary but Marxist'.[15] By 1937, in the essays published in *Fact* and *The Changing Scene*, a markedly different position is in evidence. Though reiterating his earlier belief that bourgeois culture was in a state of paralysed morbidity, he now felt that writers were moving towards a new, invigorating situation. They had divided themselves into three camps: those who advocated fascism, those who 'hoped to maintain capitalism without resorting to fascism'; and 'those who identified themselves with the working-class movement for international socialism'.[16] This is a very characteristic analysis from the perspective of the Popular Front: it isolates fascism as the reaction of minority, and suggests that the second group might conceivably be won over by the third.[17] The realignment of middle-class writers is partly a political matter, a realisation that their interests lie 'ultimately nearer to the working than to the ruling class', but it is also an aspiration to recapture the perspective that *Dead Centre* shows to be inaccessible to

---

13   Calder-Marshall 1935a. Page references are hereafter given in parentheses in the text.
14   Calder-Marshall 1935b, p. 133.
15   Calder-Marshall 1935b, p. 149.
16   Calder-Marshall 1937c, p. 115.
17   Ibid.

them, since 'the only class in this country which sees these things realistically is the working-class'.[18] These developments promised a way out of the over-specialisation and isolation he discussed in his 1935 essay through a broad, typifying approach: '[w]here the bourgeois novelists have been driven to the pursuit of the abnormal, the perverted or the minute, in order to find fresh material, the revolutionary is concerned with the normal and typical in his portraiture of society as a whole'.[19] In the same essay, Calder-Marshall made the compressed and very Lukácsian claim that '[r]evolutionary literature is objective, is classical in its interest in the type rather than the exception, is epic in its direct approach to life'.[20] In the first of these statements in particular, there is certainly a troubling potential – as there is in Fox's *The Novel and the People* – for the kind of normativity and conformism for which socialist realism, as state doctrine, is notorious.[21] But it is fair to recognise that Calder-Marshall is attempting to solve problems he had posed in the 1935 essay; the need for characters to be 'judged simply' is proposed as a method of avoiding the potentially endless circularities of 'infantile fixations'.[22] Moreover, in *Pie in the Sky*, it is clear that Calder-Marshall's idea of what constitutes 'the normal and typical' turns out to be the neurotic, traumatised, inarticulate, corrupt, mean and contradictory. The emphasis on the normality of neurotic cycles and routines, however, brings into question the validity of the claim that only the working class sees things 'realistically', since working-class and middle-class characters alike are shown to be locked in emotional patterns that evade rather than confront reality.

This tension – between an acceptance of the people 'as they are', as Dimitrov proposed, and an assertion that individual particularism could be transcended in a new perspective – manifests itself in important ways in Calder-Marshall's attitudes to language.[23] In his contribution to *Fact*, Calder-Marshall sugges-ted the centrality of language to his vision of how revolutionary fiction should work. The language of the middle class, he thought, was replete with 'abstract

---

18   Calder-Marshall 1937c, p. 241.

19   Calder-Marshall 1937c, p. 116.

20   Calder-Marshall 1937c, p. 117. Among those Calder-Marshall considered 'revolutionary writers' were Sommerfield, Storm Jameson and Ralph Bates, as well as John Dos Passos, André Malraux and Ignacio Silone.

21   Katerina Clark notes the socialist realist novel was a 'parabolic' form, the conformity of which to established patterns performed key functions in 'highly ritualized, intensely citational Stalinist society': Clark 1995, p. 28.

22   Calder-Marshall 1937c, p. 117.

23   Dimitrov 1935b, p. 21.

and Latinised substitutes for plain speech'.[24] Middle-class expression was stifled by 'the desire for euphemism, false social dignity and class conformity'.[25] What was needed to revive it was 'the alliance of writers with the working class and the recruitment of writers from that class'.[26] There is of course great naivety in this investment in the resistance of working-class language to conformism and conventionality, its apparently greater and more authentic expressive power. *Pie in the Sky* appears to work through this problem in its complex handling of language and its class implications. The 1935 essay establishes important themes that recur in *Pie in the Sky*: society's need to adjust to the end of religion; the displacement or sublimation of neuroses into political action; and the question of the writer's relationship with the wider society. In the 1937 texts, the work of a by-then self-identified 'revolutionary' writer, we see firm articulations of positions that the novel is more hesitant and conflicted about. The critical texts of 1937 articulate two demands: the first, for a rejection of the conformism of middle-class language; the second, a demand for breadth and typicality, the depiction of the 'normal'. The subplots involving the Communist characters in *Pie in the Sky*, on the one hand, and the proto-fascist Bernard Yorke, on the other, locate the main, 'typical' characters in the middle ground between these positions; implicitly, the novel stakes the possibility of a mass movement for socialism and against fascism on the fates of the unexceptional Fenner, Carder, Caroline and Henry.

Bathos and Narrative Convention

Calder-Marshall's 1935 essay is preoccupied by the consequences of a loss of religious faith, and the question of where impulses once directed towards religious concerns should now be channelled. By 1937, he claimed that the bourgeois novelist is interested in what distinguishes his characters, the 'revolutionary in what unites them'.[27] The question, however, of what shared meanings and common interests exist in a modern, secular society is one the novel is hesitant to answer. In one key episode, the isolated writer, Fenner Yorke, goes on a Tube journey that brings into focus the problems of secularised life. Fenner experiences the technology of the mass transportation system as a consuming

---

24   Calder-Marshall 1937a, p. 40.

25   Ibid.

26   Ibid.

27   Calder-Marshall 1937c, p. 117.

monster: 'Fenner put his left foot first on to smooth ribs, flowing between steel teeth, his whole weight on the growing stair', perceiving the escalator as 'heavy with hungry workers'.[28] This mass of individuals appears as 'two bands of human bodies travelling downwards like gliding angels' (260). Fenner's perspective is detached but not perceptive; what is conspicuously lacking are the authoritative, aerial perspectives of *May Day* which affirmed that novel's confidence in the clarity and compass of its vision – '*Let us take factory chimneys, cannons trained at dingy skies, pointing at the sun and stars*'.[29] There is a hint in Fenner's perspective of such a possibility in the 'gliding angels', since winged figures were often associated with such a view in the writing of the thirties.[30] But the city Fenner encounters is divested of the possibility of such sublime detachment and privileged perspectives; he ironically reflects on the mass movement of people as an expression of the modern city as de-sacralised:

> 'This is our Canterbury Pilgrimage', he thought, 'everybody going down escalators, holding in their hands copies of the *Star*, *Standard* or *News*, looking for Low, news of Abyssinia, and who won the three-thirty. This being packed into trains … is our "homeward plods the ploughman".'
>
> p. 260

Fenner misremembers the Thomas Gray line, as though to suggest that the omnivorous popular culture represented by the Tube in both its monstrous and technocratic aspects inevitably chews over or adapts the text of the past.[31] Gray's 'Elegy' was posited by William Empson as an exemplar of a certain type of pastoral in which class difference is naturalised.[32] The suggestion here, however, is of shared rites that lack shared meanings. It is not class difference that is suppressed, but the recognition of individuality: Fenner reflects that '[i]t was difficult to understand that beneath each hat a separate brain produced its rationalizations … It was difficult to realize from so many same-seeming faces going home to similar houses, each was an entity peculiar and important' (260).

---

28   Calder-Marshall 1937b, p. 260. Page references are hereafter given in parentheses in the text.

29   Sommerfield 2010, p. 25; emphasis in original.

30   Cunningham 1988, pp. 155–6.

31   The 'Low' referred to is David Low, the cartoonist who created the satirical Colonel Blimp for the *Evening Standard*; the cartoon reflected the growing anti-establishment sentiment and was a crucial part of a politically engaged popular culture in the thirties.

32   Empson 1968, pp. 4–6.

Adding to the already clichéd images, Fenner is 'slapped' in the eyes by adverts for a production of *Murder in the Cathedral* and a scrap of poster emblazoned with 'Dante's Inferno' (260), adopting the conventional image of the Tube as both an infernal monster and a central space for the dissemination of popular culture.[33] *Dante's Inferno* was the title of a 1935 film (directed by Harry Lachman) that recast Dante's epic in a modern, secularised setting, in which 'Dante's Inferno' is the name of a fairground attraction. T.S. Eliot's *Murder in the Cathedral* was the subject of an early television broadcast in 1936.[34] Thus the literary texts to which these posters seem to refer have already been converted into the reproducible products of popular culture – detached, in Water Benjamin's terms, from the domain of tradition.[35] The routine and banal expressions of a prosaic, demythologised modernity are attended by the crowd's failure to recognise and connect with one another.

The social rite of pilgrimage, the idea of an inherently meaningful journey, is bathetically (and pathetically) depreciated in the unemployed Henry's consciously futile tramp to Glasgow: 'Everybody knew there wasn't any work going … But everybody else went. It was a sort of Mecca' (341). Rather than a purposeful, ritualised progression, with its connotations of meaningful experience of space and time, the trek to Glasgow has become a desperate expression of the commonplace search for work in economic crisis. In these depreciatory allusions to religious rites, Calder-Marshall is clearly working against a certain rhetorical tendency in thirties literature – especially poetry – that adopted an aggrandising language of religion. In C. Day Lewis's *The Magnetic Mountain* (1933), for example, the 'day excursionists' are clearly depicted as on a pilgrimage out of the 'cursed towns': 'Know you seek a new world, a saviour to establish/ Long-lost kinship and restore the blood's fulfilment'.[36] The poem anticipates revolutionary possibility in these newly sacralised acts. *Pie in the Sky* features a comparable scene:

> See now the clerks change the pen for the wheel, forge out from the suburb, freighted with wife and kiddies: see the athletic bachelor start up the low-slung roadster, picturing himself the young man of advertisement, hero of a joke in the Happy Mag; or poorer, see him leap on mo'bike,

33   David Welsh attributes these two versions of the underground in the popular imagination to George Gissing and H.G. Wells respectively: Welsh 2010, pp. 65–6, pp. 144–5.

34   Iannucci 2010, p. 248; Chinitz 2003, p. 136.

35   Benjamin 2007, p. 221.

36   Day Lewis 1964b, p. 50.

goggles to eyes and cuty on the pillion. Let her out, lad, give the gong-
sters run for you money; take chance of death, you whom a desk chained
to safety five days and a half, only danger haemorrhoids.

> p. 274

While Day Lewis's day-trippers 'go out alone, on tandem or on pillion' in search
of 'a new world', the characters in Calder-Marshall's scene are in search of
the glamour of the world of advertising. Rod Mengham has described these
imperative-laden constructions, as exemplified in the early Auden, as a 'rhetoric of apostrophe' that rests on an assumption of 'exclusive, Masonic knowledge'.[37] In Jack Lindsay's poems for mass declamation, on the other hand, the
same rhetoric is used with the intention of forging a connection to an account
of history, a technique Michelle Weinroth has described as a form of the sublime.[38] But here, clearly, there is a fall into bathos – sublime's opposite, as Tyrus
Miller notes.[39] The narrative voice does not venture to augment everyday reality with the vestments of an inherently meaningful world; instead, the bathetic
fall indicates a circumscribed, banal reality.

The transactional logic of sacrifice is clearly demonstrated to be implicated
in class oppression as the unemployed Henry Bolton prides himself on having worked and made sacrifices for his family and for his country in fighting in
the First World War, while his childhood friend, Carder Yorke, father of Fenner,
fought for his own interests and became a capitalist (31). Henry's realisation
that, in fact, he has been exploited and oppressed all along, and that the emotional routines of duty and sacrifice have merely been defence mechanisms, is
extremely painful. He consciously refuses to give up the sacrificial account of
his life, even after he realises that '[i]t meant he'd been swindled, when he'd
done anything he thought was good and when he went out to fight, it wasn't
Carder Yorke was a coward and he brave, but Yorke wasn't a fool and he was.
He didn't want to think that' (339). Here, the two themes of Calder-Marshall's
1935 essay intersect: the failure of post-war reconstruction, which entrenched
division instead of channelling the emotions evoked into a project of national
transformation (the unmade 'land fit for heroes' of popular mythology), and
the lingering influence of sacralised modes of thought.[40] But there is a tension
between this account of the way that insight is forestalled by individual trauma
and Calder-Marshall's later, bluntly 'revolutionary' claim that 'the only class in

---

37   Mengham 2004, pp. 373–4.
38   Weinroth 1996, pp. 190–3.
39   Miller 2010, p. 54.
40   Calder-Marshall 1935b, p. 151.

this country which sees these things realistically is the working-class'.[41] Such a perspective is not immediately available. Moreover, despite Calder-Marshall's suggestion in his *Fact* essay that working-class speech resisted the obfuscations and repressions of middle-class language, Henry is disarticulated by his experiences.[42] He experiences something of a political revelation while he is on the road looking for work, but his power of language is crippled by the shame of being complicit in his own exploitation. He imagines telling his wife what he has discovered about his exploitation, 'But he never completed any speech because the memory of his cringing and urselicking spurting up choked him for words to say what a dam' fool he'd been all these years' (346). The novel implies that the process of recovering the power of articulation will be painful and possibly incomplete.

Failures of Articulation

Henry's resistance to the truth about his oppression raises questions of how such truths can be successfully recognised in language. Fenner, growing disillusioned with the Communism he begins the novel committed to, argues that one of the problems in persuading the mass of people to commit to a class politics is, in effect, that there is kind of security, an emotional routine, involved in being poor: 'There's sacrifice in the pinching and scraping. In being out of work there's a good reason for grumbling', so that it is possible that even if their material conditions were improved 'they would be faced with an inward lack' (73). There is an important contrast to be drawn with Sommerfield's *May Day*, in which, as I suggested in the previous chapter, the Communist slogans are figured as bringing to the surface repressed realities so as to activate a latent popular consensus. In such a process of activism Sommerfield's novel locates the transformation and realisation of the self, as in Jimmy Seton's apprehension that 'the solution of my conflicts is bound up with the fate of this mass' (213). *Pie in the Sky* seems to actively satirise such a utopian vision of communication, as the messages of the Communist characters fail to make themselves heard:

> No demonstrator shot revolutionary fire from his eyes. None was hawk or helmeted airman. Shabby drabby, lumpy and dumpy, straggly frumpy,

---

41   Calder-Marshall 1937c, p. 241.
42   Calder-Marshall 1937a, p. 40.

they shuffled along, wearing dress-me-down macs and Woolworth socks
and ordinary hats, like a poor funeral.
But there were the banners.
The Menace of Moscow
The Red Hand of Russia
FASCISM MEANS WAR
     p. 64

Here the 'hawk and helmeted airman' alludes to Auden's 'Consider this and in
our time'; aerial perspectives – those of birds and airmen – were associated with
authority and superior perspectives, as in Auden's early verse which, Keith Williams points out, combines the 'privileged perspectives of both camera-eyed
airman and sovietised Marxist in its bid for a thirties sublime'.[43] A comparable use of such winged figures appears in Rex Warner's *The Wild Goose Chase*,
published a few months after *Pie in the Sky*. Warner's novel narrates his hero's
pursuit of the wild geese which symbolise utopian possibility.[44] Ultimately the
hero, George, rejects the idealistic promise of the geese as a quixotic endeavour – as the title suggests – and commits himself instead to working practically
for revolution. Warner depreciates the possibility of a utopian unity of individual and society through bathos; the attempt by the questing protagonist,
George, to deliver a lecture on the nobility of 'fanaticism' degenerates into
inarticulacy as the audience collapses into laughter. The message cannot be
delivered.[45] The messages in the passage in *Pie in the Sky* quoted above likewise collapse bathetically into inarticulacy: the slogans declare 'Workers Unite
to Smash Fascism and War' but what the audience hears is '... Wurble blahble
flewble flurble ... Ooble Tooble Turlin' (64). Calder-Marshall is working against
the prospect of perfect, immediately radicalising articulation envisioned in
May Day, premised on the assumption that a slogan can span the gaps between
speakers and listeners. Moreover, there is no sign here of the work of tradition
and myth, which function in *May Day* to condition a certain context in which
rhetorical success – rather than bathetic failure – might occur.

    However, in its bathetic strategy, the novel is also reacting against a fictional
mode of presentation in which marchers and demonstrators were depicted as
signs not of specific social and economic problems, but of some metaphysical, transhistorical condition. In Dot Allan's Glasgow novel, *Hunger March*, for

43   K. Williams 1996, p. 9.

44   R. Warner 1990.

45   R. Warner 1990, p. 185.

example, published in 1934 at the height of popular demonstrations against Depression conditions, the march of the title appears as 'a shuffling mob trailing half-heartedly at the heels of their leaders; a mob wasting its strength in shouts of imprecation, in paroxysms of passion as objectless as they are pitiful to behold'.[46] Allan's detached characters look on and ask, wonderingly, 'had they assembled here of their own free will with the object of displaying, as Eastern beggars do, their sores to the world?'[47] This kind of awed pity is dispelled by Calder-Marshall through the descent into farce. His handling of the mass demonstration might therefore be considered a form of representational moderation, resisting the more excessive and optimistic accents of leftist fiction while also seeking to subvert a passive, spectacular mode. If this is considered as an example of the 'normal' and 'typical' portrayal Calder-Marshall advocated in *The Changing Scene*, such a strategy may amount less to a valorisation of the conventional as to a deflation of more hubristic modes of writing.

The normalisation of rhetorical failure and disarticulation in the novel means that characters' fantasies are frequently fantasies of articulation. Henry imagines himself coming before the Public Assistance Committee: 'I'll say you're all bastards and you're the biggest bastard, Carder Yorke' (33), but in reality says no such thing. Carder Yorke begins writing a revealing letter to his son, 'writing down things he had done, had thought, but hidden even from himself', but tears it up and sends a banal postcard instead (299). The significance of these language issues to Popular Front anti-fascism becomes clear in the characterisation of Carder's bullied and bullying son, Bernard, the character most afflicted by fantasies of articulation, and whose stammering represents his conflicted desire to both speak and not speak. The characterisation of Bernard demonstrates clearly the influence on the text of Calder-Marshall's interest in psychoanalysis during this period.[48] There is a clear implication in Bernard's relationship with his father that, as Calder-Marshall claims, distrust in the parent – a consequence of the breakdown of faith – would lead to a 'union of the children' taking either a fascist or a Communist form.[49] At his first appearance in the novel Bernard is rehearsing to himself an admonishment of his father for his promiscuity – 'have you no regard for ethical considerations?' – but he is completely unable to articulate his outrage when actually speaking to Carder (11). Bernard, much more than his father and brother, relies on the stability of

---

46   Allan 2010, p. 203.

47   Allan 2010, p. 370.

48   In an autobiographical piece published in 1939, Calder-Marshall described undergoing psychoanalysis in 1933: Calder-Marshall 1939, p. 100.

49   Calder-Marshall 1935b, p. 119.

the class structure to provide him with a sense of identity, and he is tormented by sexual fantasies about one of the women at his father's mill, fantasies that elide sex and speech: 'He shut out the fantasy of the barriers broken and he took her to the shade of a wall and said, "My angel, my heart's-ease, queen, queen of love, queen of all earth beauty", knowing all the time that she was trash' (251). In the figure of Bernard, inarticulacy and psychosexual wounding conspire to sow the seeds of fascism. His fantasies are those of barriers broken – barriers of class, sexual inhibition and inarticulacy – that cannot be realised because of a failure to construct an utterance that can span the gaps between classes. His failure to effectively construct discursive authority leads directly to authoritarianism: '[a]s it was, he was forced into being a disciplinarian, to avoid being a clown' (301). In a predictably Freudian manner, when he does speak his repressed aggression makes itself apparent: 'when he tried to crack a joke, for some reason there was always a second meaning to it ... a meaning which was a slight, an insult or a gibe' (303). His behaviour creates a cycle of bullying, since the more disciplinarian he becomes, 'the more justified the antagonism which had been instinctive at first' comes to seem (302). Bernard's bullying and neurotic nature has real political consequences as he becomes a figure of incipient fascism and his management causes an intensification of class tensions in the mill, resulting in an alignment of skilled and unskilled workers: 'now the enemy was within: not the competitor or rival business, but the employer, the man at the top. Even Joynson [the foreman], whose technical training had led him to identify his interests with Carder's, began to veer over to his subordinates' (302). The development described here (in a somewhat awkwardly direct manner) mirrors the Popular Front analysis of fascism as the strategy of the most reactionary of the capitalist class, producing an increase in class tensions that could be channelled into the formation of an anti-fascist front. Like Sommerfield, Calder-Marshall differentiates between his bourgeois characters to isolate the most reactionary and so indicate a space for class alliance.

Given the entanglement of language in neuroses and delusion, the question of how truth can be articulated is, unsurprisingly, a vexing one. One focus of this problem is the Communist characters, who, unlike Sommerfield's Communists, show no clearer insight into social problems than other characters, and are just as wrought by self-delusion and repression. Indeed, at points the novel invokes and satirically dismisses already clichéd socialist realist motifs: the young Communist Alexey 'stared before him – into the Future – thinking the girl's eyes shone before him like dark pools of mockery, thinking she was the girl to ride beside him on his tractor, driving a straight furrow towards the sunset' (64). The substance of Fenner's objection to Marxism is that it lacks 'psychological realism' (22), and he voices resistance to the emergent personality cult of Stalinism: 'The difference between us and the totalitarian states is not that we're more civilized, cultured or whatever, but we can't believe in the divine inspiration of human beings' (21). Fenner rails against the cultish attachment to Russia and the dishonest writing that promotes it: 'Don't read Radek's panegyrics. Read Zoshenko. He writes of the real Russia: and by God, it's dreary' (72). This anxiety about Russia is not limited to Fenner, but finds expression in the description of the atmosphere at a Communist meeting:

> Heads bent forward. Dialectical materialism. Surplus values. Imperial exploitation. Glasgow. India. The N.E.P. Rosie put sugar on the tables in cups that had lost their, Defence of Civil Liberties, handles for those who wanted it, while Comrade Deuteropopoff holding the coffee bottle, Ugh, Lansbury, Pacifism, in his hand, made more and more, If we can win over the Forces, at threepence a cup. There is no denying that the liberty of the individual is greater in Russia than … The zinc bowl of the till grew heavy with warm pennies. Zinoviev. Zinoviev. Everything was going very well. Lenin's Tomb. And the Third International. And the Fourth, the permanent revolution. Tuesday was always the busiest night of the week. Though Caesarism, the worship of emperors by eastern peoples, is not the same as reverence for world heroes, fighters for liberty.
>
> p. 26

The reference to Zinoviev attests to the growing disquiet over the increasingly conspicuous political violence in the Soviet Union, although this is not explicitly discussed in the text.[50] While Sommerfield's novel is buoyed by the optimism of the election of Popular Front governments, Calder-Marshall's is the product of a more troubling climate in which the war in Spain showed no signs of ending with a Republican victory, the violence and repression in the Soviet Union was undeniably escalating, and Mussolini had declared victory in Abyssinia. In the passage above, Calder-Marshall is clearly indicating that Communists were trying to effectively repress criticism of the Soviet Union, but that the repressed was continually and inevitably making its return. The tailing off into ellipsis of the sentence about liberty in Russia is another ironic acknowledgement of worries about the direction of the Soviet Union, as is the excusatory reference to 'Caesarism', which acknowledges the real nature

---

50   Grigory Zinoviev was executed in August 1936 following a show trial at which he was found morally complicit in the murder of Sergei Kirov, the event which occasioned the start of the Great Purge: Brendon 2000, pp. 398–400.

of Stalin's leadership even as it tries to suppress it. The question of dictatorship in the Soviet Union was much discussed in the wake of the first Moscow Trial in the summer of 1936, and commentary from the Communist left often evoked the Soviet constitution of 1936 (the so-called 'Stalin Constitution') as assurance against claims of dictatorship. Beatrice and Sidney Webb's *Soviet Communism* (1937) reproduced the new constitution in full as evidence for the legality and constitutionalism of the new phase in Soviet politics: 'It is clear that, in form, there is nothing in the constitution of the USSR at all resembling the Roman office of dictator; or, indeed, any kind of government by the will of a single person. On the contrary, the universal pattern shows even an exaggerated devotion to collegiate decision'.[51]

Stephen Spender, meanwhile, declared that Article 131, condemning 'enemies of the people', was the foundation stone of political freedom. 'Above it, the whole structure may be repressive, but it will always be possible gradually to knock away the repressive laws and establish complete political freedom.'[52] It was for the credulity of their faith in the power of the document that Leon Trotsky attacked the Webbs' book, dismissing their belief that simply producing texts and blueprints will somehow bring into being the state of affairs those texts describe:

> Instead of relating what has been achieved and in what direction the achieved is developing, the authors expound for twelve hundred pages what is contemplated, indicated in the bureaus, or expounded in the laws. Their conclusion is: When the projects, plans and laws are carried out, then communism will be realized in the Soviet Union.[53]

What the Webbs and Spender had failed – or were unable – to recognise was that, as Katerina Clark argues, Soviet official language 'no longer sought to convey real information'; it was no longer constative but chiefly 'symbolic'.[54] Although *Pie in the Sky* appeared before Spender's book, and before Trotsky's *The Revolution Betrayed* was translated, Calder-Marshall's anxieties about what was happening to language under Soviet Communism are nonetheless apparent.[55] In this light, the frequent ellipses, silences and interruptions that char-

---

51   Webb and Webb 1937, p. 428.
52   Spender 1937, p. 260.
53   Trotsky 2004, p. 228.
54   Clark 1995, pp. 30–1.
55   The first English translation of *The Revolution Betrayed*, by Max Eastman, was published by Doubleday in 1937.

acterise *Pie in the Sky* attest to a discomfort with the prospect of a totalising discourse, and directly challenge the assumption of a simple correspondence between world and word. Language in Calder-Marshall's novel is fluid and contingent; the bathetic effects of the Communist slogans are, as Miller puts it in relation to Auden's bathetic strategies, 'socially necessary', that is, they refuse to erase or repress the existence of a socially complex context in which such messages cannot be immediately or unproblematically received.[56]

The question of how intellectuals can engage with such a disunited social context, and with a society in which political consciousness may be blocked by personal neuroses, is rehearsed through the figure of the journalist Fenner Yorke. At first, Fenner demands a purely rational politics free of neurotic undertones (22), and, when that is not available, retreats into isolation and passivity (73). Finally – though the novel is never fully clear about the catalyst for the transformation – he reconnects with society through a renunciation of privileged individuality: 'Now he saw himself more clearly, as a person of great importance to himself, of lesser and lessening importance to friends and acquaintances, a useful enemy, a cipher to strangers, a foreigner to Frenchmen' (459). Fenner's realisation of the social, rather than metaphysical, construction of identity provokes something of a literary epiphany and he begins writing a novel, one which would reflect his new self-image and confront the problems of representation *Pie in the Sky* itself rehearses:

> Well, you know a wire cable is made of a lot of strands of wire twisted together. The novelist like Dickens picks out one strand and says, 'Here's this man's life'. What I want to do is cut the cable and shew all the threads interrelated ... A world full of purposes that cancel out: subject to rigid determinism yet always surprising: barbarous and yet noble: extravagant and yet limited.
>
> p. 330

Fenner imagines writing short texts strung together: 'That would get the effect I want, the large order of chaos, a mosaic of small conflicting pieces' (330). This apprehension marks Fenner's transition from being a journalist who, rather than voicing popular feeling, renders people inarticulate – Caroline tells him, 'that's why I couldn't speak: you kept strangling me with your brain' (44) – into a writer within society, perceiving a world that is prosaic and limited and yet which retains grandeur and extravagance. What is interesting about

---

56   Miller 2010, p. 51.

this vision of a fictive text is that it corresponds to Calder-Marshall's critical writing in a way that *Pie in the Sky* as a whole does not. Fenner's literary development in the final pages closely shadows Calder-Marshall's prescription for revolutionary writing published in *Fact*, in which he suggests that the novelist 'has to realize that neither he himself nor any of his characters is at the centre of the universe' in order to adopt a 'composite method'.[57] Such a method would generate a total picture of society, and, echoing Fox, follow a typifying method of characterisation.[58] The novel seems to invoke such an aesthetic goal at its conclusion as a potential solution to the problems it has raised; but the solution is only given at the level of one character's individual realisation. Indeed, Fenner himself is sceptical about whether the envisioned text could successfully break out of the routines the novel has depicted: 'Everybody hates anybody who says anything new and quite rightly. It's one more thing to be learnt: another task set to suffering humanity with no holiday to do it in' (331). Although glimpsing the prospect of a popular literary form that can speak successfully to a disunited, confused and neurotic society, the novel itself maintains a sceptical distance from its realisation.

Conclusion

Jack Lindsay suggested in 1937 that it was only through an engagement with Marxism that writers could hope to overcome their alienation from popular life, and in so doing capture something of the significance of the realist novel at the height of its powers. It is Marxism, Lindsay argued, that 'restores to [the writer] his completeness, his objectivity'.[59] Calder-Marshall is a useful example of a writer who moved from a socially engaged but consciously apolitical stance in 1935, in which he registered the need for cultural change without committing himself to it, to a self-declared 'revolutionary' position in 1937. *Pie in the Sky*, in its closing scene of aesthetic speculation, is drawn to the potential of Marxism to furnish a complete picture of reality. This closing moment suggests that, for all its scepticism, the novel ultimately keeps faith with the possibility of a collective form: but its commitment is made on the level of plot, in the form of an imaginary text. This solution retains an ambiguity largely absent from Sommerfield's version of a collective novel; *Pie in the Sky* is cut by rhetorical

---

57   Calder-Marshall 1937a, pp. 42–4.
58   Calder-Marshall 1937c, p. 116.
59   Lindsay 1937c, p. 51.

failures and ironies, by an apprehension of the contingencies of language and identity that could not obviously be solved (only repressed) by the type of realism it envisages. Calder-Marshall wrote in 1937 of the middle class moving hesitantly towards the alignment of its interests with those of the working class, and declared that 'it is to that section of the middle class and the working class that I, and a great many other writers, address ourselves'.[60] The form in which that bridging of classes and that mutuality of interests might be articulated remains, however, beyond the reach of the novel discussed here. As the next part of this book will suggest, Marxist interventions into the writing of history and the historical novel provide some of the most significant attempts at resolving the problem of how a divided society might be addressed in the name of collective action.

---

60   Calder-Marshall 1937c, p. 119.

PART 2

History and the Historical Novel

∵

History and the Historical Novel

When Georgi Dimitrov expounded the need for ideological struggle against fascism at the Comintern's Seventh Congress, he stressed the central importance of national histories and traditions, both as the stake in that struggle and as the site and means of resistance. The fascists, Dimitrov argued, appropriated national cultural traditions, 'rummaging through the entire *history* of every nation' so as to position themselves as heirs to the national past.[1] It fell therefore to the Communists and their anti-fascist allies to formulate an ideological response, to 'enlighten the masses on the past of their people in a historically correct fashion' and to 'link up the present struggle with the people's revolutionary traditions and past'.[2] The neglect of this ideological task allowed fascism to control and manipulate deeply felt popular sentiments, posing as 'heirs and continuators of all that was exalted and heroic' in the national past.[3] For the international Communist movement, this entailed the downplaying of internationalism in favour of what Kevin Morgan calls 'acclimatised internationalism', situating themselves within national and sometimes nationalist cultural narratives.[4] The French Communist leader Maurice Thorez, whose country had experienced a failed fascist coup in Paris in 1934, exemplified the new line in his declaration that, 'We claim for the working class the revolutionary heritage of the Jacobins and the Paris Commune. We do not hand over to the enemy the tri-colour flag and the "Marseillaise"'.[5]

This chapter considers British Marxists' readings and writings of English history and examines how the turn towards national cultural resources and the principle of class alliance was negotiated in non-fiction and the novel. The production of historical texts as totalising national stories served the crucial ideological function of asserting that the progressive sections of the bourgeoisie and the working class had mutual interests in the defeat of fascism. These attempts have been criticised in the strongest terms as legitimating bourgeois perspectives and suppressing the limits and contradictions inherent in

1   Dimitrov 1935b, p. 69; emphasis in original.
2   Dimitrov 1935b, p. 70.
3   Dimitrov 1935b, p. 69.
4   Morgan 1989, p. 42.
5   Remarks reported in Shepherd 1935.

them; Francis Mulhern, for example, sees the Popular Front advocacy of a common culture as essentially a regressive step, appealing in the end to '"culture" in its most familiar sense as the common spiritual inheritance of worker and bourgeois', closing off vital critical channels, while John Coombes has argued it amounted to 'functional accommodations of revolutionary theory to the cultural politics of the liberal bourgeoisie'.[6] Coombes argues that it rendered unchallengeable bourgeois cultural authority and placed few real demands on intellectuals, constructing an uncritical, undemanding defence of white, European, male-dominated bourgeois perspectives and voices. These tendencies were certainly real, and deeply problematic, often risking what Coombes identifies as the 'perpetuation of liberal elitism under the mask of "humanist" Marxism'.[7] However, I wish to suggest that in the case of some British Marxists, especially Jack Lindsay, there is by no means blindness towards this threat. A reading of Lindsay's trilogy of novels of English history, *1649: A Novel of a Year, Lost Birthright* and *Men of Forty-Eight*, set, respectively, in 1649, 1769 and 1848, reveals that Lindsay was deeply concerned with the nature of bourgeois culture, and through the recurring trope of bourgeois dissidence and radicalisation, he examined the contestation from within of bourgeois hegemony. Lindsay's novels and writings in the period are a key site of convergence for the historical preoccupations of Popular Front culture, Popular Front appraisals of the novel form, and tensions within Popular Front appeals for class alliance against fascism.

British Communists and English History

For Communists whose Party allegiance predated the adoption of the Popular Front line, the change in attitudes to British history and institutions was dramatic. While, especially in the 'class against class' period (from 1928 to the Popular Front turn), Communists had been instructed to work towards 'the creation of a distinct proletarian counter-culture anticipating life after the revolution', the emphasis now fell on an assimilationist approach.[8] This volte-face required an acceptance of the validity of non-revolutionary traditions and the treatment of popular nationalist sentiments not as symptoms of working-class incorporation but of deeply felt and potentially radical collective senti-

---

6   Mulhern 2000, p. 47; Coombes 1980, p. 72.
7   Coombes 1980, p. 80.
8   Harker 2011a, p. 17.

ments.[9] To this end, Communists attempted to construct and present through often innovative means a totalising national story organised around 'the English people' as an agent continually contesting oppression. The first major event to express this new-found sensibility was 'The March of English History', held in Hyde Park in September 1936. Looking ahead to the event, Party organiser Ted Bramley anticipated that '[w]hat will be new are the tableaux of English history'.[10] A sequence of historical scenes was constructed to retell the 'story of the English', 'from the signing of Magna Charta to the present day', clearing the way for a 'stronger and united Labour movement to lead England forward on the road to a Free and Merrie England'.[11] This event marked a key moment of development in the public presentation of Communism in Britain, which reflected the Party's efforts to move from an oppositional position to one of active engagement in public life.[12] The Communist-led mass movement is thereby imagined as a force for national salvation and the fulfilment of a national destiny: the curiously archaic phrasing echoing the 'antiquarian mythologisation' that inflected Popular Front rhetoric throughout Europe.[13] Meanwhile the mass spectacles that were mounted near the end of the decade, such as *Heirs to the Charter* and *The Pageant of South Wales*, both produced in 1939, provided a vital space in which the ideals of the Popular Front could be publicly enacted.[14] As Mick Wallis has shown in his ground-breaking work on the Communist pageants, audience participation was a key part of these events, and this participatory aspect aimed to engage audiences in a sense of history as a mass, creative process, and thus to make available to them a sense of their power in making it.[15] Two weeks after 'The March of English History', on 4 October 1936, the British Union of Fascists were prevented from marching through the East End of London. To some Communists, the united resistance, Communist-led but ultimately popular and mass in character, displayed in the Battle of Cable Street was a vindication of the efficacy of the appeal to existing popular traditions.[16]

---

9   Ibid.

10   Bramley 1936.

11   *Daily Worker* 1936a, p. 5.

12   See Wallis 1998, pp. 48–9.

13   Coombes 1989, p. 107.

14   Wallis 1995, pp. 28–9.

15   See Wallis 1994 and Wallis 1995.

16   Prominent Party intellectual Robin Page Arnot made this argument explicitly in Page Arnot 1936, p. 693.

Beneath the more opportunist surfaces of the transformations in public rhetoric, however, were important currents of thought that considered the relationship between popular politics and institutional forms. In particular, the rethinking of liberal democracy not as the apparatus of bourgeois power but as the outcome of popular struggles, so that, as Andy Croft puts it, democratic gains became 'a common ground on which anti-fascists could meet and band together', marks a key change from earlier Communist positions.[17] The Party's 1935 programme, *For Soviet Britain*, inopportunely adopted in February of that year and rendered outmoded only six months later, declared that '[w]hat the parliamentary system really is, as any worker may learn from his own experiences, is a form of political organisation which the capitalist class of Britain has worked out to serve its own needs', and which has 'not brought any real democracy to the overwhelming majority of the British people'.[18] The programme insisted that '[i]t is quite impossible for the workers to take over this machine and use it for their own entirely different purposes'.[19] By 1938, however, the Party's General Secretary Harry Pollitt was using his address to the Party's congress to articulate a dramatically modified stance. Pollitt made two claims of particular relevance here: the first, a historical claim, to the effect that '[d]emocracy means the rights won in the factories and pits for trade-union and workshop organisation', and the second, a strategic claim, in which 'democracy, even under capitalist economy, offers the best field for the development of the class struggle'.[20] At a time when liberal democracy was undergoing a genuine existential crisis, Communists worked to revive a democratic spirit, endorsing democracy as testament to the efficacy of popular political struggle and the means by which further advances might be secured.[21] The fear of democracy deprived of that spirit, of democratic form without content, is manifested in a number of important leftist novels of the period. Storm Jameson's *In the Second Year* (1937) plays out the consequences of the fascist appropriation of history evoked by Dimitrov in a near-future England; fascism is called to power in a 'bloodless revolution' expedited by fragmented resistance, apathy and nationalist demagoguery.[22] 'The State' (rather than 'the nation' or 'England' or

---

17   Croft 1990, p. 207.

18   Communist Party of Great Britain 1935.

19   Ibid.

20   Pollitt 1938.

21   For the general crisis in democratic politics in Britain, see Buchanan 2002.

22   S. Jameson 2004, p. 77. The kind of complacency Jameson's novel attacks was expressed by
       the Liberal Home Secretary, John Simon, in a 1936 speech on Britain's 'natural' resistance

'Britain') becomes an increasingly fetishised, mystical entity, detached from popular participation and consent. In a similar way, the fellow-travelling Communist Rex Warner's 1938 novel, *The Professor*, written in the wake of the Anschluss, is an unsettling allegory of the incapacities of the liberal state faced with authoritarianism: 'You refuse to arm them: you refuse to arm your own ideas', the liberal professor of the title, who finds himself made head of state, is told by his revolutionary son.[23] But this novel sees no way of activating 'the people' against the atrophy of democracy; the *polis* has lost its ability to command consent against fascism's irrational appeal. It has no intellectual resources with which to combat its usurpation.

While both Warner's and Jameson's novels express a deep scepticism about the possibility of mobilising a popular and democratic revival against the abstraction and formalism felt to be paralysing the liberal state, Communists engaged in wide-ranging and creative efforts to that end. Although the work of Antonio Gramsci was not known to British Marxists at this time, it is nonetheless instructive to note the consonance between the ethos of this project and Gramsci's sense of the 'national-popular' as a historical bloc: 'Its underlying assumption will be that a collective will, already in existence, has become nerveless and dispersed, has suffered a collapse which is dangerous and threatening but not definitive and catastrophic, and that it is necessary to reconcentrate and reinforce it'.[24] Influential readings of Gramsci have also stressed his rejection of ideology as deriving essentially from class positions. Ernesto Laclau and Chantal Mouffe derive from Gramsci instead an account of ideology as formed by the articulation of 'elements [which] considered in themselves, do not have a necessary class belonging'.[25] British Marxists' history-writing projects during the Popular Front era can be usefully considered in this light. Among the most enduring monuments of this enterprise is *A People's History of England*, published in 1938 by A.L. Morton, the son of a Suffolk farmer, who joined the Communist Party in 1928 and worked as a journalist on the *Daily Worker* from 1934. Morton's book is a crucial example of an attempt to

---

to authoritarianism, which argued that democracy was 'our own form of government: gradually developed over centuries by the genius of the British people, bone of our bone, and flesh of our flesh, the embodiment of our national character'; *Manchester Guardian* 1936b, p. 25.

23 R. Warner 1938, p. 167.

24 Gramsci 1971, p. 130. The *Daily Worker* reported Gramsci's death (*Daily Worker* 1937c), but there was no substantial engagement with his work in Britain before the late 1940s (see Forgacs 1989).

25 Laclau and Mouffe 2001, p. 68.

produce a totalising national story from a Marxist point of view, in which 'the people' – whether peasants resisting feudalism, Levellers in the English Civil War or nineteenth-century Chartists – were positioned as continually contesting exploitation and injustice. This required a sense of classes not as fixed social blocs but as formations continually being remade by the negotiation of interests. At the upper end of feudal society, for example, was not simply a concentration of power, but a site of continual contestation within the Norman legal framework.[26] Such events as the Peasants' Revolt of 1381 are read in terms of a complex of political, economic and cultural factors, a procedure that restores their definite political character by explaining them in terms of rights already won and rights aspired to, as well as existing organisational traditions.[27] Defeated popular movements, Morton argued, also have lasting effects; in the case of the 1381 rising, the peasants gained 'a sense of their power and common interests as a class'.[28]

A second important contribution Morton makes to the development of an activist perspective on history is a continued attention to the differentiation of form and content in popular politics. Morton stressed that such developing consciousness found expression in the forms that were available to it. From this position, the popular movements of the past could not be dismissed for their failure to conform to models that were not at the time available, nor mystified as distant and esoteric. In the sixteenth-century Pilgrimage of Grace, though 'in form' a 'reactionary, Catholic movement of the North', Morton found the means of expression for a much wider range of grievances among the dispossessed that made up its rank and file.[29] Likewise, the Labourers' Revolt of 1830 was not just a reaction against mechanisation, but the form of expression of a much more diverse range of dissenting positions.[30] Morton's English story, therefore, is a narrative of popular activism, of political knowledge gained in struggle and gradually articulated through available forms. The development of capitalism was continually contested; as against the theoretical elitism and vanguardism of the Third Period, Morton suggested that a fully developed theoretical critique of capitalism was not necessary for effective resistance. William Cobbett, he noted, lacked the ability to fully grasp the problems he decried, and his remedies took the form of a dream of 'an impossible return' to a 'largely

---

26   Morton 1992, p. 56.

27   Morton 1992, p. 102.

28   Morton 1992, p. 103.

29   Morton 1992, p. 142.

30   Morton 1992, pp. 319–20.

imaginary golden age'; Cobbett nonetheless used the resources available to him to articulate a political situation: his 'clear, simple conception of politics gave his demand for democracy, for Parliamentary Reform, a directness and an application to the desires of the masses'.[31]

While John Coombes has argued that Popular Front perspectives on history largely retained a narrative basis in a liberal, bourgeois account of 'progress' as gradual evolution culminating in the liberal state, much emphasis in Morton's *A People's History* is placed on the popular contestation of that course of development, even while asserting that such movements were, for historical reasons, necessarily defeated.[32] Edgell Rickword and Jack Lindsay's anthology of radical texts, *A Handbook of Freedom*, subtitled 'A Record of English Democracy Through Twelve Centuries', marks an ambitious attempt to document and anthologise this national popular culture of dissent that is not attached to one particular class.[33] The title of the anthology seems to have concerned the Party hierarchy as presenting a challenge to Emile Burns's *The Handbook of Marxism*, and thus to Burns's canonical selections from Marx, Engels, Lenin and Stalin.[34] Rickword's introductory essay, 'On English Freedom', announces the editors' intention to record not only the courage and energy of past radicals, but also their 'clear insight into, and articulation of, the conditions which at each stage in our history could bring nearer the life of freedom and good fellowship'.[35] At the core of the text's purpose is the need to demonstrate that victories have been won against vastly superior powers. As Rickword makes clear, this knowledge is intended to empower ordinary people to frustrate the march to war.[36] 'On English Freedom' is a key statement of the recasting of democracy integral to the Popular Front. Rickword's argument is a radical one, figuring the struggle for political rights as analogous to the struggle to make the land of England inhabitable:

---

31   Morton 1992, p. 318.

32   Coombes 1989, pp. 72–4.

33   *A Handbook of Freedom* was republished during the war under the title *Spokesmen for Liberty*.

34   Hobday 1989, p. 168.

35   Rickword 1941, p. vii. Rickword and Lindsay's anthology, with its emphasis on the agency and political consciousness of ordinary people, and its implicit rejection of a perspective of class consciousness as an intellectual construct to be received from without, prefigures the seminal work of E.P. Thompson in *The Making of the English Working Class*. Thompson's famous preface echoes their historical practice: E.P. Thompson 2002, pp. 8–13.

36   Rickword 1941, p. vii.

The freedom we possess had to be won by centuries of endeavour, as the land itself was wrested from forest and swamp; and just as the land without constant care will revert to waste, so the legal sanctions which support our freedom are effective only so long as we are energetic to maintain them not merely as principles but as fact.[37]

The articulation of an ethics of activism as the founding principle of culture as well as of democracy is not, of course, unproblematic; it most certainly runs the risk of effecting the kind of repression of class difference that Nick Hubble names as the 'pastoral' content of Popular Front texts.[38] It elides intellectual and productive labour, on the one hand, risking legitimating economic labour as a necessary security for 'freedom' while simultaneously offering an undemanding valorisation of intellectual labour to the same ends.[39] On the other hand, the elision of the specific legal structure of the state at a particular moment with 'freedom' in the abstract, risks a pastoral turn. Rickword's writing on culture is marked by an equivocation between a patrician rejection of mass culture and a populist figuring of 'the people' as the repository of values resistant to capitalism. Capitalism has 'depressed the cultural level of the masses of the people', excluding them from the making and appreciation of art, rendering them consumers rather than 'partners in its production'.[40] This cultural disenfranchisement leaves the masses 'condemned' to a 'seat at a trashy film', with its connotations of, at best, disempowered, impoverished passivity.[41] But, at another point, the masses are differentiated from a minority fully incorporated into capitalism: 'the competitive mentality infects only the fringe of the population which is in contact with the market'.[42] J.B. Priestley's enamoured review of A Handbook of Freedom, published in the Daily Worker, is itself

---

37 Rickword 1941, p. xxi.

38 Hubble 2009, p. 184.

39 Rickword's contribution to The Mind in Chains, a text squarely aimed at an intellectual readership, certainly bears out the depoliticising work of the analogy between forms of labour, arguing that, 'It is not the possession of ample leisure that creates a flourishing culture, as the briefest visit to Mayfair will convince, but participation in the constructive work of society'; Rickword 1937a, p. 247.

40 Rickword 1936b, p. 1.

41 Rickword 1941, p. x. Although Philip Bounds reads this tendency to denigrate mass culture as 'pandering to [their fellow intellectuals'] most virulent prejudices', in Rickword it forms part of a wider argument about the alienation of labour and the narrowing of cultural production: Bounds 2012, p. 99.

42 Rickword 1941, p. xii.

something of an object lesson in the depoliticising tendency of populism to reduce popular movements to minimal and consensually accepted demands: 'Peasants who wanted something to eat ... Fellows who would like some small say in the government of their own country ... People who thought a bit of education wouldn't do them any harm'.[43]

The anthology, however, does attempt, through its selections and organisation, to avoid the implication that the purpose of economic labour is to create the conditions for 'culture' in its elite sense, and thereby to avoid pastoralising the relationship between the intellectuals and the working class. It positions literary figures alongside contemporary, often popular voices: Shakespeare alongside an anonymous poet; Marlowe alongside the evidence of an informer; John Locke next to popular song.[44] The text remains a useful index of an important line of thought in the Popular Front formation: a wide-ranging conception of 'culture' as production, rather than in its narrower sense as accumulation of 'great' works and achievements. The anthology transmits a cultural heritage not only in terms of great works of art or the 'rational' evolution of a particular political form, but rather the variegated and conflicted processes in which those forms are produced. Although fraught with limitations – particularly the way that the national frame tends to automatically exclude those who would call its validity into question – it seeks to figure history as an open, creative process and, in making dissent the heritage of 'the people' in a broad sense, articulated across class lines, it attempts to create the ground for individuals to willingly align themselves with the Popular Front formation.[45] The understated radicalism of Rickword and Lindsay's method perhaps becomes clearest in their documentation of the English Civil War. With very minimal commentary or explanation, they reconstruct the complex discursive environment in the war, creating a sense of a much more open and indeterminate moment than Morton's more firmly narrativised style allows. The anthology reproduces Dig-

---

43   Priestley 1939, p. 7.

44   Rickword and Lindsay 1941, p. 101, p. 95, p. 170.

45   The exclusion of challenges to the privileging of English and European experience is indicated by the fact that the national frame can encompass William Wordsworth's 'To Toussaint L'Ouverture', dedicated to leader of the Haitian Revolution against slavery and French imperialism, which is quoted as part of Rickword and Lindsay's documentation of the internationalism of the English Jacobins (p. 233), but not the writings of L'Ouverture himself. The year before Lindsay and Rickword's anthology appeared, C.L.R. James published *The Black Jacobins*, his study of L'Ouverture and the Haitian Revolution, and a fierce exposition of the imperialist limits of the French Revolutionary values of liberty and equality (James 2001).

gers, Levellers, tracts, letters and pamphlets, soldiers' songs, court reports and contradictory accounts: what is lost by what Morton calls the 'historical jus-tification' for the defeat of the radical forces.[46] This opening of the historical moment as a site of conflict and negotiation is crucial to Lindsay's strategy in his historical novels.

The Historical Novel of the Popular Front

An important theoretical statement by a British Marxist on the role of the historical novel in the Popular Front is Lindsay's 1937 article, 'The Historical Novel', published in the American leftist cultural journal, *New Masses*. Lindsay explicitly links the 'great weapon' of the historical novel to Dimitrov's call to ideological struggle, endorsing the form as a means of bridging the gap between a popular readership and a national historical narrative: 'Now, with fascism raising everywhere demagogic cries of reactionary nationalism, there is no task more important for the Communists in each country than to make clear that they stand for the true completion of the national destiny'.[47] He goes so far as to argue that in Marxist hands the historical novel becomes 'the highest form of historical composition'.[48] Early in 1937, Lindsay approvingly reviewed Ralph Fox's *The Novel and the People*; he supported especially Fox's account of the heyday of the realist novel, and cited the book as an indicator of the way to 'get back to seriousness, to resume the great tradition on the new level of conflict'.[49] Lindsay's comments on the novel, and especially on the historical novel, are very consonant with Georg Lukács's simultaneously written theorisation of the historical novel.[50] In 1938, a special issue of the Soviet journal *International Literature* appeared on the subject of historical fiction. The issue featured a long article by Lukács on Walter Scott – which together with a second part published a few issues later made up a substantial part of the first chapter of *The Historical Novel* – in which Lukács describes the intertwined processes of the emergence of the historical novel and the 'qualitative' transformation by which history becomes mass experience, giving the people 'the opportunity

---

46   Morton 1992, p. 215.

47   Lindsay 1937d, p. 16.

48   Lindsay 1937d, p. 15.

49   Lindsay 1937c, p. 51.

50   Lukács' essays on the form were, however, not collected as *The Historical Novel* until after the war. See Connor 2014, p. 353.

to realize that their entire existence is historically conditioned'.[51] The major factor in this transformation was the French Revolution, but the fact that the first great historical novels emerged in Britain is explained in terms of its post-revolutionary culture; Scott's distinctive contribution was that he could 'channel this newly-awoken historical feeling artistically into a broad, objective, epic form'.[52] Jack Lindsay gives the same account of the genesis of the form: 'It was as a product of the French Revolution that the historical novel arose; it came straight out of the new sense of history created by the social turmoil. Scott is the greatest figure'.[53] Lindsay claimed in a much later reflection on his development in respect of historical fiction that, 'Near the end of the 30s I read Lukács on Scott, and felt that his analysis clarified further what I was seeking to do'.[54] This is quite plausible given that Lindsay contributed to the English and Russian editions of *International Literature*, and his novel *1649* was reviewed in the Russian edition in 1938.[55] The date of publication of the *New Masses* article (early January 1937) suggests, however, that the congruence is a matter of coincidence, of comparable responses to intellectual and political challenges, rather than of direct influence. In what follows, I do not proceed from the assumption that Lukács's work directly influenced Lindsay's historical fiction; however, the symmetry between their respective conceptualisations of the form is significant, and Lukács's more developed and sustained analysis provides a useful framework for interpreting Lindsay's work.

Jack Lindsay's English Trilogy

While sharing important common ground with Lukács, Lindsay did begin to elaborate a distinctive system of political aesthetics during an intense period of intellectual activity from 1936, when he converted to Marxism, breaking with

---

51   Lukács 1938a, p. 63. The essay drew responses from British Marxists Sylvia Townsend Warner and T.A. Jackson, which were published in the journal's next issue, together with Lukács's response. The curious nature of their dialogue with Lukács, which is less concerned with the question of the genre of the historical novel than it is with Lukács's handling of Scott's nationality, is dealt with in the next chapter.

52   Lukács 1938b, p. 73.

53   Lindsay 1937d, p. 15.

54   Lindsay 1984, p. 369.

55   Lindsay's presence in the Russian edition is referred to by Gruliow 1939.

the modernism of his earlier phase.[56] The central premise of this system is a theory of alienation, and its determinants are a theory of culture as production, a politicised elaboration of the Aristotelian trope of recognition, and an investment in the category of totality.

Lindsay prefaces *Lost Birthright*, the second novel in the English trilogy, with an epigraph from Hegel's *Aesthetics* on the relationship between art, history and the popular. Lindsay cites Hegel's assertion that 'art exists not only for the closed circle of the few who have the advantages of an education, but for the nation as a whole', and extends this claim into 'the outwards aspect of historical reality', which is necessary in order that 'we may feel ourselves at home'; so that '[the] historical becomes our own'.[57] This appeal to a totalised history as a means of ending the homelessness of alienation usefully condenses his concerns in the trilogy. For Lindsay, this homelessness, this exile from a common home, originated in the break-up of the communal lands and the communities predicated on them. Lindsay's thinking turns on a politics of loss, of the appropriation of 'that which should have been held freely in common'.[58] History is the working out of this loss. The evolution of social, political and cultural forms was dynamised by enactments of lost commonality: 'All history is the tale of the efforts made by ruling classes to dominate and destroy the communal forms of living created by the workers'.[59] These communal forms, once detached from their social basis in the common lands, took on more abstracted forms, manifested, for example, in myth and religion.[60] As capitalism developed, more and more people experienced this dispossession, creating a mass group poised, eventually, to overthrow that system.[61] Moreover, although he stressed the way that this loss pervades and plays a determining role in human culture, it assumes new forms with the evolution of society: '[a]bsolute loss', he wrote, will 'in every age bear on inspection the pattern of the age's social content. It

---

56   Lindsay (1900–90) was the son of the Australian artist and writer Norman Lindsay, who was for a time a major influence on him. He emigrated to Britain in 1926. The main source for biographical details is his autobiography, *Life Rarely Tells* (1982).

57   Lindsay 1939c, p. v.

58   Lindsay 1969, p. 256.

59   Lindsay 1939b, p. 6.

60   Lindsay's study of John Bunyan (1937) for example explores the ways that the mythic and allegorical content of Bunyan's work relates to this process of primitive accumulation, and to the Civil War intellectual and political culture more generally. The writing of the Digger Gerard Winstanley, for example, gained its force from 'the perfect law of liberty (the common birthright) and the rule of imposed law': Lindsay 1969, p. 74.

61   Lindsay 1969, p. 37.

is not loss in a void'.[62] This is a unifying principle and the key dynamic in his writings on England first articulated in his poem for mass declamation, 'not english?' (1936) and his popular pamphlet, *England My England: A Pageant of the English People* (1939). The poem 'not english?' proceeds by a logic of counter-formation that dispossesses its listeners of their membership of the national group, before re-forming them as the oppositional constituency of the 'not eng-lish' through the figuration of the nation as appropriated creation of labour: 'what little of it was ours in desperate toil/ was taken'.[63] Out of this point of recognition of loss emerges the solution of the text's conflicts in the form of slogan, 'Workers of the World'. England functions in the poem, as Ben Harker argues, as a 'blurred, submerged and immanent counter nation conceived as synonymous with resistance to British capital'.[64] The poem attempts to illumin-ate a tradition of dispossession, in which the defeated are transfigured through the continually reinvigorating practices of tradition. Likewise, the pamphlet *England My England* is rhetorically organised around a continuous struggle between property, conceived as originating in the theft of the common lands, and 'the people', 'two Englands that lie starkly divided all through our history'.[65] Drawing on the trope of inheritance, but turning it away from its implication in the transmission of property, the text transmits responsibility through transhis-torical solidarity: 'for you inherit, not only their physical strain, but also their struggle, the world which they created, the rights for which they fought and died'.[66] The rhetorical effect of the short pageant-like scenes is a homogenisa-tion, an emptying out of detail, so that popular movements become the story of 'the countless unknown who rose in the great insurrections or died in small hopeless outbursts in the lean years of oppression'.[67] In both the pamphlet and the poem, the national frame serves as the mediating device through which this loss – this alienation from a common home – could be seen and concep-tualised.

Bound up with this account of an original exile is Lindsay's conception of cultural form, and especially of 'mass' form. Concepts of 'the mass' and 'the common' are central to his historiography. In his *A Short History of Culture* (1939), he concluded that 'always out of the productive group, the mass, has evolved the dynamic point of structure from which all cultural advance, in art

---

62   Lindsay 1969, p. 87.
63   Lindsay 1936 p. 356.
64   Harker 2011a, p. 25.
65   Lindsay 1939b, p. 26.
66   Ibid.
67   Ibid.

or in science, is made'.[68] It is in production that man 'objectifies' himself, in all cultural production from tool creation onwards.[69] There is an advance, or attempted advance, here from Rickword's pastoralised theory of culture as a form of labour towards a theory of structure. Past cultures, Lindsay argued in the journal *Poetry and the People*, bore out two impulses: 'A mass-impulse and the working out of that impulse among the leisured classes. The masses, chained down to the drudgery of unending toil, could never develop in detail the cultural impulses which they generated'.[70] This formulation decouples the origin of cultural productions from particular economic conditions, thus rejecting the notion that the culture of the ruling class merely articulates its dominance. Instead cultural texts bear more complex ideological content that includes revolutionary impulses emerging from different social levels. This is important for Lindsay's reading of bourgeois culture, but it also marks an important attempt on his part to theorise the progressive content of bourgeois culture that other British Marxists, such as Ralph Fox, tended to take as given. However, although this formulation marks a significant innovation, it could, as we shall see, legitimise a prioritisation of bourgeois dissidence and an assumption of working-class passivity, denying to working-class movements a specific class content. This tendency arises from Lindsay's central claims about the nature of the bourgeois epoch. The destruction of feudal society brought, for a time, the possibility of mass democracy: 'Advancing from a thesis that society was a contract in which all authority was merely a delegation which could be called to order, the democratic spirit gradually challenged all the actual manifestations of the power-rule'.[71] Crucially, however, that development was curtailed, in England, by the all-pervasive success of capitalism, so extreme as 'to suppress to a large extent the creative forces rising out of the productive advance'.[72] What was lost was a perspective of difference that residual feudalism has provided, but which once destroyed left the masses in England with no way of recognising their conditions. The 'creative centre' passed over into countries where capitalism's success was more isolated, in which 'the financial mechanism was sufficiently isolated from the general run of social life as to be something visible'.[73]

---

68   Lindsay 1939a, p. 376.
69   Lindsay 1976, p. 430.
70   Lindsay 1938b, p. 14. Lindsay took up editorship of this journal at about the time of compiling *The Handbook of Freedom*: see Lindsay 1982, p. 782.
71   Lindsay 1939a, p. 305.
72   Lindsay 1939a, p. 438.
73   Lindsay 1939a, p. 348.

In a late reflection on his political and aesthetic development, Lindsay recalled his turn to the historical novel in the early 1930s:

> I saw the individual caught up in a complex pattern of social, economic, political mediations. (I did not yet use the term of Lukács, but it best explains what I was working to.) The mediations somehow came together in a dynamic moving unity ... Never in quite the same way even in the same person at different moments, though there was an ultimate unity of the self. At moments the compacting or unifying element predominated, at other moments the contradictory or unbalancing elements asserted themselves and there was profound and lasting conflict, which carried on till a new balance emerged.[74]

This passage demonstrates Lindsay's formulation of historical process and specifies an essentially Lukácsian model of totality as infinitely mediated and expressive – present in every moment of the process. But a critical difference of emphasis is also brought into view: Lindsay's intense stress on the imbalance of the moment of crisis, on those phases of 'profound and lasting conflict', is in some tension with the tenor of Lukács's arguments in the thirties which emphasise continuity, the struggle in the everyday, so that popular movements are perceived as 'necessary continuations and intensifications of normal popular life'.[75] These are not mutually exclusive positions, but Lukács's emphasis reflects, more strongly than Lindsay's, a climate in international Communism that prioritised immediate defence over long-term transformation.[76]

In his autobiography, Lindsay describes his intellectual struggle during his period of conversion 'to hold true to the existential moment, in which the unexpurgated colour and richness of experience is alone preserved'.[77] This commitment to the specificity of the moment, carried over from his earlier engagements with Kierkegaard's work especially, shapes the novels. Much of the intensity of the novels derives from this stress on individual commitment, a

---

74   Lindsay 1984, p. 368.

75   Lukács 1976, p. 361.

76   Lindsay made this point in aesthetic terms in his late work *The Crisis in Marxism*, in which Lukács's position on realism is criticised on the grounds that it resists penetrating into 'the point where the effective unity of the system seems threatened by the intrusion of all sorts of imbalances and disruptions. This is the revolutionary moment when the result can only be a breakdown or the creation of the new centre of living, a new totality'. Lindsay 1981, p. 46.

77   Lindsay 1982, p. 771.

drive to hold individuals to account to the demands of their historical moment. Lindsay described the cognitive moment in which the individual gleaned the nature of their historical situation by an elaboration of the Aristotelian concept of recognition that he found expressed in socialist novels like Sommerfield's *May Day*. In that moment, a new, socialised subjectivity was realised: 'Recognition appears as the point where the shell of the old self cracks and the new self is born, breaking into new spaces of activity and achieving fullness of social contact.'[78] The crises in the novels – the English Revolution, the revolutionary period of the late eighteenth century, and the momentous year of 1848 – are configured not in terms of a mechanistic breakdown, but in terms of moments of choice, in which the acts of individuals combine to create social change, but also – just as importantly – as moments in which choices are not made and changes fail to occur, leading to the tragedy of 1848 and the 'great divide of bourgeois triumph'.[79]

What was lost in that divide was a critical standpoint from which to view society as a whole, a standpoint suppressed by the levelling and homogenising of capitalism.[80] It was precisely this standpoint that, for Lindsay, the Popular Front promised to restore. A complete history, a truly national narrative, was, Lindsay thought, available in the thirties in a new way as a result of the anti-fascist struggle and the advancement of the Soviet Union: a new conception of 'the people' as a homogenous audience; 'a conquering class which can rightly arrogate to itself the terms of the "whole"'.[81] In reading Lindsay's novels, I wish to bear in mind Lukács's arguments in the final chapter of *The Historical Novel* for the Popular Front's role in restoring to possibility the classical form of the historical novel, acquiring its objectivity, breadth and progressiveness from the 'standpoint of popular life'. This standpoint 'alters the perspective which historical novels have of the future', generating a new novel that can 'discover

---

78   Lindsay 1937b, p. 837.

79   Lindsay 1956, p. 19.

80   Lindsay 1939a, p. 348.

81   Lindsay 1937a, p. 516. Lindsay's sense of what was at stake in the Popular Front was, however, always Soviet-oriented, and became more so as the decade progressed, so that, in *A Short History of Culture*, written at the time of the outbreak of war, Lindsay imagines the transformation of historical perspective less in terms of popular anti-fascism than in terms of the glorification of the Soviet Union: 'we can bear to look back on that terrible past, to look into the terrible present, because of that voice, which is now the voice of the working classes and their allies all over the world, the confident voice of the millions of the Soviet Union'. See Lindsay 1939a, p. 388.

entirely new tendencies and features in the past'.[82] And yet there is an important tension between this investment in the energies of popular life mobilised
against fascism and Lindsay's reading of historical moments in terms of crisis
and rupture. In his *New Masses* article, Lindsay endorses the function of the
historical novel in terms of stability and continuity, asserting its utility in 'sift-
ing and absorbing all that is positive in past achievement, in establishing the
continuity of tradition and stabilizing culture'.[83] His commitment to the form
in these terms continually interplays with his desire to recognise the revolutionary moment as indeterminate and conflicted. That interplay is marked by
intense political pressures as the drama of the thirties played out in the defeat
of the Spanish Republic, the Hitler-Stalin Pact and the outbreak of world war.

1649: A Novel of a Year (*1938*)

Lindsay's autobiography identifies as his motivation for the turn to novels of
English history the desire 'to use the novel to revive revolutionary traditions'.[84]
For Lindsay revolutions in history always have a dual aspect: they advance productive activity, intensifying the division of labour, while also creating the conditions for a new unity. In his study of John Bunyan, Lindsay argued that during
the English Civil War there were two revolutionary forces: one that was individualist and which was 'to build bourgeois industrialism', but also another, 'the
new coherence resulting from the productive advance'.[85] The relation between
these two forces, and the emergent antagonism between them, is the central
dynamic of his Civil War novel. Lindsay's argument foreshadows Christopher
Hill's later proposition that there were two revolutions in seventeenth-century
England: the 'bourgeois' revolution that succeeded in establishing the 'sacred'
rights of property, as well as 'another revolution which never happened, though
from time to time it threatened'.[86] This second revolution, Hill argues, existed as a 'counter-culture'.[87] This counter-culture manifests itself in Lindsay's
novel in the gestures of resistance made by the Levellers and the Diggers, and
especially in the depiction of the trial of John Lilburne, and while ultimately
the novel asserts the historical necessity of their defeat, it suggests that such
acts of defiance were not simply tragic gestures, but the means of carrying the

---

82   Lukács 1976, p. 420.
83   Lindsay 1937a, p. 16.
84   Lindsay 1982, p. 781.
85   Lindsay 1969, p. 18.
86   Hill 1975, p. 15.
87   Hill 1975, p. 341.

revolutionary content of the defeated side forward into the future through the structure of 'Recognition'. In this, however, Lindsay's thinking was in some tension with more orthodox readings of the English Revolution.

In the novel's opening scenes, the act of regicide which marks the end of a social order predicated on absolute monarchy appears to the uncertain, troubled crowd as by turns banal and intensely symbolic. The act marks not the onset of a new order but a hiatus, a breakdown, rather than, in Lukács's terms, an intensification of normal life: 'They waited, they accepted, they remained silent. They were neither eager nor depressed. They waited'.[88] The king reads a speech, and yet, 'the crowd couldn't hear' (13); he 'kept making unintelligible gestures' (14). This communicative breakdown indicates an end to Charles's absolutist function as 'the sole repository of national-social unity'[89] and the beginning of a period of profound conflict; the fight, as Andy Croft puts it, 'to determine the sort of victory the people had won'.[90] The import of the event cannot yet be enunciated: '"Everything", said Ralph in explanation, jerking his head round to indicate the whole scene. "Do you realize ... we, the People of England ..."' (8). In Lindsay's terms, the sudden rupture cannot yet be 'objectified' in word and narrative, and the plotline concerning the Leveller characters entails a quest for precisely this verbal objectification through the establishment of the *Agreement of the People*. Arising from the radical interruption of the communicative culture is the necessity of a new form of utterance.

Encountering the People

The novel is structured through multiple perspectives and short chapters, interspersed with original documents. The method creates an indeterminacy that brings into focus what is elided by the discourse of the victors. The question of what kind of narrative can be constructed from these fragments is explored through the central plotline, in which the former New Model Army soldier Ralph Lydcot joins the Levellers in their pursuit of popular consent for *The Agreement of the People*. Christopher Hill described the importance of the concept of popular sovereignty – the *vox populi* – during the period, and Lindsay examines the effect of the destruction of the commons on the coherence of the popular voice.[91] The 'people' as constructed by this text does not yet exist: the community in language that it designates is a hypothesis only. The yeoman Will Scamler, another Parliamentarian veteran, finds on his return from the war

---

88   Lindsay 1938a, p. 1. Page references are hereafter given in parentheses in the text.
89   Lindsay 1969, p. 17.
90   Croft 1990, p. 208.
91   Hill 1975, pp. 34–5.

that his perception is changed: 'when he now looked across the field, he saw England, not a private patch of the summer' (116). The soldiers' involvement in the first conflict to function as a 'mass experience' makes available a new perspective on history. Will and Ralph try to narrate their wartime experiences, but the heroic register is only briefly introduced before being interrupted by ellipsis and uncertainty: '"Do you remember ..." the first good cause. "Godscods, Ralph ..." "I tell you, Will ..." "Do you remember ..."' (57). The narrative of the war that might have served as a national story that could unify opposition to Cromwell's dictatorship resolves into silence. The idea of the nation enters the characters' conceptual vocabulary through their experiences and serves to inform a radical democratic ideal hypothesised in the Leveller declaration, transforming Ralph's perception so that, 'The voices he heard were not those of blackbirds ... they were the voices of peasants in the ale-house or under the hedge' (239). But the disjunction between this and the Levellers' rhetoric is apparent: 'The voice was there, speaking, desired, awaited. But could it speak loud enough and soon enough?' (240).

The coherence and audibility of that voice, and the national constituency it might represent, is vitiated by economic conditions. The people have been ruined by the financial crises following the war so that the 'ditches of England were filled with outcasts, yeomen driven off the land, disbanded soldiers who could find no work bankrupt tradesmen and journeymen' (238). This dispossession is central to Lindsay's account of the failure of the English Revolution to restore the 'birthright' of the people: the inability of the radicals to make efficient challenge to the advancement of enclosure and the deflection of 'natural' rights onto the rights of property. The disappearance of the land held in common had destroyed the sense of 'union' as a basis from which such a challenge could be organised (238). While John Lilburne believes that *The Agreement of the People* will 'bring into being the first free Parliament since the Norman Conquest', Chidley retorts that 'We must remember that there is no people in the sense in which you use the world' (132). For the *Agreement* to pass from a speculative expression to popular representation, to become an authentic collective utterance, requires the transformation of economic conditions by capitalism so as to create a new unity in labour. In this, Lindsay reiterates Marxist readings of the Levellers as a historically premature force. The interpretation of the Civil War, and the politics of the Levellers particularly, was identified by Raphael Samuel as the 'gravitational centre' of Marxist historical thinking in the thirties and forties.[92] A.L. Morton wrote that the Levellers' role was essentially path-

---

92   Samuel 1980, p. 84. The politics of seventeenth-century England were a central concern

breaking, 'to carry the movement to positions which could not be permanently held' but which were nonetheless crucial for further advance.[93] Christopher Hill argued that 'the Levellers never represented a sufficiently homogeneous class to be able to achieve their aims'.[94] Ralph Lydcot's turn to commerce is in this sense to be seen not as an abandonment of the revolution but a pursuit of the necessary conditions for its full realisation. The division of the text into multiple perspectives and incompatible accounts refuses to suppress this divided social context, the unification of which only became possible, Lindsay felt, in the thirties.[95]

As the revolutionary momentum of the Levellers is broken, Ralph Lydcot withdraws from active politics, a measure that precipitates a loss of critical perspective: the effect of the loss of hope is a contraction of his vision from the general – the national and popular – to the immediate and specific: he finds he can no longer face the phrase 'a free England' and 'wanted to escape all generalisation and live in some immediate objective – the cornering of the tin supply' (312). The apparent contraction of his vision is attended by a sharpening sense of international context through the lens of commodity production: 'Cotton, dye-galls, aniseeds, corodovans, wax, grogram, camlets, carpets, gems from India, indigo, spices from Arabia, mohair and raw silk. What did he know about the world from which these various things came, paid for by the exports and tin? ... He wanted to travel' (454–5). Ralph's Levelling instincts are displaced into this other form of equivalence and equality. These 'various things' become the mediators of Ralph's understanding of the world. The England of labour, briefly brought into view by his experience of the mass conflict of the war, is displaced by the world of things. The loss of the national scale in this scheme, which moves directly from the local to the international, suggests the Popular Front endorsement of the nation state as a form in which capitalism could be resisted. Ralph's abandonment of the idea of a free English nation enables him to blindly facilitate the development of the commercial empire.

---

of the Communist Party Historians' Group, which grew out of a meeting at Marx House in 1938 called to discuss a new edition of Morton's *A People's History of England* (Schwarz 1982, p. 44). The key interventions and discussions on this subject, by Christopher Hill, Rodney Hilton, Victor Kiernan, Maurice Dobb and others, are collected in Parker 2008.

93   Morton 1992, p. 215.
94   Hill 1955, p. 51.
95   Lindsay 1937a, p. 516.

Levelling

In suggesting that the underlying cause for the Levellers' failure was a lack of a developed social base, Lindsay at one level echoes other Marxists, such as Morton and Hill, who were exploring the 'bourgeois' revolution of the 1640s. However, Lindsay is concerned with the cultural and textual consequences of that failure. The novel depicts a moment of early capitalist modernity in which modern cultural forms begin to circulate, and the Levellers' *Agreement* is implicitly figured as a unifying alternative to the fragmentation of narrative those forms entail. This current in the novel is most clearly seen in the figure of the Puritan apprentice, Roger Cotton, who experiences an intense crisis of faith, a search for the 'absolute' (44) that is no longer available after the execution of the monarch inaugurates a phase of radical contingency. His initial revolt is against his employer, Mr Bagshaw, who has 'collected a pack of down-and-out authors who, for a glass of wine, a plateful of meat, and half a crown, would knock off a pamphlet, a ballad, or a hack-translation, even a treatise on history or science' (71). Most distressing to Roger is Bagshaw's scheme of selling texts of popular sermons, 'Paper obtained on credit; half the book put out to a printer to save time' (70). Roger is repelled by the levelling process that reduces ideas and texts to equivalent commodities and empties them of their signifying power – a reality becoming prosaic. The breakdown between, on Roger's reading, Word and world emerges from, but also participates in, the advance of the capitalist mode of production. His appalled confrontation with the degradation of text induces a quest to objectify the contradictions manifested there, conditioning him as a listener so that, at Lilburne's trial, '[Lilburn's] words gripped Roger; they seemed aimed directly at him' (476).

Roger's commitment to the Diggers is an extension of his revolt against the corruption and abstraction of text: he is formed by nascent capitalism into an oppositional figure within it. His quest is for a sure gesture that might counteract the ambiguity of modernity; in the Digger Everard he finds, 'The words and the voice so eager and assured before the unmoved listeners; the eyes unfathomably burning. That was what he wanted; that certainty' (204). Likewise, in Gerard Winstanley he finds the unity of word and gesture that overcomes the rupture he apprehends as the foundation of commerce: 'The penetrating gentleness of his voice, the quiet benediction of his hand, filled Roger with a balmy certitude' (209). But in both cases Roger is forced to confront the failure of the 'certainty' manifested in the Diggers to make contact with social reality. While his involvement in the Digger commune assuages his sense of alienation arising in commerce, this labour cannot overcome his alienation from his 'species-being', in Marx's sense, which makes itself felt in his relationship with his wife.[96] He is tormented by his inability to subsume his sexual drive to his sense of a social body in which all are separate but equal: 'The desire to take the body of another, he said, was only part of the greedy spirit of discontent and hate' (309). This attempt to repress causes a disjuncture between word and gesture: 'he could feel the garters above her knees and the soft movement of her thighs as he knelt there; and the gesture which he had meant as one of simply brotherly affect ceased to be so easy, so unequivocal' (309). The 'certainty' seemingly embodied in the Diggers fails when confronted with Roger's divided being: his bad faith.

It is useful, at this point, to consider Georg Lukács's somewhat enigmatic comments about 'capitalist prose' that appear in his thirties writing on realism. This form, for Lukács, inscribes the bourgeois order as the natural way of things, and frames the entrenchment of bourgeois power as inevitable. 'Capitalist prose', Lukács suggests, becomes dominant after the 'heroic' phase of bourgeois history, in which the bourgeoisie was still the objectively progressive force, in the sense that, as A.L. Morton put it, 'they could not fight for their own rights and liberties without also fighting for the rights and liberties of all Englishmen and of humanity as a whole'.[97] For Communists working for a Popular Front, the 'progressive', indeed heroic, past of the bourgeoisie was a rhetorical lynchpin of the appeal to alliance. 'Capitalist prose' is the product of the schism between bourgeois class interests and wider society: '[t]he rule of prose set in after the heroic period because objectively the only result of the people's colossal heroic efforts was the replacement of one form of exploitation by another'.[98] Capitalist prose in so far as Lukács defines it, then, is perspectival, and to some degree temporal: the vanishing of the revolutionary future from the bourgeois perspective ensured that revolutionary outbursts could only appear as aberrant and 'episodic'.[99] The posited supersession of that perspective by the perspective of the Popular Front, the 'standpoint of popular life', would, Lukács thought, spell an end to the epoch of 'capitalist prose'.[100] Lindsay's novel may be seen to be writing back into the moment of bourgeois victory

---

96   Marx 2000a, pp. 88–9. Lindsay did not read the *1844 Manuscripts* until about 1941; however, he acknowledged the consonance with his own work in the thirties in a later reflection on his development: 'Though [in 1936] it was to be some five or more years before I learned of Marx's 1844 manuscripts and began to study them, to make some use of their idiom, I had on my own reached their positions': Lindsay 1976, p. 433.

97   Morton 1992, p. 194.

98   Lukács 1976, p. 420.

99   Ibid.

100   Lukács 1976, p. 419.

the contestation of that closure, not just from the forces of reaction without but from more radical positions within: to acknowledge, in literary terms, that, as Lukács argued in 'Realism in the Balance', 'historical necessity neither implies justification of what actually exists ... nor does it imply a fatalistic belief in the necessity of historical events'.[101] But while the novel may thus resist naturalising bourgeois dominance, in doing so it also threatens to jeopardise the very idea of a 'progressive' bourgeoisie. This predicament brings into view a central contradiction in the historical premises of the Popular Front.

Lindsay's pamphlet, *England My England*, while accepting the necessity of the victory of the Cromwellian forces and the defeat of the Levellers, nonetheless clearly positions itself on the side of the 'plain-spoken revolutionaries who stood up and told Cromwell to his face what the poor people of England expected and meant to have'.[102] Although the pamphlet was generally well received by Communists, this apparent refusal to valorise the Cromwellian victors caused some concern among Party critics. Idris Cox criticised Lindsay for 'so serious an underestimation of Cromwell's objective role in unleashing the forces of revolt against caste and privilege'.[103] Christopher Hill, meanwhile, foreshadowing the argument he would make in his seminal essay 'The English Revolution 1640' published the following year, suggested that Lindsay had not made due efforts to show that Cromwell and the parliamentary leaders 'were members of a class that was then progressive leading a national struggle against intolerable economic and social and political conditions'.[104] In *1649*, the scepticism towards Cromwell as a progressive force is even more pronounced. The Leveller Ralph Lydcot's turn away from the 'good old cause' is a response to Cromwell's shooting of Leveller soldiers, who had mutinied over Cromwell's planned invasion of Ireland and their unmet political demands, at Burford in May. Lindsay draws on a contemporary report to describe the act in terms of a unity of gesture and word: ' "Shoot me", [the mutineer] said, "when I hold out my hand to you". He held out his hand and they shot him' (261). Hill argues that the shooting of the mutineers 'made a restoration of monarchy and lords ultimately inevitable'.[105] But Lindsay's use of the contemporary account, in a novel preoccupied with language and gestures, restores a symbolic, even heroic, power to the soldiers' actions.[106] The soldiers' deaths are

---

101   Lukács 2007, p. 45.
102   Lindsay 1939b, p. 31.
103   Cox 1939, p. 7.
104   Hill 1939, p. 127.
105   Hill 1955, pp. 52–3.
106   The young Lukács wrote of gesture in terms of this kind of commitment: 'Perhaps the

inevitable, but their conduct is chosen. The contemporary source, reproduced in *Spokesmen for Liberty*, describes the mutineers as 'looking [the soldiers] in the face till they gave fire, not showing the least kind of terror or fearfulness of spirit'.[107] This strange, haunting moment in the novel epitomises the violence of success while giving form to the minimal power and agency that is graspable even by the defeated. The emphasis falls not on the heroic energies of the bourgeoisie in their development of the productive forces, but instead on the immediately repressive disavowal of its revolutionary ideology. But we might equally understand this moment, in the terms offered by Lukács, as figuring one of the privileged moments in which the 'inner poetry' of life interrupted and briefly transcended the levelling effects of capitalism as formalised in 'capitalist prose'; that form intimated in Ralph's paratactic description of the world of commodities (454).[108]

The central dramatic episode of *1649* is the trial for treason of the Leveller John Lilburne, and Lindsay's writing here is also an exemplary use of his trope of recognition. The Lilburne trial provides the occasion for realising the hypothesis of the *Agreement of the People* within available forms. Lilburne is a levelling agent who expresses the positive side of the 'levelling' Roger finds so degrading. The depiction of his imprisonment suggests a national and popular leader in whom the fate of the people is concentrated: 'lifting his hand, saying aloud, "I shall not be ensnared", he felt the old strength flowing back ... till he stood up, up, all over England' (265). Lilburne's conscious merging of himself with the people of England gives rise to a moment of recognition of his situation, and the articulation of commitment:

> The end was not yet. He said to the night, not in any vanity (for it was of himself as the voice of the surging struggle that he spoke; himself as England): Until Lilburne is broken, liberty is not lost. They may kill, but not break me.
>
> p. 269

But Lilburne's defence takes the form of an appeal to the law and the constitution and eschews the extra-legal power he could invoke in gesture: he 'knew

---

gesture – to use Kierkegaard's dialectic – is the paradox, the point at which reality and possibility intersect, matter and air, the finite and the infinite, life and form'; 'In a word, the gesture is that unique leap by which the absolute is transformed, in life, into the possible': Lukács 1974, p. 29.

107   Quoted Rickword and Lindsay (eds.) 1941, p. 145.

108   Lukács 1970, p. 127.

that if he so wished, with the raising of a hand he could smash the court and chase the learned judges out of it' (462). It is this choice – the choice to fight on the basis of the law – that is represented as heroic. The court attempts to prevent him from reading the text of the law (486) so that the act of enunciating already existing rights is itself both gesture and praxis. For Lindsay, the greatest evidence that radical gains could be made and freedoms defended within existing state and legal frameworks came from cases of trial by jury, in which the jury had acted as 'defender of liberty' against the misuse of the law.[109] As in the representation of the shootings of the Leveller soldiers, Lindsay draws closely on the contemporary report of the trial.[110] While the regicide that opens the novel moved the revolution into unprecedented territory – Edgell Rickword noted that the execution was 'public and ceremonial', 'for it could not be called legal' – the Lilburne trial upholds the text of the law against its corruption.[111]

Lilburne stands metonymically for the people as yet unformed as political subject. Where the radical act of the regicide is severed from its origins in human agency – even the politically aware characters cannot explain it – Lilburne is shown making an active choice in full awareness of the limitations of the moment. The text of the law ceases at this moment to be an abstraction and comes into force as a concrete realisation: momentarily, there is a convergence of legality and legitimacy, and therefore an intimation of the abolition of the generative contradiction within capitalism. Recognition, in Lindsay's specialised sense, is the narrative outcome of the Lilburne trial. Roger finds that 'he had never before seen the whole struggle, the righteous man arrayed against the great ones of the world, in so stark and noble a form' (490). The 'heroic pattern' of the struggle 'came home to him with tremendous force, clarifying his personal conflicts' (490). Gesture, it is suggested here, can give form to the perception of totality occluded by the bourgeois perspective represented by Ralph's traumatised retreat into the immediacy of commerce. Roger is transformed by the end of the novel into a literary intellectual; in showing that the revolutionary promises of the Levellers are not destroyed but transformed, carried into the future in different forms – France appears on the horizon at the novel's end – Lindsay writes back into the history of the novel an account of its origins in resistance to the 'levelling' of commercial exchange. This device carries into the history of the form not only the bourgeois mode of 'capitalist

---

109   Lindsay 1939b, p. 47.
110   The proceedings of the trial are available at http://constitution.org/trials/lilburne/lilbur ne1.htm.
111   Rickword 1978b, p. 179.

prose', as Lukács calls it, but also its dialectical counterpart: the heroic, ecstatic mode born of religious revolt against the degradation of the world.

The significance of the trial to the form of *1649* has tended to be overlooked by critics reading the novel in terms of Lindsay's emphasis on the 'mediocre' heroes, Roger and Ralph. The *Daily Worker* saw in the Levellers the image of the modern Communist Party, and subsequent critics have tended to read the novel for political parallels.[112] The trial of Georgi Dimitrov, in whose 'moral grandeur and courage' Ralph Fox saw a paradigm of the new literary hero, is certainly a presence in Lindsay's novel, as Jan Montefiore points out.[113] However, within the wider system of Lindsay's thought, the trial combines symbolic gesture with political praxis. The paradox of the events of 1649 is the discharging into social life of two forms of levelling: the freeing of the forces of commodity capitalism and a legalistic principle of democracy. Once mobilised, both forces generate their own momentum. In his re-writing of that history, Lindsay offers an account not just of the onward march of capitalism's cultural forms but also the formal possibilities of resistance.

Lost Birthright (*1939*)

1649 ends on New Year's Day, 1650, with a letter from Oliver Cromwell in Ireland affirming his belief in the divine justice of the conquest (561–2). Near the end of the trilogy of English historical novels he wrote in the late thirties, one of Lindsay's characters (a Chartist) makes explicit what is implicit in his earlier work:

> The English Revolution against Charles I went on mounting democratic-ally until the point when Cromwell turned its forces into the subjugation of Ireland; then came the collapse of democracy. Ever since then we have been fighting to regain the British liberties that were lost by the conquest of Ireland.[114]

The implication is that the catastrophe of the conquest of Ireland turned revolution into counter-revolution almost immediately, but Lindsay's vision of the revolutionary year writes the contestation of that conclusion by the Level-lers' mutiny and John Lilburne's defence of the law. However, there is a notable

---

112   The *Daily Worker*'s reviewer wrote that the novel 'has for its hero a Party, the Levellers', and that readers 'see the Party in all its aspects': 'Martin Marprelate' 1938, p. 7.

113   Montefiore 1996, p. 152; Fox 1979, p. 121.

114   Lindsay 1948, p. 388.

ambiguity in this quotation over whether it articulates a historical argument, or if it is instead to be taken as another rendering of the 'lost birthright' trope, another inflection of 'absolute loss'. This problem comes into focus in *Lost Birthright*, the second instalment of the English trilogy. *Lost Birthright* is set in 1769, and the gestures of resistance that inscribe the Levellers' defeat with power and agency are shown to be less available in the more mediated capitalist environment of the late eighteenth century. Meanwhile, the novel form and its generic conventions – as well as other cultural hallmarks of bourgeois society – are shown to be intimately bound up with the production and mediation of subjectivity in capitalist society. The result is a novel preoccupied with questions of the figuration of capital, and with the question of how a perspective of totality can be reached.

The 'lost birthright' occupied a privileged position in Lindsay's thought; it recurred through history as the mythic image of what had been unjustly taken, 'that which should have been held freely in common', manifesting itself in changing forms over time.[115] In *Lost Birthright*, the 'birthright' is invoked to dynamise several interlinked plots. At the first level is the story of two middle-class brothers, Harry and Valentine Lydcott (the surname thus linking them to the Leveller Ralph in *1649*), who find that their inheritance has been misappropriated and set out to restore their fortunes. For Valentine, accompanied by his friends Kit and Julian Fane, this quest takes the form of an attempt to unjustly secure wealth, initially by gambling and fraud and, when that fails, through the murder of an elderly distant relative in a bid to claim his estate. Simultaneously, the novel narrates the unravelling of the character of Julian Fane during his own pursuit of his origins. By contrast, for Valentine's brother, the disillusioned scholar Harry, a pursuit of security takes him through several failed marriage schemes before leading him into the radical political movement around John Wilkes. Through this activist position he is able to recognise the real nature of what has been lost in a way his brother cannot.

Figuring Capital

The section of Rickword and Lindsay's *Spokesmen for Liberty* that covers the period in which *Lost Birthright* is set takes its title from Oliver Goldsmith's 'The Deserted Village': 'Wealth Accumulates and Men Decay'.[116] Central to the novel is the process of accumulation. Accumulation is shown to involve speculation and gambling, in which Valentine and his friends are involved while trying

115   Lindsay 1969, p. 256.
116   Rickword and Lindsay (eds.) 1941, p. 169.

to recover Valentine's lost birthright. As David Harvey describes, the process of speculation causes money to be withdrawn from circulation and hoarded as capital, and the physical presence of money is replaced by the fictitious currency of credit and debt.[117] The connected dynamics of accumulation and the crisis in circulation are understood by Marx as integral to the founding of the national debt and the modern state. This debt is characteristic of the modern (bourgeois) state: 'Public debt becomes the *credo* of capital'.[118] This process is given form in *Lost Birthright* in the figure of the libertine Lord Hawkins, who proposes an Enclosure Bill by which he intends to pay off his gambling debts through dispossessing the rural workers, and the scheme is presented as a gambling away of 'the ancient communal rights' of the rural people.[119] The insidious and pervasive nature of this development serves to undermine the perspective of difference necessary to successfully oppose it.

Lost Birthright represents a crisis in circulation in which the withdrawal of capital, its vanishing into private accumulation, leads to paranoia, distrust and a fetishisation of physical contact with the money form: Valentine and his friends obsessively and violently seek 'not the money in the banks' but 'the gold coins that you can touch and see' (326). Meanwhile the uncle, a formerly radical merchant, asks the middleman Mendoza to act as his agent in investment: 'I want to keep my hand in, to have the feel of the market' (193). The privileging of presence, sight and contact reflect the anxiety of alienation more generally, and may be read as an acknowledgement on Lindsay's part of the connection between the form of the novel and the rise of empirical epistemology.[120] Lindsay's novel ironically undercuts the form's empiricist basis as the 'truth' of that reality continually disappears into the networks of advancing capitalism, and the characters' pursuit of the present and tangible is shown to be a reflex response to a capitalist reality becoming increasingly intangible and decentred, revealing thereby the epistemological limits that constituted the novel in its early phase. The novelistic tropes of 'fate' and 'luck' are shown to happily conspire in this obfuscation. Following the discovery of Mr Lydcott's murder, a farcical quest for his will ensues, in which his various distant relatives imagine themselves in a Gothic novel: 'It feels like the Mysteries of Udolfo' [*sic*] (492). Another relative is thrilled by its prosaic narrative potential: 'What could be more dazzling than the discovery of a miser's treasure on the scene of his midnight murder? The newspapers would be full of it' (486). The satiric

---

117   Harvey 2010, pp. 111–12.
118   Marx 1990, p. 919.
119   Lindsay 1939c, p. 247. Page references are hereafter given in parentheses in the text.
120   Later this connection was influentially examined by Ian Watt: Watt 1957, p. 7.

use of Gothic and adventure conventions lays bare their function in mediating the bourgeois characters' perception of their activity: they perceive the quest not in terms of the real ambition of advancing their control of capital but instead as part of a romantic, individualist adventure.

Lindsay's perception of the connection between novelistic form and the dynamics of capitalism is demonstrated most acutely in the figuration of Valentine's friend, Julian Fane. In Julian, Lindsay coordinates a quest for roots with an account of capital's origins in primitive accumulation, merging two forms of illegitimacy. In his *A Short History of Culture*, Lindsay considered the origin-quest, whether directed inwards (as in *Tristram Shandy*) or outwards (as in *Tom Jones*), to be an inflection of the 'wandering theme' that was the central dynamic in all narrative literature, and which arose in the break-up of the communal settlement and the privatisation of property.[121] Julian is psychologically traumatised by his abandonment as a child, which he understands in terms of disinheritance and exile from his true self, driven by the blind force of 'accumulative anguish' (327). His sense of having been stripped of his 'birthright' is a feeling of being stripped of identity; 'what I have lost is not money, it is my real self' (329), and the documents that might have proved his claim to both have been burnt. Like Valentine, he fetishises the physical commodity of money in circulation, seeking 'not the money in the banks' but 'the gold coins that you can touch and see' (326). This fixation with the physical presence and immediate encounter with the money form is one strand of the novel's critique of empiricism as an inflection of commodity fetishism. The quintessential mode of eighteenth-century bourgeois philosophy is explicitly linked to the disorientating experiential conditions of burgeoning capitalism: a valuation of presence and direct contact at the very moment when such encounters themselves become scarce commodities. In Lindsay's taxonomy of symbols, the circle and the line are the principles of movement; Julian's circulation is however a sign of the disconnection between the principle of advancement and the principle of renewal.[122] He feels himself in circulation around a centre that is both feared and desired: 'like a slow whirlpool he was caught in the tide of this confession', the momentum of which would 'swing him into the crushing foam-fury at the heart of the circling' (203). For Julian, the miser and his hoard represent the birthright from which he has been dispossessed – the irretrievable truth about himself. Part of Julian's trauma is his belief that his mother was raped, and he displaces this traumatic belief about his origins on to the

---

121   Lindsay 1939a, pp. 444–5.
122   Lindsay 1939a, p. 79.

hoarding Mr Lydcott. This trauma presents itself in the figure of 'A hairy hand, say, when you're asleep, coming in through the window' (326). This is a terror of seeing with sudden clarity the body as a whole: 'a touch, yes, you understand, coming out clear and terrible' (326). This 'hand', which represents the coercion from which Julian originates, as well as the illegitimacy of capital itself, may be read as the double of the central metaphor of political economy, the invisible hand that supposedly directs the forces of individual greed into the general interest of the social body. Adam Smith's *The Wealth of Nations* (1776) is a product of the period in which the novel is set, and the metaphors Smith carried over from physiocratic models of the social and economic body suggest themselves.[123] As Susan Buck-Morss has shown, the development of capitalism in the late eighteenth century necessitated the development of conceptual means of 'envisioning' capital as it became impossible to visualise except by means of representation as a consequence of the crisis in circulation *Lost Birthright* depicts.[124]

In the figurative system of political economy, the 'social body' is the organising metaphor, and 'the public finances are the blood that is discharged by a wise *economy*, performing the functions of the heart'.[125] Julian's obsession with circulating money echoes this image: 'It's movement, swung in the star-net, flowing like blood. There's the heart pounding away, out of sight, locked up, but the blood flows' (326). In the murder scene Julian conflates money with blood, 'As if gold, not blood, would pour from the wound' (331). He comes to believe that Mr Lydcott raped his mother, concentrating his trauma of being dispossessed and identity-less into the killing of the hoarder. His fear of the 'hidden hand' suggests a repressed knowledge that, as Smith's schema cannot admit, the body for which the hand stands is not a 'civilised' one.[126] Furthermore Julian's own function in the text is that of a malevolent version of the 'invisible hand': lacking a sense of self or a fortune of his own, he controls through indirection. He contrives the murder of Mr Lydcott, deciding that 'the other two must do the killing. Then his power would be complete' (330). As a malevolent manager he merges with the increasingly invisible operations of capital to the extent that Valentine eventually realises 'I've just taken you on credit. The bill's overdue. What the devil are you?' (521). His self-identification with money, the 'radical leveller' that 'extinguishes all distinctions', leads inexorably

---

123   See Adam Smith 2007, pp. 293–6.

124   Buck-Morss 1995, p. 445.

125   Jean-Jacques Rousseau qtd. Buck-Morss 1995, p. 445; emphasis in Buck-Morss.

126   Buck-Morss 1995, p. 450.

to the dissolution of the self.[127] In this concluding image, Lindsay demonstrates the non-fulfilment of the trope of recognition, as Julian becomes unrecognisable through identification with the form whose origins cannot be revealed. Although Valentine experiences a partial revelation, it leads only to a scuffle with Julian in which they pull each other to their deaths in the Thames (527), an accidental and pointless struggle that starkly contrasts with the images of elective heroism in *1649*, which were read above in terms of a moment in which the defeated are able to recognise the minimal power available to them. Here, however, the mediations of capitalism occlude a perspective of totality which could reveal such a possibility. Julian's filiation to the allegiance-less, endlessly mobile commodity leaves no point of stability from which such a gesture could be made.

'Wilkes and Liberty'

The narrative thread in which Julian is destroyed by the radical uncertainties of capitalist society provides a counterpoint to Roger's partially successful quest for a sure unity of word and gesture in *1649*. As in that novel, *Lost Birthright* features an overtly political plot in which a bourgeois figure leads a popular movement whose demands transcend the interests of the bourgeoisie. It is through the political activism of the emerging capitalist, John Butlin, and the dispossessed scholar, Harry Lydcott, that Lindsay explores the ways in which the democratic struggle might supply that insight. Butlin is drawn to industry because it appeals to his empirical sensibilities: it is 'solid and understandable' (400); he has a 'horror of abstract ideas' (399) – ideas like those that terrorise Julian Fane, originating in primitive accumulation, and which Butlin finds reassuringly excluded from the world of trade. Once again Lindsay is using the form of the novel to expose the bases of bourgeois authority, rather than to reinscribe them. The prospects for the liberalisation of trade push Butlin into the movement gathering around John Wilkes agitating for reform. The Wilkite movement at one level was adopted by the rising middle class as a way of curtailing the power of parliament in order to liberalise trade and, at another level, by newly organised groups of the working class in pursuit of a range of more radical aims. While in *1649*, however, the courtroom scene suggested that such radical demands could be acknowledged before the law, and gains made within the existing legal system, in this novel such a possibility recedes as a consequence of what Marx describes as the 'alienation' of the state through

---

127   Marx 1990, p. 229.

the specialisation of its legislative bodies.[128] Butlin feels the political conflict dwindling 'when compared with the scientific and economic movement' (442). Politics becomes a question of 'the application of technique' divorced from history (especially the bourgeoisie's revolutionary history), from 'memories of the Roman Republic and of ancient Tyrannicide' (442), expressing how, in Marx's terms, the political revolution 'abolished the political character of civil society'.[129] Through this process of amnesia and naturalisation the market comes to appear autonomous. The novel thus attempts to capture what Lukács called the 'tragic' dialectic of the bourgeoisie – that with each specialisation it became less able to see the whole.[130]

Lindsay clearly wants the plebeian, rather than the capitalist, element of the Wilkite agitation to stand against the limited, class-interested epistemology suggested by Butlin. But the popular movement – and Lindsay's handling of it – is ambiguous. In *England My England*, which Lindsay interrupted *Lost Birthright* to write, he acknowledged that Wilkes's campaign had little to do with the working class – their involvement was 'essentially an emotional movement' without 'clear political aims' – but also that 'it gave a powerful impetus to revolutionary emotions among the workers'.[131] In *Spokesmen for Liberty*, Rickword and Lindsay reproduced a range of texts from the period including extracts from Wilkes's articles in the radical newspaper *The North Briton*. Wilkes appealed in Parliament for a 'more just and equal representation' of 'the body of the English people'.[132] But the state form, shown to rationalise bourgeois perspectives, could not deliver that representation. The rhetoric of the Wilkite campaign rested on the mythic figure of the 'Freeborn Englishman' and reveals the severe problems inherent in a politics of unity addressing itself to a national character. E.P. Thompson describes how Wilkes and his supporters understood the concept of national liberties primarily in terms of property rights, but the campaigns elicited a much wider range of issues through its malleable language: 'Even Old Corruption extolled British liberties; not national honour, or power, but freedom was the coinage of patrician, demagogue and radical alike'.[133] Both Thompson and George Rudé note that the persistence of

---

128   Marx 2000b, p. 62.
129   Marx 2000b, p. 63.
130   Lukács 1971, p. 65.
131   Lindsay 1939b, p. 42. Lindsay refers to breaking off the writing of *Lost Birthright* to write the pamphlet in Lindsay 1982, p. 786.
132   Rickword and Lindsay (eds.) 1941, p. 201.
133   E.P. Thompson 2002, p. 83.

the concept in popular ideology lay in part in its appeal to xenophobia.[134] This is unavoidable in the recurring references to 'corruption', 'blood' and the rights of Englishmen not to be 'slaves' in the *Spokesmen for Liberty* documents. In *Lost Birthright*, this accent is not suppressed: Harry reads of a strike at the East India Company at which the agitators compared the actions of the Crown to that of a 'pack of aliens'; an 'insult to the common sense of free British merchants' (179). To read this rhetoric, as Lindsay seems to want to do, as another variation on theme of the loss of what should be held in common risks emptying it of specificity; real losses and gains, different levels of oppression, become blurred.[135]

But Lindsay also wants to argue that the wider popular movement transcended the narrowness of the expansion of trade. The voices of demonstrators are called up in the manner of the oral style of *England My England*: 'Stand out, Dick Nicholl, rope-maker, and have your say' (264). This convocation produces a pageant-like quality in which these voices, drawing very closely on original sources, describe their occupation of the spaces of London and their carnivalesque humiliation of authority: 'We struck the Austrian ambassador ... took him very courteously out of his coach and chalked [the Wilkite sign] 45 on the soles of his shoes' (262). Coupled with this extra-legal gesture of popular power is, however, a cool statement of democratic defiance: 'Then they expelled J. W. from Parliament ... and we keep on re-electing him' (268).[136] But this section is in the past tense, recalling the voices of the previous year; in the novel's present moment, Lindsay's handling of his plebeian characters is more uncertain, and is characterised by the strong intervention of the omniscient narrative voice. This is marked in one short, enclosed scene describing the fate of the peripheral rural characters, Rose and Will, who 'play no further part in our tale, but we can spare their small lives a glance' (413). These characters, 'who had lost the land and the village-community, and yet had found no other bond of toil' (413), are presented as merging with the urban working class and its politics: 'Their voices sound among the other voices. *Wilkes and Liberty!* Give them a thought before they drift down Holborn-way, trickles in the great tide surging on' (431). The implication is that the loss experienced by workers in the eighteenth century could find no immediate outlet, no form in which to be articulated. The result was a situation in which the bourgeoisie could continue

---

134   E.P. Thompson 2002, p. 71; Rudé 1995, p. 55.

135   Lindsay 1969, p. 256.

136   The accounts Lindsay draws on for this section were probably those published by Edmund Burke (Burke 1800). Another likely source is Horace Walpole's *Memoirs of the Reign of King George III*, which recounts the treatment of the Austrian ambassador much as Lindsay describes – but from the point of view of the mortified Walpole (Walpole 1845).

performing its progressive function of destroying feudalism without needing to transform society as a whole. In this enclosed scene, Lindsay describes this contraction of possibility, but there is an unwillingness or inability to give form to these characters' perspectives; they disappear into the highly aestheticised undergrowth of history. Although Lindsay affirms their entry into the radical oral tradition configured in 'not english?', a kind of pastoral silencing takes place, leaving their perspectives inaccessible.

By contrast, as these characters dissolve into background, the bourgeois Harry Lydcott becomes more solid, and the narrative more clearly one of bourgeois political radicalisation. Harry, as a disinherited and dispossessed bourgeois, is able to acquire through contact with working-class politics the perspective of difference that Lindsay saw as essential for opposition to capitalism, and which the working-class characters can no longer access (413). But Harry's switch in perspective is largely an elective one that valorises middle-class identification with working-class causes based on a questionable analogy between individual privation and class injustice. Harry's 'suffering sense of desertion and injury made him particularly susceptible to the tale of mass-deprivations which [the radical weaver] Eastman told' (426). Individual experience is thus presented as the privileged locus of radical politics; the ruined bourgeois is better able to understand class injustice than those who routinely suffer it. The metaphor of the 'lost birthright' of the novel's title is intended to act as the ground by which these different deprivations can be mediated by figuring them as elements of a common inheritance of humanity. Harry's yearning for his birthright transforms itself from an image of property into that of the misappropriated 'common inheritance of the Land' (531):

> Strangely, he felt it was the earth, this thing of birdsong and of furrowed fields of labour, that he had lost; his inheritance which he had never owned yet which now smelt so agonizingly in his nostrils with the tang of loss.
>
> p. 410

But this fulfilment of the recognition trope overshadows, and seems to trivialise, the resolutions of other plotlines. The weaver Eastman, Harry's guide in the struggle, is, like the other working-class characters, dissolved into the historical background as he is sentenced to be hanged. His death is disclosed prosaically as the 'one darkness on the scene' amidst Harry's rapture of political revelation (530). Harry concludes the novel with a feeling of commitment to 'the innermost spirit of life, human life' (533), but unlike in *1649* this feeling, articulated through interior monologue rather than through a gesture of commitment,

seems disconnected from any real promise of justice for the working-class characters. The popular element tends to appear as an ahistorical counter-culture
continually waiting to be discovered by the disenfranchised bourgeois character. From one (Lukácsian) point of view, Lindsay's narrative therefore privileges and exaggerates the significance of the atypical bourgeois intellectual
over characters more directly conditioned by the central historical forces of the
age.[137]

Some of these tensions were detected in an otherwise favourable *Daily
Worker* review of the novel, which noted the 'structural difficulties' and a
tendency for the writing to 'sink into banality' or 'over-wrought effects'.[138] But
it is worth recognising how Lindsay's overall approach in this novel relates to
the Popular Front context. The attempt to ground the text in an assertion that
alienation is operative at all levels of capitalist society is legible as an attempt
to give political weight to the broad rhetoric of the Popular Front appeals to
common interests. The emphasis on bourgeois dissidence, while problematic,
considered the prospects for class alliance in particular conjunctures. However,
the novel's moment of writing, in which the historical tragedy of the thirties
approached its climax as the war in Spain drew to its bleak conclusion and a
new world war loomed, may be a reality the novel is avoiding in the curiously
optimistic manner of its conclusion: 'How good life was' is its final note (532).
Lindsay's marginalisation of Eastman at the moment of his death, so that he
makes no gesture of defiance in the manner of the Levellers of *1649*, also refuses
him heroic power. In 1939 such glorifications of sacrifice may have seemed
outmoded.

Men of Forty-Eight (*1948*)

Men of Forty-Eight, written during the early months of the Second World War,
but not published until 1948, completes the English trilogy. Lindsay's description of the writing process in his autobiography conveys something of the
immense strain under which he was working: 'In those bitter days of the
phoney war, with the feeling that at any moment hell would be let loose, I
strove to let myself go and to pack my deepest emotions about alienation
and the class-world into the novel'.[139] The tensions within this formulation
('strove to let myself go') suggest the imperatives imposed by the intensity of
the moment. The moment of 1848 and that of 1939/40 threaten to collapse

---

137   Lukács 1976, pp. 32–3.
138   'R.K.' 1939, p. 7.
139   Lindsay 1982, p. 789.

into one another as the plot tracks the increasingly hopeless wave of upris-ings across the continent. 1848, the 'year of revolutions' and of the publica-tion of *The Communist Manifesto*, is evoked in Marxist discourse as a turning point both in the bourgeoisie's historical trajectory and in the conditioning of the novel form. For Georg Lukács, the bourgeoisie 'for the first time fights for the naked continuance of its economic and political rule'.[140] This crystallisa-tion of class interests, Lukács argued, occluded the totalising perspective that characterised classic realism and generated instead the antinomies of literary naturalism and expressionism.[141] Ralph Fox likewise argued that after 1848 the bourgeoisie's progressive vocation was terminated so that 'one could resign oneself to the long process of social decay and destruction of civilization by this stupid and miserly bourgeoisie, with its wars, its narrow nationalism and its bestial greed'.[142] The final chapter of Lukács's *The Historical Novel* is organ-ised around the claim that the Popular Front provided writers the possibility of ending the genre's retrograde, post-1848 phase.[143] It is the moment of 1848 that the Popular Front novel, as Lukács envisions it, must redeem. Lindsay's Popular Front novel of 1848, then, is of particular interest as something of a test case for the relationship between Marxist theory and literary practice during the years of anti-fascist cultural organisation.

Lindsay's novel ambitiously attempts to encompass the grand drama and tragedy of the revolutionary year that Eric Hobsbawm considered to combine 'the greatest promise, the widest scope, and the most immediate initial success, with the most unqualified and rapid failure' in modern European history.[144] Eschewing the multiple plotting of the previous novels, this text focuses on one English bourgeois character, Richard Boon, who, somewhat improbably, becomes involved in the February and June Revolutions in France, the Chartist movement in England and, finally, the Vienna Uprising, the last stand against the entrenchment of empire. The chronotope of the single year creates a cer-tain symmetry with *1649*: in both novels the revolutionary advance of the year's early months is tempered by reaction by the year's end. As in *1649*, the novel

---

140   Lukács 1976, p. 202.
141   Note, however, Raymond Williams's discussion of the inadequacy of this summary ac-count in relation to English novels in 'Forms of English Fiction in 1848': R. Williams 1984, pp. 150–65. Tony Pinkney points out, furthermore, that in Britain the upheavals of 1848 led to a reaffirmation of classical principles rather than an emergent modernism: Pinkney 1989, p. 7.
142   Fox 1979, p. 81.
143   Lukács 1976, p. 420.
144   Hobsbawm 1997, pp. 27–8.

begins with the contestation of the narrative of historical events. This contest-ation is dramatised in the clash of voices describing the February Revolution in Paris. A collective voice is constructed, designed to challenge the objectivity of authorised accounts of history and to displace them with a polemical call to responsibility. This voice sets itself in competition with 'those discreet gentle-men, the Liberal historians'.[145] The revolution and the reality of class struggle it reveals cannot be countenanced by that mode of apprehending history, thus forcing it into the subjunctive: if 'the moment of lightning' had not happened, 'how nicely and amicably' things would have worked out (38). The antagonistic collective voice of 'the People' asserts the authority of experience – 'you weren't on the streets' – in order to insist on responsibility: 'The hell with you, gentle-men of the Liberal Opposition. You can't sneak away like the old king with the sawdust trailing out of the belly of his punctured dignity. We're not going to give you the breathing-space for your intrigues, your evasion of responsibility' (41). Contrary to John Coombes's assumption that Popular Front writing is grounded in essentially liberal and progressive coordinates, the liberal view of history is here cited as directly implicated in the repression and disavowal of the events of February, its conception of progress annulled in that moment.[146] The account of the events in February draws directly on Marx's *The Class Struggles in France* (1850), but the rendering of the voice as one of collectivity and partisanship asserts the possibility of a kind of engaged, factually grounded historical writ-ing that avoids the antinomies of subjectivity and objectivity.[147] This voice, however, only briefly re-emerges in the June Days and disappears with the pro-spect of revolution, projecting its potential speculatively into the future. The question of what narrative might be excavated from the ruins of 1848 becomes a central formal problem in the text.

Bourgeois Dissidence

The focalisation of the novel through one bourgeois character leads David Smith to deem the novel a failure, 'a left-wing history textbook, with large chunks of unassimilated material'; a failure attributed to the inappropriate-ness of Boon as a focal point for the subject matter, particularly with regard to the largely proletarian Chartist movement.[148] In *England My England* Lind-say acknowledged that Chartism was a working-class movement, and so his

---

145   Lindsay 1948, p. 38. Page references are hereafter given in parentheses in the text.
146   Coombes 1980, pp. 72–4.
147   Marx 2000c, pp. 42–3.
148   David Smith 1978, p. 110.

choice of classed narrative perspective is significant.[149] Although the central positioning of Boon does at points produce a diminishment of the agency of the working-class characters, the novel reveals the limits of Boon's (bourgeois) individual agency in respect of class injustice more strongly than *Lost Birthright*. Faced with the reality of crisis, his dilemma is, in Lukács's terms, the choice to either recognise a new period or sink into apologies for declining capitalism, and so his predicament mirrors that of the anti-fascist intellectual.[150]

Initially Boon's efforts take the form of individualised exercises of power, for example, when Boon beats an agricultural contractor who employs gangs of children to work in the fields (87).[151] Lindsay uses this moment to demonstrate Boon's inability to bring about justice through the disciplining exercise of his own class power. His father immediately stops his allowance, containing Boon's revolt by indicating the limits of his independence (89). The attempt to exercise political power through the nexus of personal relationships is shown to be misguided for the working-class characters too; the rural workers in his home village are reluctant to rise against their conditions because of the residually feudal ties that lead them to see their predicament in terms of their personal relationships with individual members of the landed gentry (239). Boon's attachment to the working class shifts uncertainly from romanticism to commitment as he comes to terms with these limits, and these shifts are indicated in the series of gestures he feels impelled to make. Echoing the gothic imagery of the *Communist Manifesto*, he makes a denunciatory speech at a village fête on the subject of 'Modern Ghosts and Suburban Spectres', telling the audience that 'you are surrounded by the emaciated shapes, the men and women on whom you feed day and night' (405), revealing at last the secret at the heart of the 'interminable family anecdote' that is England (71). These acts of defiance, however, arise from no personal hardship: Boon undergoes no great *loss* – that most crucial experience in Lindsay's thought. In this regard, he can be usefully contrasted with the protagonist of another Popular Front-era Communist novel set in 1848, Sylvia Townsend Warner's *Summer Will Show* (1936). In that novel, the central character, Sophia Willoughby, a wealthy English woman, is set on the path to Marxism in the ferment of the June Days by her experience of the loss of her husband (to his mistress, a Jewish storyteller) and her children (to smallpox). Sophia pursues her husband and mistress in revolution-

---

149   Lindsay 1939b, p. 52.
150   Lukács 1976, p. 28.
151   In James Barke's *The Land of the Leal*, it is the young worker Jean Ramsey who does exactly this; an act of revolt, in her case, against gender and class power: Barke 1950, pp. 58–9.

ary Paris with the aim of becoming pregnant.[152] While Sophia's revolutionary development is figured as naturally arising from her English grasp of political economy and her unromantic, 'prosaic' temperament, Boon is motivated in *Men of Forty-Eight* by a feeling of inner significance, a convergence of existence and meaning. In the February Revolution, he feels a sense of grandeur, that 'the least gesture of common life was as richly suggestive as the hieratic ceremonials into which thousands of years of dream-terror, dream-release, had imprinted their pattern' (110). What he finds in the reports of the spring uprisings is the possibility of actualising that prospect of a life imbued with heroic potential.

Boon's rendition of the trope of bourgeois dissidence results not in solidity, as in *Lost Birthright*, but in dissolution. Quite aware that he is no 'demonic hero' capable of revolt against the levelling process of capitalism (378), his eventual death is preceded by a self-erasure experienced while reading the *Communist Manifesto*, 'drifting into moments of sheer blankness when it seemed that some obstinate force inside himself simply took a sponge and wiped his mind empty' (361). All that is solid melts into air: 'The result is that I am not human at all; I am approaching the stage where I will fade off in a whiff of marshgas, leaving only my clothes and boots for the dustmen to remove' (361). Lindsay wrote later that there was a 'cultural break' in mid-nineteenth-century England that occurred as a consequence of the extreme success of industrial capitalism, and in Boon Lindsay figures this closure of possibility.[153] While he toys with writing a book, giving the 'concrete picture of the year' (425), his death in another failed rising forecloses the prospect and suggests the abolition of the bourgeois as subject of history. Yet this only announces what has been written into the text all along: the very instability and lack of solidity of Boon's character, such that his own voice and his own perspective can never be unambiguously identified.

Irony and Insight

Men of Forty-Eight depicts the hardening of the bourgeois state in a manner that contrasts with the earlier novels' explorations of the efficacy of popular resistance within the state apparatus. For Marx in the *Eighteenth Brumaire*, the establishment of the bourgeois state after 1848 amounted to a loss of innocence: 'The fruit fell into [the bourgeoisie's] lap, but it fell from the tree of knowledge, not from the tree of life'.[154] The bitter knowledge Marx invokes here pervades the novel. Boon and his political educator, the Chartist Scamler, attain

---

152   S.T. Warner 1987, p. 99. Page references are hereafter given in parentheses in the text.
153   Lindsay 1956, p. 19.
154   Marx 1973, p. 158.

an apparently absolute lucidity in their readings of the events unfolding. The lack of struggle in the acquisition of these insights does strain the credibility of the characterisation; but in another way, a lack of ironic distance is a refusal to exculpate the characters. Up until April, an ironic distance imposes itself between readers and characters, but the failure in that month bestows on characters a prescience of what is to come. Failure makes itself felt as a saturation of knowledge attributed to the characters themselves. Scamler in particular often seems to proleptically address readers facing another crisis: 'Our failure – the working-class failure this year – has doomed the world to colossal wars of empire rivalry' (388). Lukács writes of the bourgeoisie of 1848 experiencing a kind of last flowering of insight, 'a last brief, irretrievable prime of humanity', like Hegel's Owl of Minerva. It is possible to read Lindsay's ascription of seemingly excessive clarity to his central characters in these terms.[155]

Irony is the dominant mode of Sylvia Townsend Warner's *Summer Will Show*, as Sophia's stern, empirical respect for money and 'pious respect for property' (177) are continually undercut by the unfolding of history, and her gestures of defiance resolve into powerlessness.[156] But Sophia, unlike the 'romantic' revolutionaries with whom she aligns, survives the revolt to end the novel reading the *Communist Manifesto* in a state of confirmation and clarity (406). In Lindsay's version of bourgeois dissidence in 1848, however, this certainty precedes Boon's revolutionary action, and its value is thereby brought into question. Boon experiences 'a sustaining certainty' at the novel's outset that precedes his efforts to rationalise it, and which he takes to coincide with his vision of a unity of intention and act, an end to the ambiguity so troubling to Roger in *1649* (39). The novel's ironic climax is the revelation, at the novel's conclusion, of the circumstances of Boon's participation in the February Revolution. This revelation comes in the form of a 'confession' made in a letter to his lover Mary that he sends from Paris on the eve of the June Days. The letter reveals Boon's own evasion of responsibility, having driven his lover to attempt suicide. These two chronological scales – that of the calendar year and the longer frame of Boon's own life – interact in Boon's attempt to relate his own past to the rhythm of history.

The confession reshapes Boon's revolutionary perspectives. His merging with the crowd is reframed as an attempted absolution, an evasion consequent

---

155   Lukács 1976, p. 28.

156   Her lover Minna is shot dead by Caspar, the illegitimate son of her uncle, whom her husband has enrolled in the Gardes Mobiles arraigned against the revolutionary forces (S.T. Warner 1987, p. 383). It is Sophia's own status as a 'lady' that saves her from execution (S.T. Warner 1987, pp. 380–1).

on his loss of innocence and his ethical awareness of his actions. The 'confession' stages a confrontation with Boon's past at the very moment that his class breaks with its own and commits the 'crime' it will be forced to evade. Boon's working through of his own past injustice enables, at a personal level, the acceptance of responsibility that the bourgeoisie cannot take on at the political level. This substitution articulates a humanist and ethical symmetry, but the price paid is a destruction of the self. Boon's pursuit across Europe of the revolutionary storm he equates with absolution results in a loss of personal historical coherence. At the barricades in Vienna, 'The whole world was dissolving ... How long was it since he had left London? He tried to remember exactly, to recall each day in succession, but the events wouldn't fall into the right order; he found himself forcing them into arrangements that worked for a while then fell to pieces' (438). The temporalities of individual experience and history no longer coincide.

It is the failure of the (working-class) Chartist movement that makes Boon's death inevitable and causes the ironies that constitute the realist novel to dissolve. After his experiences in France he is unable to reconcile himself with an England from which the prospect of revolution, 'the ending of all class forms', has vanished, and a complete alienation interposes itself: 'A vast sense of homelessness had descended on him ever since he had landed' (359). Boon feels this condition of exile is a consequence of his position as an outsider-revolutionary, in contrast to the proletariat for whom, Boon thinks, 'the enclosing pressure, by giving them both an immediate goal and a basic resistance, obliterates, at least in part, the bewilderment of failure and sets them steadily, however imperceptibly at first, on the road to the next burst of open conflict with the evil thing' (359). There is an echo in this of the 'standpoint of popular life', the perspective of universal, rather than *class* liberation, and yet the qualifiers in this sentence undercut its confidence. Where in spring he had felt a romantic excess, 'an irrepressible overflowing of united energy' (133), here that hope is tempered by the experience of revolutionary failure. The resulting phrasing encloses the image of revolutionary outpouring with the prosaic syntax of realist restraint. The failure is mirrored in Boon's renewed quest for an adequate gesture:

> There are moments, he thought, when the gesture must be made ... The English working class had failed the world, bitter as the realisation was. Well, at least the Chartist core would make a gesture, would die tonight for the honour of their class. He strode along in time with the joiner. Life was good.
>
> p. 393

The gesture referred to is the doomed Orange Tree Conspiracy, after which leading Chartists were tried and transported.[157] While left-wing histories produced in the thirties ascribe the collapse of the movement to misguided leadership and immature forms of organisation, Lindsay's stress on the idea that the Chartists 'had failed the world' is distinctive.[158] If the phrasing attributed to Boon seems glib, and the Chartists' deaths too readily accepted as necessary acts of penitence, this is a sign of the difficult convergence of ethical and political currents in the novel. Lindsay's Hegelian view of history is that of an unfolding of class struggle that can be formalised as a narrative immortalising the dead as participants in a unified struggle for human community: a story in which '[a]ll the fights of the people are defeats but the last fight' (330). But this sense of history's shape is tempered by an existentialist emphasis on individual choice, and the moments of 'recognition' in the novels all involve a negotiation of these two currents. Where, especially in *1649*, the radical gesture was framed in terms of a recognition of limits – of what action was available in full view of historical realities – the excess of knowledge in *Men of Forty-Eight* means that no delimitation, no realistic confrontation with possibility, occurs.

The excessive knowledge granted to Boon and Scamler threatens to destroy the irony constitutive of realist characterisation. There is, frequently, no apparent tension between Boon's interiority and the external world; his perspective on his historical moment is totalising.[159] However, where in the earlier novels, especially *1649*, the limits of individual knowledge and agency constituted the possibility of radical acts, the very lack of this dialectical tension here underpins Boon's inability to meaningfully act in the world. What Boon is not is Frédéric Moreau, anti-hero of Flaubert's *L'Éducation Sentimentale*, whose life, as Jay Bernstein argues, is meaningless because it is conditioned by the failures of 1848.[160] Lindsay and Lukács both considered Frédéric a cipher for frustration. Lukács argued that Frédéric's 'interiority possesses no lyrical power of scorn

---

157   See Chase 2007, pp. 326–30.

158   See, for example, Morton 1992, p. 377. In a piece for the *Daily Worker* commemorating the centenary of Chartism, Ness Edwards described the movement in more ambiguous terms as 'a blind, unsuccessful attempt to perform in Britain what, at a similar juncture of political development, was successfully performed by the working class movement in Russia': Edwards 1939, p. 2.

159   As Jay Bernstein argues, reading Lukács's *Theory of the Novel*, irony may be the 'master-practice' of the novel form; a 'constitutive, form-giving structure' that avers the division between man and world in modernity: Bernstein 1984, pp. 185–6.

160   Bernstein 1984, pp. 121–2.

or pathos that might set it against the pettiness of reality'.[161] Lindsay's own hero of 1848 inverts this pettiness through an excessive romanticism, the prose saturated with an inner quality of rhapsody, 'an irrepressible overflowing of united energy' (133), that fails to be formalised by an adequate act and resolves in the pathos of Boon's death in Vienna. For Boon, no retreat from failure is possible: 'There is no return', he thinks (438); 'There was to be no leaving-alone' (423). Boon's subjectivity, formed in the February Revolution and promising new content for the bourgeois subject, cannot withstand the closing down of possibility announced by the June counter-revolution.

Conclusion

Boon's campaign in Vienna links him with the anti-fascists of the thirties, a parallel made explicit in Lindsay's prefatory 'Note', which quotes a German politician in 1848 denouncing Polish national rights, and notes the consonance with Nazi policy.[162] The Vienna Uprising entailed a mutiny by Viennese troops ordered to put down a nationalist movement in Hungary, and in 1937 Philip Ormond wrote in the *Daily Worker* of the parallels between this incident and the anti-fascist struggle.[163] There are resonances too with the brutal suppression of popular and socialist resistance to incipient fascism in Vienna in February 1934.[164] In another strong echo of the anti-fascist struggle, Boon is haunted by 'scraps of memories about Munich' (424).[165] Boon's death in the suppression of the Vienna Uprising asserts the importance of national liberties and commemorates internationalist participation in the struggles for self-determination. The shifting of attention in *Men of Forty-Eight* onto central Europe and the question of the fate of the Germanic countries has obvious contemporary significance: the prospect of a 'federation of equal republics' (428) is an unrealised dream of a different Europe, a different way that history might have moved.

---

161   Lukács 1978, p. 125; echoed in Lindsay 1939a, p. 367.

162   Lindsay 1948, pp. vii–viii.

163   Ormond 1937, p. 4.

164   Stephen Spender's long poem *Vienna* commemorates these events: Spender 1934.

165   As Eric Hobsbawm writes, 'The Munich agreement of 1938 perfectly demonstrated [the] combination of confident aggression on one side, fear and concession on the other, which is why for generations the very word "Munich" became a synonym, in Western political discourse, for craven retreat': Hobsbawm 1995, p. 146.

CHAPTER 4

The vision here, as elsewhere in the novel, is uncomfortably clear and prescient. The historical distance between 1848 and the moment of reading is therefore not a safe distance – indeed, it feels like no distance at all. The novel's historical situation, a moment in which Lindsay found 'paralysing contradictions' as British Communists negotiated a dilemma over the respective demands of anti-fascism, defence of the Soviet Union, and the pursuit of socialism at home, must be addressed.[166] In the early phase of the war, Lindsay felt himself to be 'odd man out' as he disputed the Moscow-imposed line that the war was an 'imperialist' conflict that Communists could not support, arguing instead that 'the situation would develop the war along anti-fascist lines' and should therefore be supported.[167] In the literary sphere he felt that writers at this point abandoned political engagement as the anti-fascist front failed, and thus many advances made were lost. That moment, which Lindsay would later scathingly describe as a 'renunciation by so many writers of an active creed of humanism', is invoked through a stress on responsibility and commitment even against necessary defeat.[168] Yet Lindsay acknowledged the intense difficulty of maintaining faith after the end of the war in Spain, and his realisation that the working class were not going to defend the Soviet Union during the 'phoney war'.[169] Boon is not innocent and is fully aware of the imminence of death, a courageous stance that partially cancels out, but is also itself partially cancelled by, the banality of death when it occurs. The ambivalence Boon feels over whether it is better to 'live as a slave' than accept 'this murdering, this will to death' (438) reflects the more morally troubled environment of the incipient Second World War.[170] The lyrical description of a Victorian Christmas and Scamler's resumed domestic romance with Prue enclose Boon's act, leaving it, and the possibility of revolution, simultaneously enclosed in the past and projected into the future.

---

166 Lindsay 1956, p. 59. For a detailed account of the conflicts and developments in Communist Party thinking at this time, see Morgan 1989, pp. 105–33.

167 Lindsay 1982, p. 791.

168 Lindsay 1956, p. 44. It must, however, be noted that this book appeared in 1956, the year in which the world Communist movement was fractured by the revelations of the 'Secret Speech' and by the Soviet suppression of the Hungarian Revolution. Lindsay, who unlike many remained loyal to the Party, may be referring as much to the perceived betrayal of those who left the Party during that year as to the ostensible subject of 1939/40.

169 Lindsay 1956, pp. 64–5.

170 The link with Spain is evident in the fact that Boon's phrasing inverts the well-known declaration of Dolores Ibárrui ('La Pasionaria'), 'Better to die on your feet than live on your knees' (see Dellinger 2013, pp. 285–315).

There is much, therefore, in the conclusion of Lindsay's English trilogy that is consonant with the tone of valediction, regret and ambivalence that characterises the literary responses of many thirties writers to the outbreak of the war. After Boon's death, the final pages of the novel can only look forwards to what Ralph Fox called the 'vulgarity of Empire', and to the wars accurately prophesised by Scamler.[171] The motif of the cyclical year resumes to affirm an eventual spring, but the novel's 'perspective of the future', as Lukács calls it, is much weaker than that of its forerunners.[172] While Boon's death is a banal accident, reflecting none of the calculated minimal agency of the Levellers in *1649*, he announces the significance of his dissidence as a defection from his class, declaring himself 'not English' (429). In this qualified manner, Lindsay admits the bourgeois radicals of 1848 into his narrative of English radical tradition given form in his poem for mass declamation, a work intended, in 1936, to speak to the new mass audience that would rise against fascism.[173] If that audience had not asserted itself in 1940, the novels nonetheless attempt to recover, in their complexity, the course of development of capitalism in England, and the crucial moments in which the outcomes – both of 1848 and of the 1930s – were contested. In one sense, however, Lindsay's faith in the future he saw instantiated in the Soviet Union was rewarded: while *Men of Forty-Eight* received little critical notice in Britain, the success of the Russian translation resulted in an invitation to visit the Soviet Union for the first time as part of the Pushkin jubilee in 1949.[174]

---

171   Fox 1979, p. 81.
172   Lukács 1976, p. 418.
173   Lindsay 1936, p. 357; and Lindsay 1937a, pp. 511–17.
174   Lindsay 1982, p. 801.

PART 3

Class, Nation, People

••

CHAPTER 5

James Barke and the National Turn

In the last chapter, Jack Lindsay's novels were read as thematically unified by a sense of the 'loss' of what should be held in common, and the mutating forms that deprivation took. As I suggested, however, Lindsay tends to posit bourgeois dissidence (radicalism from within the dominant class) as a privileged trope that risks marginalising and excluding working-class experience, and thereby reinforcing the normative position of middle-class voices and perspectives in the form of the novel. The English inflection of the Communist national turn proposed in 1935 could, as we saw in Chapter One in relation to Ralph Fox, sanction a brushing aside of anti-imperialism and a reinstatement of triumphalist, Eurocentric humanism. The following two chapters consider the Popular Front engagements of two writers who fall outside the normative position of this perspective: James Barke, a Glasgow shipyard engineer, and Lewis Jones, a working-class Communist activist from the Rhondda Valley. Both draw on the historical experiences of the working class in their communities to produce novels that examine the relation between the particularity of that experience and the world-historical events of the thirties. In both writers, we find a valorisation of community resources of resistance as weapons in the struggle against fascism. The question of the meanings of 'the nation' and 'the people' and of the viability of a national story as a means of mobilising elements without definite 'class belonging', in Laclau and Mouffe's terms, come into focus.[1] This chapter considers the 'national turn' outside England, and examines Barke's *Major Operation* (1936) and *The Land of the Leal* (1939).

The National Turn (1): British Questions

The national turn among English writers could produce a certain troubling indifference to or deferral of the problem of imperialism, as well as a generally unquestioned elision of 'England' with 'Britain'. But for writers who were not English, who emerged in different national traditions, and for whom the claims of a national culture could not be unproblematically separated from the

---

1   Laclau and Mouffe 2001, p. 68.

claims of political independence, the national turn presented problems. There
was considerable ambiguity in Dimitrov's Seventh Congress address about precisely what constituted the distinction between 'bourgeois nationalism' and
the newly endorsed 'proletarian' nationalism.[2] Developments in Europe after
1933 meant that questions of the right of nations to self-determination and
sovereignty had to be addressed in however pragmatic a fashion. One such
pragmatic response can be seen in Rajani Palme Dutt's argument, made shortly
before the adoption of the Popular Front strategy in January 1935: 'We do not for
a moment exclude military defence against Fascism – *on one condition*, and one
condition only, namely, that we have country to defend. We shall defend Workers' Britain, as an integral part of the World Workers' Republic, of the future
World Soviet Union'.[3]

Although the 'national' turn resonated most strongly in terms of cultural
and historical, rather than more narrowly political, emphases, the Communist Party of Great Britain did engage with questions of the status of Wales and
Scotland within Britain.[4] Morgan, Cohen and Flinn suggest that this engagement predated the Popular Front line, and that as early as 1934 a preliminary
draft of the Party's programme *For Soviet Britain* included the proposal for 'a
federal republic of Soviet Britain', but this phrase was removed as a result of
Moscow's objections.[5] The Party did, however, make efforts to mobilise Scottish and Welsh national cultures against fascism, but attempted to do so in
cultural terms without addressing questions of national autonomy. Communists in Scotland were encouraged to make alliances with nationalists but, as this
chapter describes, Scottish Communists themselves expressed hostility to the
idea, while in Wales nationalist support for the Franco regime in Spain would
certainly have prevented any such alliance being contemplated.[6] The Party's
increasing interest in Welsh culture during the late thirties may seem oppor-
tunistic, but to some extent the Party was taking the initiative by marking out
a place of Welsh culture within the global anti-fascist struggle. A brief compar-
ative glance at the *Daily Worker*'s coverage of the Welsh National Eisteddfod in
1932 and 1938 brings this shift into view. In 1932, Idris Cox, probably the most
prominent Welsh Communist in the thirties, condemned the event for its elitism and lack of popular appeal: 'All the songs, choral tests, poems, and dramas

2   Dimitrov 1935b, pp. 70–1.
3   Dutt 1935, p. 17; emphasis in original.
4   Morgan, Cohen and Flinn 2007, p. 205.
5   Ibid.
6   Morgan, Cohen and Flinn 2007, p. 209. For Plaid Cymru's attitude to Spain, see Stradling 2004,
    p. 34 and H. Francis 1984, p. 97.

are divorced from the real life of the people', and '[u]nderneath the glamour and ceremonial of the National Eisteddfod are the vicious claws of grasping profit-mongers who suck the lifeblood of the working class'.[7] By 1938, however, the event could be figured as 'a symbol of the devotion of the "common" people to the finer products of the mind at the price of great material sacrifice'.[8] In 1938, shortly before the Munich Crisis, a bilingual pamphlet on Welsh culture, *The Lore of the People* [*Llên y Werin*], appeared, co-authored by Arthur Horner (the president of the South Wales Miners' Federation, who encouraged Lewis Jones to write fiction), Will Paynter and Glyn Jones, representing the South, and Jennie Hughes, T.E. Nicholas and J. Roose Williams representing the North. In this atmosphere, the defence of the culture and freedom of Europe's minority nationalities had acquired a new urgency. The pamphlet argued that the Eisteddfod was 'a truly national and democratic institution'; national in 'the widest sense', because at the event 'Welshmen of all parties and sects gather together in friendly emulation to enrich the national culture'; and democratic, 'for it owes nothing to State encouragement, and little to the patronage of the wealthy, and has been built up by the efforts and sacrifices of the common people of Wales'.[9] The rhetorical move here in many ways echoes the reframing of democracy outlined in the previous chapter, marking a shift from the condemnation of the repressive tendencies of the form to the valorisation of its popular credentials. This is part of the broader move, characteristic of the Popular Front formation, to work within existing forms – often forms, like the pageant, closely associated with the reproduction of conservative ideology – and to consider how elements within dominant discourses could be articulated differently.

The National Turn (II): Critical Voices

Although, as discussed below, there are problematic attitudes to Scottish and Welsh national questions expressed by some English writers, it is not the case that Communists in those countries were necessarily keen to involve themselves in questions of the national status in their home nations. The idea that national traditions of struggle and national cultural forms could be turned towards the objectives of the Popular Front without addressing

---

7   Cox 1932, p. 2.

8   Wyn 1938, p. 2.

9   Communist Party of Great Britain (South Wales District) and Communist Party of Great Britain (North Wales District) 1938, p. 3.

political questions of national autonomy was inevitably fraught with problems. In November 1936, *Left Review*'s 'Scotland' issue provided something of a case in point. The contributions by Scottish writers themselves will be considered in due course, but here it is worth assessing Edgell Rickword's contribution, 'Stalin on the National Question'. Responding to the recent Welsh Nationalist arson attack on a British Government bombing school on the Llŷn peninsula,[10] Rickword wrote that,

> A recent case of alleged arson in Wales must have opened many people's eyes to the existence of national problems not only in the colonial dependencies of the British Crown, but actually within the boundaries of the Mother Country herself.[11]

This apparent 'discovery' of national tensions within Britain led Rickword to look to the model of the Soviet Union, in view of 'the successful solution of the minorities problem' there, for guidance.[12] Rickword quoted at some length both from Stalin's 'Marxism and the National Question' (1913) and his 'Report to the 16th Congress of the CPSU' (1930), but the line of argument only draws attention to the problems with Stalin's definition of a nation: 'A nation is a historically evolved, stable community of language, territory, economic life, and psychological make-up manifested in a community of culture'.[13] This is of course to evade the issue of political self-determination entirely. While affirming the positive action of the Spanish Popular Front government in granting autonomy to the Basque and Catalan peoples, Rickword's aim appears to be to deflect the question of any similar turn in Britain, which Rickword felt would represent a 'deviation to the Left'.[14] That nationalisms within Britain were a distraction from the greater project of anti-fascist action, and that Scottish (and Welsh, and Irish) cultural traditions could be celebrated and mobilised without any reference at all to questions of political constitution, brings to the fore the difficulty of separating what Fox called the 'truly national' from the 'merely national-

---

10   Nationalist sentiment was ignited by the Government decision to locate the school on the site of Penyberth, a farmhouse associated with patrons of the arts in Wales. Thus opposition was mobilised on the grounds that the decision represented an outright attack on Welsh culture. See Powell 2002, pp. 159–60.

11   Rickword 1936a, p. 746.

12   Ibid.

13   Stalin, 'Marxism and the National Question', qtd. Rickword 1936a, p. 746.

14   Rickword 1936a, p. 749.

istic'.[15] At root is the issue of whether the idea of the nation can be detached from its imperial and chauvinist connotations and rearticulated in such a way as to provide a base for class alliance.

An example of this problem, which has bearings on the theorisation of the novel, can be found in *International Literature* in an exchange between Georg Lukács, Sylvia Townsend Warner and T.A. Jackson in 1938. The two-part essay on Walter Scott adapted from the first chapter of *The Historical Novel* that Lukács published in the journal in 1938 fails to bestow any relevance to Scott's national identity. Lukács uses 'England' and 'Scotland' interchangeably, or as presenting no important political differences:

> As a typical English gentleman, by tradition and mode of life closely connected with the gentry and the bourgeoisie, Scott has a deep sympathy for the independent and self-respecting medieval English and Scotch burghers and for the independent and free peasants.[16]

To the first part of the article, Sylvia Townsend Warner responded with the complaint that Scott's relationship to national questions had been misrepresented by Lukács, and that furthermore he had overlooked their relevance to the national question both in Britain and the Soviet Union:

> Strongly conscious of his nationality, proud of his country's history, Scott was yet quite comfortable, so to speak, in the United Kingdom. He is the most important example that a minor nationality can be blended into a compound state, without either servility or the chauvinism of racial theories; and as such, Scott is relevant to the question of national minorities.[17]

Lukács's subsequent response to Townsend Warner brushed off the question as beyond the concerns of his article. Jackson however intervened in Lukács's defence. He conceded that Lukács had misunderstood Scott's national status, but, just as Soviet constitutional politics are impenetrable to the British critic, so to the Soviet writer, 'in all but exceptional cases the specific distinctions between English, Scottish and Welsh are of negligible moment'.[18] In response to the tension between these two positions – being neither able to admit

---

15   Fox 1979, p. 23.
16   Lukács 1938a, p. 61.
17   S.T. Warner 1938, p. 100.
18   Jackson 1939, p. 69.

the importance of Scott's nationality nor to dismiss it as entirely irrelevant – Jackson takes the extraordinary step of amending a passage from Lukács in the following manner:

> Through historical research in the entire past of England [and Scotland] he tried to discover the 'middle' road, to find the 'mean' between the two contending extremes, English [and Scottish] history furnished him with comforting examples; the most embittered [national and] class battles, where sometimes one and sometimes the other came out victorious, resolved, in the long run, in some 'mean' spacious enough to enclose and reconcile both hostile elements.[19]

This episode is to be understood as a literary debate between three writers, none of whom can be assumed to be voicing an official Party line, but which nonetheless brings into focus the difficulty posed by the national turn. Jackson is attempting the type of mediation so central to Lukács's work, a process by which immediately incommensurable forms of social relations (such as national or class divisions) are shown to be in fact elements of the social totality. The fact that Jackson's amendment does serious damage to the coherence of the passage – so that the duality of class struggle becomes conflated with an undefined 'national' struggle – underscores the point that it is not possible to simply impute national content in the manner Jackson supposes. He describes his intervention as a 'quantitative' addition that makes a 'qualitative' enhancement – but this is already to suppose that 'nation' and 'class' express analogous forms of social *category*, overlooking the constitution of class as a *relationship* of exploitation. Lukács's theory of mediation does not suppose that all types of societal relation are in fact identical or analogous, rather that they can be understood as parts in a whole complex of relations.

A second useful example of the difficulties presented by a tendency to assume that national cultures can be unproblematically assumed into a general 'front' of struggle is to be found in Jack Lindsay and Edgell Rickword's anthology, *Spokesmen for Liberty*. The editors include a number of texts by nationalist writers while seeking to evade specific questions of national autonomy. John McLean, James Connolly, and Cunninghame Graham all feature, but the editors' introduction relegates questions of Scottish, Irish and Welsh national movements to a footnote:

---

19   Jackson 1939, p. 72. All parentheses are Jackson's.

> No single volume could adequately show the heroic resistance of Welsh, Scots and Irish to the encroachments of the English Crown, of the many nations of Asia and Africa to that of the capitalists; but we have proved that the English people are not guilty of all the blood shed by their rulers ... The surnames under our later extracts: Jones and O'Connor, McLean and Connolly, reveal the co-operation in a single aim which is building the basis for the free communities of tomorrow.[20]

This comment is obviously aiming to mediate the specifics of national struggles so that they are read as part of a universal project of emancipation from capitalism. The effect however is rather closer to Jackson's modification of Lukács, in the sense that the need to assert that national struggles are part of a total project is emphasised in a way that ends up denying any specificity to those struggles. Lindsay and Rickword's handling of the Connolly text they present suggests that their evasion of national autonomy is deliberate – and, furthermore, that the 'single aim' can only be brought about through coercion. Although they present their selection, titled 'The Only Enemy', as drawn from an article in *Forward* published on 22 August 1914, the text is in fact spliced together from two different pieces: one published on the date given, and the other published on 15 August 1914. The created text seems to argue for a 'patriotism' that is not 'the patriotism of capitalism'; echoing the ideal of an alternative form of nationality and national loyalty at the heart of Rickword and Lindsay's project.[21] But to make Connolly's voice consonant with that ideal it is necessary to omit the clear call to national struggle in the texts appropriated. The edited text reads, '[t]hat which is good for the working class I esteem patriotic', but the full sentence in Connolly's 15 August article is, 'That which is good for the working class I esteem patriotic, but that party or movement is the most perfect embodiment of patriotism which most successfully works for the conquest by the working class of the control of the destinies of the land wherein they labour'.[22]

---

20   Rickword 1941, p. xvi, fn.
21   Connolly (22 August), qtd. Rickword and Lindsay eds. 1941, p. 386.
22   Connolly 1914.

'There is no Scottish National Question'

The *Left Review* 'Scotland' issue referred to above featured a debate between the novelists James Barke and Neil M. Gunn. Although lifelong friends and correspondents, Gunn was stung by an earlier article by Barke, commemorating their mutual friend Lewis Grassic Gibbon, in which he argued that 'Scottish nationalism is largely inspired by the superior race-theory of the Gael and the current demagogy of Major Douglas. The identity of [Neil M.] Gunn's nationalist ideology is with that of Aryan theoreticians of Hitler fascism'.[23] Gunn responded to Barke's criticism from an anti-imperial position, with the argument that a Scotland that does not have autonomy cannot participate in the international struggle.[24] In a manner comparable to the organic and primitive communist imaginings of Rickword and Lindsay, Gunn believed that the culture of the Gaelic speakers had been originally a primitive communist one. For Gunn, that precedent was a central part of the imaginative struggle for a better Scotland.[25] Barke, however, had no time for this idea, and positioned the nationalist cause as a distraction from the real issue, about which he is emphatic:

> It was Capitalism that enclosed the common lands of England. It was the self-same Capitalism that destroyed the Highlands as the land of the Gael, broke the Lowland peasantry and drove them into the factories and mines. It is capitalism that's destroying beyond all hope of resurrection An Gaidhealtachd.[26]

Where for Gunn national culture is something ideally embodied in the national past, for Barke it is a site of constant struggle, something continually being made and remade. There is no point of harmony in the distant past: 'Every worth-while national characteristic has been the work and the inheritance of the Scottish people – even when they have been bedevilled in denial and (temporary) repudiation'.[27] Where Gunn's Gaelic culture represents a static otherness, an unchanging counterpoint to the modern world, Barke's model of culture is a dialectical one, with Scottish writers and thinkers in continually recip-

---

23   Barke 1936a, p. 221.
24   Gunn 1936, p. 736.
25   Gunn 1936, p. 737.
26   Barke 1936b, p. 744.
27   Barke 1936b, p. 743.

rocal relationships with other cultures.[28] Barke's article, however, balances a rejection of nationalist politics as middle-class affectation with an articulation of a national and popular perspective consonant with Dimitrov's conception of ideological struggle. Thus 'the nation' and 'the people' both become synonymous with resistance to capitalism; in William Wallace, Barke argues, 'the concept of the nation reached its (then) highest expression', since '[a]gainst the warring and mutually antagonistic feudal overlords whose one guiding principle was their own aggrandisement he set the republican commonality of "the people"'.[29] This conception of 'the people' is the locus of the culture in need of defence: 'All that is truly national, all that is best and worthy of preservation in the various national cultures is the heritage of the workers and peasants concerned, of the class in whose hands the future lies'.[30] Barke concludes on an impeccably Popular Frontist demand for intellectuals to ally with the workers if they are 'genuine humanitarians', 'real lovers of their country's best traditions' and haters of 'Fascist barbarism'.[31] The article is perhaps the best example of a non-English British Marxist negotiating the national turn by emphasising national traditions as a weapon against fascism and denationalised capital, marking out a common ground on which members of different classes could align.

James Barke, *Major Operation* (1936)

The *Left Review* debate articulates a position on national cultural questions that Barke had been working out for some years, and which is being worked through without being fully resolved in *Major Operation*, published, after a series of delays, two months before his *Left Review* article appeared.[32] Although the novel has been read by Gustav Klaus as a symbolic enactment of the Popular Front, I argue here that the novel demonstrates Barke's struggle to reconcile himself with the new line.[33] The central plotline of the novel is a

---

28   Barke 1936b, p. 741.

29   Barke 1936b, p. 742.

30   Barke 1936b, p. 744.

31   Ibid.

32   Barke's papers suggest the delay was caused by his publisher's worries that an obscenity suit could be brought as a result of the 'Erotic Nocturne over the Second City' section: see F.T. Smith, TS, to Barke, 25 April 1936, Box 6A, James Barke, Special Collections, The Mitchell Library, Glasgow.

33   Klaus 1998, p. 19.

variation on the theme of middle-class radicalisation; a ruined businessman, George Anderson, finds himself sharing a hospital ward with a leader of the unemployed, Jock MacKelvie, and this extended encounter provides a political education that sees Anderson enter the labour movement before, like James Seton in *May Day*, being killed in a clash between demonstrators and police. I will suggest here that the novel shifts between a mode of 'subaltern modernism' and a more realist narrative of radicalisation. The novel may be understood as rehearsing Barke's conflicted attitudes to the principle of class alliance and to the national turn, and his effort to identify a conception of 'the people' and 'the nation'.

Known in later years primarily as a scholar of Robert Burns, Barke's cultural influences were nonetheless extremely wide and international in range. Barke at least in private expressed antipathy towards *Left Review* in particular, and a number of central Popular Front figures besides. In a revealing exchange written as he was working on *Major Operation*, Barke declares *Left Review* a pale imitation of the work of Soviet cultural theorists:

> I think my next effort [i.e. *Major Operation*] will be the goods. There is no question it will be translated. The [*Left Review*] is tripe – and pretty awful at that. We have nobody who can formulate literary theory (say) like Averbakh, Bezimensky, Radek, Libedinsky, Frichte, Brik, P.C. Kogan, Gorbatchev, Shkolvsky, Polonsky. Or Pilnak, Fedin, or the very sensible Gladkov. But we have such hoodlums as [Ralph] Fox and Mrs [Amabel] Williams-Ellis. On the other hand West and Garman are good. And of course there's myself![34]

Barke's very un-Scottish and un-British list of enthusiasms did not sit easily with the cultural formation around *Left Review*, and his difficulty in reconciling himself to a non-sectarian politics did not go unnoticed. *Major Operation* was praised in the *Labour Monthly* for its vividness of description, Aitken Ferguson declaring that 'it is a book which will appeal, and ought to be on the library shelf of every Labour man in Britain'.[35] Others, however, found it

---

34 Barke, TS, letter to 'Arthur', 21 November 1935, Box 4B, James Barke Papers, Special Collections, The Mitchell Library, Glasgow.

35 Ferguson 1936, p. 643. Ferguson's admission of the novel's political significance reflects his own movement from the 1920s, when under the pen-name 'Clydebank Riveter' he wrote regularly to the *Weekly Worker* to attack its cultural coverage, which he saw as an indulgence of fellow travellers (Croft 1990 p. 36, and Morgan, Cohen and Flinn 2007, p. 206). Barke's reference in *Left Review* to 'a Clydeside engineer' who understands national

a cause for concern. In a letter to Barke, John Strachey said he liked the hospital scenes, and though he considered the first part of the book first rate, he found the rest 'decidedly sectarian'.[36] Strachey does not elaborate on precisely what he found sectarian in the novel, but Barke's technique of narrating his middle-class character's progression to Communism through an overwhelmingly traumatic physical and mental collapse was perhaps not in keeping with an ethic of inclusivity and voluntary alliance rather than coercion.

Barke's difficulties with a politics of alliance should be seen in the context of his paradoxical status as a non-Party member, who nonetheless played the role of, and was treated as, an orthodox Party Communist by his fellow writers.[37] His correspondence with Lewis Grassic Gibbon particularly bears out this self-characterisation. In September 1933 he was writing to Gibbon in an uncompromising mood:

> No doubt you'll have formed the opinion that I am a hopelessly intolerant doctrinaire. And I believe I am. Toleration belongs to the period of toothless liberalism. The class struggle takes on ever more brutal aspects. To stand aside from the conflict is no longer possible – either you stand by the working class and its heroic vanguard the Communist Party or you take your stand (directly, indirectly or benevolently neutral – it doesn't matter which) with Fascism.[38]

In early 1934 Gibbon was playfully deriding Barke's political orthodoxy, enthusing about *The Free Man* journal,

> which is going to be revived into an 18-page sheet where all kinds of innovators – communists, douglasites, anarchists – are going to raise hell. Not orthodox from your point of view, but great fun ... An idea: write the editor and ask him for a column a week to be headed 'From the

---

questions better than a university graduate could be an allusion to Ferguson's persona (Barke 1936b, p. 741).

36   John Strachey, TS, to Barke, 16 October 1936, Box 4B, James Barke Papers, The Mitchell Library, Glasgow.

37   John Manson's thorough investigation into the formality of Barke's Communist commitment appears in Manson 2006, pp. 5–11. Manson concludes Barke never formally joined, and my own research on Barke's papers revealed nothing to contradict this.

38   Barke, TS, to Lewis Grassic Gibbon, 5 September 1933, Box 4B, James Barke Papers, The Mitchell Library, Glasgow.

Communist Point of View' or under some such title. Say I asked you to. He'll probably be delighted, and you can do agitprop through a boorjoy [*sic*] sheet.[39]

This dynamic, in which Barke articulated an unyielding line against Gibbon's more eclectic and continually shifting positions, while Gibbon cheerfully mocked Barke's intransigence, characterised the relationship between Barke and Gibbon until the latter's untimely death, aged 34, in February 1935. This dialogue continued, however, after Gibbon's death in Barke's novels, which revisit and revise aspects of Gibbon's work. *Major Operation* in particular is a novel in dialogue with Gibbon's *Grey Granite*, published in 1935.

Gibbon's major work, the trilogy *A Scots Quair*, published between 1932 and 1935, was a source of inspiration and frustration for Barke. Barke had written to Gibbon to express his displeasure with *Cloud Howe*, the second part of the *Scots Quair* trilogy:

> It was a disappointment to me. For me, the grave and fundamental weakness in Cloud Howe is your attitude to the Seggert spinners, symbol of the industrial proletariat. Herein your attitude (and it certainly can't be your 'real' attitude) is that of the semi-socialist-cum-half-spewed-Fabianintellectual. I find it very trying.[40]

He repeated this argument in an unpublished extended version of his *Left Review* appreciation of Gibbon: 'Certainly his sympathies are with the spinners. But it is the sympathy given and felt from above the battle'.[41] His attitude to *Grey Granite*, the final part of the trilogy and the least critically acclaimed, was more mixed. Although claiming in a letter to Gunn that, 'Its "line" is right – or very nearly so. It showed the way out – not *a* way but *the* way',[42] he elsewhere suggested that Gibbon lacked the 'essential and vital knowledge' to carry off the

---

Lewis Grassic Gibbon, TS, to Barke, 18 February 1934, Box 4B, James Barke Papers, The Mitchell Library, Glasgow.

Barke, TS, to Lewis Grassic Gibbon, 5 September 1933, Box 4B, James Barke Papers, The Mitchell Library, Glasgow.

Barke, TS, 'A Critical Appreciation of A Scots Quair', undated, Box 9B, James Barke Papers, The Mitchell Library, Glasgow. This essay was intended for a tribute volume which was never published.

Barke, MS, to Neil M. Gunn, 20 November 1934, Box 4B, James Barke Papers, The Mitchell Library, Glasgow. Emphasis in original.

novel.[43] But he nonetheless commended the trilogy in Communist terms as 'a worthy forerunner of [the] novel that will be written by workers, for workers, expressing the hopes, ideals and aspirations of workers'.[44]

Critical readings of *Grey Granite* have tended to focus on the connotations of the novel's title and link them to the representation of the younger Ewan Tavendale's Communist commitment, which appears unshakeable and ruthless. Angus Calder links the granite of the title to the certainties of Presbyterianism,[45] but it refers equally to the creed 'clear and sharp as a knife' that Ewan finds in Communism.[46] The grey granite that appears in Gibbon's essay 'Aberdeen' represents austere stoicism: 'a grey glimmer like a morning North Sea, a cold steeliness that chills the heart'.[47] Ewan's ruthlessness caused consternation; John Lehmann considered him 'too humourless, and at times even priggish',[48] while the *Daily Worker* criticised what it took to be the representation of Communists as 'figures of unbending steel which never smile', 'which is the old idea of a Communist'.[49] This 'old idea' of the Communist is implicitly contrasted with the Popular Front conception of the Communist as an ordinary participant in popular life.

Barke's *Major Operation* takes up Gibbon's images of steely necessity, but it tries to detach them from their association with austere, elitist Communism in which the ends always justify the means. Barke appropriates from Gibbon a metaphor of the city of Glasgow as a moribund monster in need of radical intervention, drawing on Gibbon's essay, 'Glasgow' (1934):

> But there (as elsewhere) the physicians disagree – multitudes of physicians, surrounded by anxious groups of the ailing patient's dependents. A brief round of the various physicians convinces the investigator of one thing: the unpopularity of surgery. The single surgeon orating is, of course, the Communist.[50]

---

43   Barke, TS, 'A Critical Appreciation of A Scots Quair', undated, Box 9B, James Barke Papers, The Mitchell Library, Glasgow.

44   Barke, TS, 'A Critical Appreciation of A Scots Quair', undated, Box 9B, James Barke Papers, The Mitchell Library, Glasgow. This passage also appears in Barke 1936b, pp. 220–1.

45   Calder 1982, p. 104.

46   Gibbon 1998, p. 495.

47   Gibbon 2002a, p. 111.

48   Lehmann 1935, p. 90.

49   *Daily Worker* 1937a, p. 7.

50   Gibbon 2002b, p. 105. John Manson offers a suggestive account of the way that the metaphors of surgery, the knife, and the personification of 'History' that are prevalent in

The knife; the affliction of the body politic; the heroic surgeon: these are the organising metaphors in *Major Operation*, and have shifting significance in the context of 1936. Barke's title resumes Gibbon's use of the figuration of the Communist as surgeon, making a necessary, thoroughgoing intervention rather than, like Ramsay MacDonald in a searing essay by Gibbon, placidly waiting for the 'beast' of capitalism to evolve.[51] Alongside these connotations, Barke may also have had in mind C. Day Lewis's *The Magnetic Mountain* (1933), 'It is now or never, the hour of the knife,/ The break with the past, the major operation'.[52] It is likely, too, that Barke was alluding to William Bolitho's lurid 1924 account of conditions in Glasgow, *Cancer of Empire*, which warned that revolution would break out on the Clyde if living conditions did not improve. Together, these associations point firmly towards revolution as the only solution to an ailing social system at a moment in mid-1936 when such rhetoric was being muted in favour of immediate defence against fascism.

Major Operation is, at its outset, militantly urban and civic in its focus, accepting Glasgow's imperial status as 'Second City of the Empire'. The city appears separated off from its national context, formed by the dynamics of international capitalism and the global exercise of power. Its inhabitants are always 'citizens' – 'Mr No-Mean-Citizen of No-Mean-City', an ironic nod to another Glasgow slum novel.[53] In keeping with its urban and metropolitan compass, the novel is stridently modern and, indeed, deliberately modernist in its frame of reference; it may indeed be considered an example of what Michael Denning calls the 'subaltern modernism' that emerged around the world among working-class writers after 1917.[54] The most memorable passages in the novel construct a collective voice of the street, a playful, politically charged urban mode that revels in the promiscuity of popular culture and the unstoppable creativity of history: 'Sure hadn't she a form like Venus! Who was

---

Gibbon's writing on Communism also recur in writing from the left across Europe in the thirties and forties. In the thirties, these images signify auspiciousness and opportunity, but later come to signal the ways that people are annihilated *en masse* by impersonal historical forces: Manson 2008, pp. 44–50.

51   See Gibbon's essay, 'The Wrecker: James Ramsay MacDonald'. In this piece, Gibbon attacks MacDonald's 'hazy inability to grasp at the flinty actualities of existence', a failure which manifests itself in an evolutionary, rather than a revolutionary, understanding of historical change; MacDonald waits for the ailing dinosaur of capitalism to evolve. Gibbon 2002f, pp. 150–1.

52   Day Lewis 1964a, p. 62.

53   Alexander McArthur and H. Kingsley Long's *No Mean City*, published in 1935.

54   Denning 2006, p. 720.

Venus anyway? Oh yeah! The world moves on. Time's a certain-sure go-getter'.[55] The many Joycean echoes and allusions in *Major Operation* have been noted elsewhere, and Barke himself saw the connection with Joyce as a potential selling point, once again complicating the assumption that writers on the left were uniformly anti-modernist.[56] I will suggest here, however, that the novel is conscious of the limits of modernism and ultimately seeks to move beyond them. Denning's claim that the texts of 'subaltern modernism' tended to be 'curiously ahistorical, and rarely produced the temporal and spatial sweep of grand historical fiction or generational epics' may be an indicator of the motivation for this shift.[57] *Major Operation* is not 'ahistorical', but it is quite conscious of modernism's potentially ahistorical tendencies, and seems to be toying with that tendency, articulating a scepticism towards the historical narrative nonetheless interlocked with a deep preoccupation with it. The first half of the book in particular regularly evokes the passage of time and resists nostalgic attempts to grasp the receding past:

> There aren't enough brain cells in the human mind to store all the lumber of the past. The machine vibrates so terrifically that the cells can hardly keep anything in. Name of a footballer: name of a film star: name of a Derby winner. Lost a couple of bob – or won ten! But 1066 and all that ... The world moves on. My cutie's due at two-to-two ... TO-DAY.
>
> p. 109

In this fast-paced, forward-moving modernity, the meaning of older cultural forms comes into question: 'Mass productions, mass culture, mass gutter journalism – what could Loch Lomond mean?' (108). A narrative voice warns that, 'The bonnie banks had had their day in the consciousness of drawing-room ballad writers. The world isn't a drawing-room any more for the Gentlemen of Culture' (108). The novel critically represents two positions in relation to Scottish history. At one pole, what Tom Nairn calls the 'cultural sub-nationalism' of Scotland is conspicuously satirised in the 'city folks' with their 'kilts and

---

55   Barke 1955, p. 108. Page references are hereafter given in parentheses in the text.

56   Cunningham 1997, p. 13 notes the Joycean resonances of the novel. Writing to his publisher to defend the novel prior to publication, he wrote that, 'If James Joyce is mentioned, many of the critics will be careful to point out that James Barke can't hold a contraceptive to James Joyce. But on the other hand a large section of the reading public will be interested in the link up. Ditto for Zola'. Barke, TS, to F.T. Smith at Collins, 28 April 1936, Box 6A, James Barke Papers, The Mitchell Library, Glasgow.

57   Denning 2006, p. 721.

their bastard Gaelic', who have bought a version of Scottish history as 'a super-ficially attractive semi-Celtic tartan ragstore twilight' (81).[58] The characterisa-tion of cultural nationalism as 'superficial' positions it, in terms of the novel's metaphors, as unable to deal with the deeper problems that require a 'major operation'. In the Eastern Infirmary, representatives of Scotland's past are dying away: the old crofter, William MacDonald, is 'dazed, lost and isolated' by being uprooted from his farm (160). His presence in the hospital is the result of the intervention of a Marchioness who has taken a historical interest in him since he conforms to her romanticised notion of Gaelic culture (162). This doomed attempt at preserving a dying culture reiterates Barke's argument in his note on Gaelic culture: 'The death rattle of Gaelic culture may be amplified by all sorts of bodies and committees. They delude themselves, however, in thinking that by doing so they are performing an act of resurrection'.[59] These notes were writ-ten in response to a request from Gibbon, who quoted from them at length – describing Barke as 'a remarkable Anglo-Gael' – in his essay 'Literary Lights', part of *Scottish Scene*, a collaboration with Hugh MacDiarmid and an important meditation on Scottish modernity.[60] Resurrection of the dead and the preser-vation of the dying are impossible in the scheme of the novel. Another patient, Peter MacGeechan, is likewise lost, both in the hospital and in the modern world; he is 'a survival from the past: a patriarch of the Scottish peasantry: a Scottish Hebrew' (170). He and the other patients 'might have belonged to dif-ferent countries, divided by mountains and a waste of seas' (169). The figuring of these histories as mutually incomprehensible brings into question the exist-ence of a common culture and the possibility of a national narrative. At the other pole, the quintessentially middlebrow playwright Fred Rowatt represents the abandonment of history altogether; for Fred and his friends 'history had no significance … they were not even interested in the superficial pageant of Scot-land's historical effects' (81), seeing themselves instead as the 'fruit and cream of a great Empire' (62). Rowatt's plays are 'nothing very deep and nothing very clever' (61); a shallow contemporaneity that, like nationalist kitsch, fails to get to the root cause of the crisis.

The implicit problem the novel poses is how to establish a relationship with history that is neither a fetishised attachment to the past nor an amnesiac mod-ernism in the context of the emerging Popular Front emphasis on national cul-

58   Nairn 1981, p. 156.
59   Barke, n.d., 'Note on Gaelic Culture', Box 4B, James Barke Papers, The Mitchell Library, Glasgow. Undated, but mentioned in Barke, TS, to Lewis Grassic Gibbon, 4 November 1933, Box 4B, James Barke Papers, The Mitchell Library, Glasgow.
60   Gibbon 2002d, pp. 135–6.

tures and class alliance. It is with this central problem in mind that the novel's modernist elements must be read, rather than in the context of an assumed schematic opposition between modernism and realism. Valentine Cunningham in particular has focused on one section, 'Red Music in the Second City', to argue for a Bakhtinian reading of the novel as rejecting Stalinist 'puritanism' in favour of the officially forbidden jouissance of modernism.[61] As previous chapters have suggested, it is an overestimation of the clarity of the official Communist line during this period to assume, as Cunningham does, that there was any particularly clear proscription of literary experiment. Cunningham's reading also overlooks the relationship between this experimental section and the novel as a whole. 'Red Music in the Second City' toys with modernist images and stylistics to represent the street life of the city: 'I'm only trying to find my feet in the flux of time: paddle my own canoe in the stream of consciousness: make ends meet: solve the jig-saw: earn an honest livelihood', declares one of the many voices, echoing, as Keith Williams notes, Joyce's 'Dooleysprudence' (123).[62] Another voice toys with overturning the boundaries of high and popular art: 'Wonder what Mrs. Bloom would have thought about Mae West? Or Mae West about Marion Bloom?' (122). The section represents a heteroglossic rendering of the speech of the city, demonstrating a plurality of discourses and dialects each suggesting its own limits and obfuscations in order to deauthorise discourses of cultural power. These playful reversals of authorised distinctions lead Cunningham to suggest the section presents us with a 'classic carnival on the Bakhtinian model'.[63] This, however, overlooks the fact that 'Red Music' marks a turning point in the novel, and the shift in tone at the end marks the onset of crisis and a halting of the dynamic, carnivalesque energy. Earlier in the novel, the streets are shown to be sites of class coexistence, of civic identity: 'Over the entire City the object of the patrol was the same: there was an identity of interests between the middle-class and the working-class: the desire to be in the stream of life' (85). 'Red Music' opens the second 'book' of the novel, set eight years after the first – in the mid-thirties – and shows that illusion of identity breaking down as the crisis stagnates the 'stream of life.' The title of the second book is 'The Wheel of the Wagon is Broken', and 'Red Music' represents the transition from movement to stasis. The spectre of unemployment turns the mutability of urban life into an unsettling loss of identity: 'Father's got the sack from the water works, the brick works, the rivet, bolt and nut works' (125),

---

61   Cunningham 1997, p. 17.

62   K. Williams 1991, p. 184.

63   Cunningham 1997, p. 16.

while a chorus of middle-class voices drifts towards authoritarianism: 'What we need is a strong hand at the helm. (Chorus: We need a strong hand at the helm!)' (125). The street carnival, pulled along by the consoling and relatively levelling effects of post-1918 consumerism, becomes something else, a claustrophobic, dispossessed and fractious mass.

In 'Red Music in the Second City', Cunningham argues, 'the people ... is speaking'; however, the collective voice is shown to be a surface phenomenon which is fractured by the crisis at the section's conclusion.[64] The novel must therefore look elsewhere for its means of popular representation, for another way of articulating popular fears and desires. The crisis causes another form of social mixing to emerge as the somatic effects of the downturn on the collective and individual bodies of the city gather the principal characters together in the Eastern Infirmary. In contrast to the novel's earlier, celebratory evocations of the passage of time – 'Forward O Time: on wheels and foot. Pause, and the century flashes past: for the century hasn't got There – yet' (50) – for George Anderson and Jock MacKelvie, the temporary vitality of work (for Jock) and prosperity (for Anderson) gives way to the longueurs of illness and extended convalescence: 'Never had time dragged past so slowly, with such tedium' (292).[65] The slowing down of time (or, in Bakhtinian terms, the switch from the chronotope of the street to that of the infirmary), stretches out what has previously been presented synchronically. George Anderson's Leopold Bloom-like stream of consciousness, with its digressions and non-sequiturs, identifies him with the aforementioned voice in 'Red Music' trying to find its feet in the flow of time, 'make ends meet: solve the jig-saw: earn an honest livelihood' (125). He finds, however, that no such solution is possible: 'His mind process had been jig-sawed: scattered' (148–9). The stream of consciousness is no longer a mark of the novel's modernist bearings but rather a symptom arising in economic conditions, and the central subject of the remainder of the novel is the long process of the recomposition and rehabilitation of Anderson's thought processes. The agent of this process is Jock MacKelvie, and his techniques in the 'major operation' are a linguistic overpowering of Anderson and an enforced lesson in history. Against Anderson's 'state of agitated confusion' (292) in which he finds himself quite unable to 'discipline [his thoughts] in any way' (290), is ranged the stabilising and disciplining force of MacKelvie's 'ordered and controlled' mind (292).

---

64   Cunningham 1997, p. 7.

65   *Forward O Time!* was the title of a socialist realist novel by Valentin Katayev, published in English by Victor Gollancz in 1933, the title of which had in turn been appropriated from Mayakovsky's *The Bath House*.

MacKelvie's function in stabilising language and providing an authoritative discourse is again overlooked by critics anxious to emphasise the novel's modernist credentials. While Keith Williams has noted Barke's 'Joycean delight in puns', as in Jock MacKelvie's transition from 'red leader' to 'Red leader', the novel is not wholeheartedly engaging in such linguistic play.[66] It is keen to relativise certain kinds of monologic speech, particularly the voice of the BBC, which is defamiliarised as a synthetic dialect, 'broadcasting the Geneva Lullaby' in its artificial language: 'Just a nice voice, you know: wethah fawcaust' (375). Working-class speech too is shown to be fraught with obfuscation: in the infirmary, the working-class patients are just as adept at obscuring unpleasant realities through such euphemisms as 'Shanghai Express', meaning operating table, and 'domino', meaning death, as the medical professionals whose official language is intentionally unintelligible to the patients ('duodenal carcinoma'). This serves the important function of distancing the novel from the more naïve endorsements of working-class language found in the early *Left Review* as characteristically immediate, honest and authentic.[67] Crucially, though, the 'red leader' Jock MacKelvie is able to switch linguistic codes and mediate between these variously incomplete discourses, able to speak authoritatively to the doctors and translate the language of the surgeons for the other patients (202; 300). This ability ensures that MacKelvie's discourse is apparently total and without fractures. Anderson realises that if MacKelvie's political discourse is compelling, 'and there didn't seem to be any loopholes', then 'it was going to be difficult not to be a Red' (316). Ideology becomes common sense; Anderson finds that 'the phrases [begin] to trip off his tongue' (317).

This rhetorical overpowering is effected through lessons in the violence of history; both the violence of the past – 'How do you think the Highlands of Scotland were laid bare? By the bloodiest terror' (340) – and of the present – 'Mass murder, mass sadism, mass torture' (406). Anderson is disabused of his illusions about Scottish history and recognises that there was 'no need to go out of Scotland to trace the bloody human pulp of history' (422). MacKelvie's therapeutic intervention aims to 'inoculate' Anderson against the 'virus' of fascism to which the collective middle-class voices are succumbing (376–7). Even when Anderson is converted, however, he fails to attain the linguistic authority of MacKelvie, as when he finds he 'could not bring himself to shout a slogan'

---

66   K. Williams 1991, p. 183.
67   Exemplified by Brown 1934, pp. 76–7; but also echoed in Montagu Slater's argument, 'The speech of the men "at the hidden foci of production", workers and technologists, craftsmen and peasants, is the air a live literature must breathe': Slater 1935a, p. 127.

at a demonstration (401). Anderson is, in the course of MacKelvie's rhetorical assault, left with nothing, and struggles to assimilate MacKelvie's own values. In this sense, MacKelvie's discourse is poised between authoritative and internally persuasive, in Bakhtin's terms, and this equivocation might reflect the unresolved tensions in Barke's attitude to class alliance.[68] Anderson commits himself to Marxism in a state of absolute loss; the internally persuasive force is ambiguous in its sheer destructiveness. The novel itself seems conscious of this issue, which is, at root, a question of under what conditions the middle class can commit themselves to working-class politics. As in other Popular Front texts, this problem of conversion is raised in terms of conditions of discursive reception. Anderson 'had been in the mood to listen to Mac-Kelvie. But would he have listened to him had he not been forced to listen?' (365).

This ambiguity over the nature of Anderson's conversion is integral to the novel's central political tensions and ambiguous resolution. Anderson's trajectory is one of abject personal loss. Gustav Klaus rightly points out that, 'if it takes an ordeal such as Anderson goes through to make sections of the middle class susceptible to the idea of the popular front, it seems pretty hopeless from the start'.[69] The novel has little time for the notion that there were progressive resources within bourgeois culture waiting to be activated: Anderson's 'major operation' is twice described in terms of a 'liquidation' of his past (365; 491). In both cases, it is clearly implied that such a procedure is both the aim of radicalisation and a commendable achievement. Having surrendered every aspect of himself to MacKelvie's rhetorical conquest, Anderson's commitment fails to produce a new political subjectivity, so that he remains an outsider to the movement he wishes to belong to, concluding the novel, with grim predictability, being beaten to death saving MacKelvie from police violence (490). What is not offered within this narrative is a conception of ideology that detaches it from a particular class, a move that would appear necessary if the aspirations of the Popular Front were to be successfully extended through wider society. Ideology is shown to be naturalised to the point of embodiment; Bessie, Mac-Kelvie's sister-in-law, had 'rebellion in her bones' (282). This essentialism, which is to a significant extent written into the novel through its central corporeal metaphors, suggests that Anderson's conversion could never be fully complete; his 'constitution' remains essentially bourgeois (458). However, constitutional discourse could equally work in the opposite direction and affirm that the

---

68   Bakhtin 1981, pp. 345–6.
69   Klaus 1985, p. 123.

body, capable of suffering and vulnerable to violence, is the common ground that transcends class difference; intermittently, the novel points this way, as when Anderson is physically sickened by the thought of the suffering visited on 'the helpless bodies of the German workers' (406). Although the essentialist valence is the more commonly emphasised in *Major Operation*, the ambiguity nonetheless leaves space for another position to begin to emerge near the novel's conclusion. This other possibility is given clear articulation by Mac-Kelvie:

> The armed forces – apart from the brass hats of all ranks ... We are the armed forces. We are the army, the navy, the big guns, the aeroplanes, the munitions. We are the Nation. If we take our power, openly and firmly, realising clearly what we are doing and what we want, who the hell's to gainsay us? We can win the day, win the future for peace, right, justice, equality, for ... all fundamental human decency, without shedding a drop of blood.
>
> p. 343

Here, a quite different mode of political activism and subjectivity is suggested, not attached to a particular class position, but rather suggestive of that 'republican commonality' evoked in Barke's *Left Review* article.[70] There would, in this formulation, be no obvious need for a 'liquidation' of the past, or for the kind of conversion ordeal that Barke/MacKelvie inflicts on Anderson, or, indeed, for the bloody narrative conclusion of the novel as a whole. In place of rhetorical domination, MacKelvie offers here a language of persuasion; even the ellipses and semi-rhetorical question suggest a more open, negotiable discourse. A more Popular Frontist accent is suggested in the descriptions of the final mass demonstrations, in which the various contingents from the regions of Scotland draw on their own local traditions, giving the event 'a national character' (483). There is a suggestion that the popular, mobile, urban mode of the 'Red Music' section, broken up by the Depression, might be renewed by the invigoration of mass activism: 'Here was movement, activity. An end of passivity, wrangling and sectarian dispute' (477). Significantly, it is also at the novel's close that the previously unfailing lucidity of Jock MacKelvie is shown to meet a limit: 'What had Anderson thought as he stood over his body with that banner? MacKelvie would never know' (494). Together, these concluding moments suggest a softening of the novel's politics, and the possibility of another mode

---

70   Barke 1936b, p. 724.

of writing, in which authority is not concentrated in the single, idealised 'surgeon', and in which past histories might not need to be 'liquidated'. The novel is awkwardly poised, however, between indicating these possibilities and committing to them.

James Barke, *The Land of the Leal* (1939)

Major Operation, therefore, may be read as imprinted with the difficulties Barke found in the transition to the Popular Front. The history that is revealed to Anderson is not articulated as a tradition of resistance with which to align, but rather a history of barbarism and injustice of which he can hope only to absolve himself. Barke's next novel, published in May 1939, a few months before the outbreak of war, represents a marked departure. Charting the history of one working-class family over a century, the novel narrates a long process of class formation from rural Galloway to the Glasgow of the thirties, restoring to view those histories of rural labour and struggle that *Major Operation* jettisons as inaccessible to the urban working class, and seeks to articulate them within an anti-fascist discourse. Michael Denning has identified an important shift in proletarian writing worldwide during the thirties and forties away from the 'curiously ahistorical' tendency of 'subaltern modernism' towards a 'larger historical sensibility' that emerged in 'the resistance narratives of anti-fascist and anticolonial wars' and which became fully developed through the 'recognition that the new proletarians of the century were not simply factory workers and tenement dwellers, but were migrants from the countryside'.[71] *The Land of the Leal* bears out this tendency through its emplotment of one family's history of dispossession, migration and labour; a process of class formation and of developing class consciousness: the process, that is, by which a peasantry becomes a proletariat. In its closing chapters, the family saga becomes an anti-fascist fiction, and the projection of a continuum of struggle through which the family's tradition of resistance eventually opens out into the world-historical struggle against fascism gives the novel recognisable epic resonances, conforming, in some ways, to the type of novel imaged in the final chapter of Lukács's *The Historical Novel*, which would inherit in some degree the unity, breadth and popular significance of earlier epic texts.[72]

---

71   Denning 2006, p. 721.
72   Lukács 1976, p. 419.

The anxieties and delays that dogged the publication of *Major Operation* meant that when it appeared it was out of step with novels like *May Day* which had absorbed the Popular Front line more clearly. Although Barke's publisher was concerned about *The Land of the Leal* proving 'redder' than its predecessor, the novel instead demonstrates a shift to a more accommodating position, especially in its final chapters.[73] The transitions in Barke's thinking during the period he was working on *The Land of the Leal*, which he completed in December 1938, are evident in both his public and private writing. His *Left Review* article clearly signalled that he now considered Scottish national identity – conceived as a body of popular tradition – to be deployable against fascism. This element strengthened after the Munich Crisis of September 1938. Late that year he wrote to Neil Gunn:

> But whatever happens, the next ten years in Europe are going to be Hell. But one immediate result of Munich has been for me a terrific strengthening of my never weak Scottish sentiment. The Scottish people must cleanse themselves of the shame, the bitter, humiliating shame of Chamberlain and Munich.[74]

This rhetoric of national shame and national humiliation also characterised Barke's public responses to the Spanish Civil War. On several occasions, Barke declared that the war made particular claims on Scottish writers as heirs to a tradition of struggle. In a speech written for Scottish PEN in March 1938, Barke exhorted Scottish writers to continue their tradition of fighting for intellectual liberty by fighting fascism:

> The Scots have a great and noble tradition in the fight for liberty and free-dom. We must not sully that tradition now in our keeping. The traditions of Wallace, or Barbour and Blind Harry, aye, even of the good Lord James, of Ramsay, Ferguson and Robert Burns: of men like Cunninghame Graham and Keir Hardie and the great and glorious John MacLean, are our traditions: our noblest and best traditions.

---

73 Barke wrote to his agent, David Higham, on 24 January 1937: 'But you can see how nervous [F.T.] Smith is, how thoroughly English the delicately worded hint that they don't want a political autobiography: the fear that the Land of the Leal may turn out to be even 'Redder' than Major Operation'. Barke, TS, to David Higham, 24 January 1937, Box 6A, James Barke Papers, The Mitchell Library, Glasgow.

74 Barke, TS, to Neil Gunn, 28 November 1938, Box 4A, James Barke Papers, The Mitchell Library, Glasgow.

> Are we Scottish writers – we whom ... Stalin has designated 'Engineers of the human soul' – to lag behind the hundreds of brave and courageous Scots from the mines, the factories, the universities and the derelict areas – and all Scotland is almost that – who are fighting for the people of Spain?[75]

Barke here adopts a classically populist rhetoric that first uses pride in national prestige to rouse his listeners to a positive sense of their own history, and then attempts to shame his readers through the moral example of working-class participation in the conflict. *The Land of the Leal* may be considered Barke's own response to the call he issues here; the novel is concerned with the question of what Scotland's 'noblest and best traditions' are, and seeks to identify them as arising in the historical experience of the Scottish people from the break-up of the peasant communities with the coming of capitalism to the modern traditions of the labour movement.

There is much in Barke's *The Land of the Leal* that recalls Lewis Grassic Gibbon's *A Scots Quair*; both are concerned with a long history of dispossession and evolving modes of resistance. Gibbon's essay 'The Land' celebrated the rural workers as

> the masters who feed the world! ... And it came on me that all over Great Britain, all over Europe this morning, the mean fields of France and the fat pastures of Saxony and the rolling lands of Roumania those rulers of the earth were out and about, bent-backed to plodding toil, the world's great Green International awaiting the coming of its Spartacus.[76]

While Gibbon seems in this text to position these workers as a kind of unchanging moral authority, Barke's novel, beginning in the mid-nineteenth century and recounting the experiences of three generations as they are displaced first by the collapse of the crofting economy, then by the agricultural depression in the Borders, before finally ending up in the Glasgow of 1938, narrates the development of a historical and national consciousness, and the ultimate transposition of the 'Green International' into a 'Red' one. In his 'Note' to the novel, Barke commented that, 'The spiritual validity alone remains historically

---

75   Barke, MS, Draft Speech, 'The PEN and World Affairs', 19 March 1938, Box 2A, James Barke Papers, Mitchell Library, Glasgow. See also 'The Refugees in Spain', letter co-signed by Barke and other prominent Scottish authors: J. Allan et al. 1938, p. 18.

76   Gibbon 2002c, p. 87.

accurate'.[77] Raymond Williams has noted the centrality of this sense of a spiritual history of resistance and defiance to Gibbon's trilogy; where, however, *A Scots Quair* suggests that tradition is finally ending, as Chris Guthrie dies and Ewan Tavendale – a more troubling and ambiguous character than Williams admits – leaves Scotland for Communist Party work in London, *The Land of the Leal* finds it continued, on a new level, in Spain.[78] The hopes and dreams of the old peasant community do not die away irrecoverably as they do in *Major Operation*, but are rather translated into new objectives, given material dimensions, with the coming of urban modernity. This is in one sense the process by which the novel's memorialising function enables the transformation of the past, so that 'by a strange and melancholy paradox, the moment of failure is the moment of value; the comprehending and experiencing'.[79] But Barke is determined too to continually reassert the tragedy of waste and frustration that those moments of failure signify, producing, in the end, an ambiguity about the death of one of the family's sons in Spain.

The peasant community is characterised by a biblical sense of timelessness and of the uninterruptable cycle of labour: 'Always the earth had called for human hands. Always it would be so' (17). This notion of labour as a fundamental condition of existence is the foundation of the 'faith' of the gigantic and tyrannical patriarch, Tom Gibson. But at the periphery of his consciousness is 'The Dragon of Capitalism [that] devoured in a decade a generation' (17). Dimly aware of the 'dragon', he nonetheless believes 'the Lord would deal with it' (17). But Tom's faith is rooted in his belief in the right to work the land, enabling him to feel a kind of belonging outside the property relation of capitalism: 'He belonged to the land and the land belonged to the Lord' (17). Tom's labour is presented at the level of his consciousness as supplying a 'deep and elemental satisfaction', and as un-estranged: 'He worked on the land as a Beethoven or a Michelangelo worked at his art' (70). This vision of unalienated, virtuosic labour is ironically undercut by the novel's narration of the coming of capitalism; Tom Gibson may think that 'the land' is his, but his conception of spiritual ownership must necessarily confront and be overcome by the reality of expropriation that makes the land neither his nor the Lord's. But the evolution of that sense of a natural right to the land, and of the 'absolute loss' that Jack Lindsay posited as such a central factor and dynamic in human culture, is at the novel's

---

77   Barke 1950, p. 10. Page references are hereafter given in parentheses in the text. The 'Note' is dated 19 December 1938, two months after the Munich agreement.

78   R. Williams 1975, pp. 323–4.

79   Lukács 1978, p. 126.

heart.[80] The traditional song 'Bonnie Galloway' recurs throughout the novel and is described as giving form to the agricultural workers' sense of the right to their land:

> Bonnie Galloway, indeed! Little did they see of its splendour and beauty. They knew its confined and restricted and much-husbanded acres. But the excess of their toil on its individual fields made the land dearer to them. Despite all the landlords and petty farmers it was *their* land: it was *their* home. No one had more right to sing its beauty and praise. If there was sadness in their song, that was the way of all songs of a land that was toiled and worked over in blood and tears.
>
> p. 109; emphasis in original

The loss of the homeland suggested here, and the moral right to life on the land, is the novel's central theme as well as the motivating force of Barke's central characters' economic migrations. Exile from and return to a homeland is of course a traditional epic theme; the novel, for Lukács in *The Theory of the Novel*, emerged in the condition of 'transcendental homelessness', the impossibility of return.[81] The severed connection between work and home, labour and property, is felt as an outrage by Tom's daughter Jean: 'the sweat and blood o' the Gibsons are in they fields – they should be ours ten times ower – aye, a hunner times!' (510). The next generation, Jean and David, are continually portrayed as fanatically, even heroically, hard workers (179), a commitment that initially seems to be rewarded with the stability of a home. But the stability is illusory; Jean and David's exceptionality is figured as out of step with history as 'mechanised inventions and devices' force the people from the land (192).

Thus the settlement is broken up, a trauma that generates a sense of loss and longing reverberating down the generations, but also a historical process, the means by which a specific class consciousness can be achieved. This is the passage from the knowable to what Benedict Anderson describes as the 'imagined community', the 'imaginary' aspect of which is the means by which individuals perceive themselves to be linked to members of the community they never meet in person.[82] What links the various episodes in the novel and gives the text its coherence is Barke's figuration of the way the same desires and longings occur across history in transposed forms. For Anderson, the 'idea of a soci-

---

80   Lindsay 1969, p. 87.
81   Lukács 1978, p. 41.
82   B. Anderson 2006, p. 6.

ological organism moving calendrically through homogenous, empty time is a precise analogue of the idea of the nation, which also is conceived as a solid community moving steadily down (or up) history'.[83] In *The Land of the Leal*, the movement from the face-to-face community of the crofters to the modern and urban society of Glasgow is marked by precisely this movement from homogenous to calendar- and clock-time and, moreover, by an emerging sense of the national and global context often transmitted to characters through newspapers.[84] But Barke is keen to stress that this imagining is by no means an easy process. David Ramsay's father realises that, 'Folks are beginning to get their eyes opened. I see in the *Mail* that the jail's packed out in Greenock because the sailors refuse to sail in their coffin ships. That spirit will spread' (51). But the relentless demands of labour ensure that spirit is 'dulled and blunted' (54). In the early sections, the repetitive nature of rural labour was tied to a sense of cyclical time, and to a sense of an immanently meaningful world: 'From every thorn bush the song went forth, a paean of praise, that the earth had been born yet again' (72). But this cyclical, enclosed world is also resistant to historical perspective: 'For the overwhelming urgency of calving obliterated any pleasant thought of the morrow' (72). The demands of labour mean that repetition, rather than the passage of time, dominates the characters' experiences during the rural sections of the novel.

Barke's ironic narrative style, continually foreshadowing characters' fates, partly supplies that historical sense that is unavailable to them. It is also a key point of difference with Gibbon's *A Scot's Quair*, perhaps the major innovation of which was the construction of a narrative voice that spoke convincingly from within the community, emulating the rhythms and patterns of popular speech.[85] Barke's narrative voice, however, distances itself from characters at important dramatic moments, reframing them in perspectives the characters themselves cannot access. When the young Jean Ramsay is sent on an errand at night, the narrative voice intervenes to reveal that, '[e]ven at the end of her days that were to be long and arduous, Jean remembered that night', and though she was not afraid, 'Fear was to come later in life' (39–40). The narrative continually glances ahead, warning of greater hardships to come and in this sense priv-

83   B. Anderson 2006, p. 26.

84   Anderson notes the function of newspapers as a form of 'imagined linkage' forging such communities: 2006, p. 34. Barke makes the same argument in his *Left Review* article, suggesting that the Scottish identity promoted by the nationalists is a creation of 'the English dailies': Barke 1936b, p. 741.

85   For a politically engaged account of Gibbon's style in *A Scots Quair* that situates the trilogy in contemporary debates around language, realism and nation, see Ortega 1981.

ileging the relationship between reader and narrative voice, defusing suspense by positioning readers and narrator in a position of superior knowledge. But irony more widely also performs the important political function of indicating the limits of characters' consciousness and acknowledging the hidden forces shaping their lives. The peasant farmers perceive the events they read about as 'movements and events far removed from their influence. The Civil War in America – or the latest speech of William Ewart Gladstone – or the Mayor of Birmingham, Joseph Chamberlain' (83). These references are ironic, since all have important implications for the characters' lives. The Civil War in America was linked to Scotland through its trading ports and through the shipbuilding industry in Glasgow, where around 40 percent of the ships involved in the conflict were built.[86] William Gladstone's introduction of Home Rule for Ireland invigorated political agitation for Scottish independence, and Joseph Chamberlain mobilised Scottish Unionists to defeat the Second Home Rule Bill. In *The Land of the Leal*, these connections cannot be made by the characters until much later on. History is not a violent intrusion, as it is in Gibbon's *A Scots Quair*, rather it is a network of connections to which only the younger, urban generation of characters gain access.[87]

This ironic mode becomes less pronounced as the novel progresses, and the direct authorial interventions are limited to the first two generations of the family. The narrative voice positions itself therefore in a position of totalised understanding, beyond the uncertainties of modernity, the 'everlasting uncertainty and agitation' that Marx describes as inherent in the bourgeois epoch, and which appear in the idiom of Barke's novel as the 'cauld' and 'care' to which his title alludes.[88] It falls to each subsequent generation to retell and reframe the experiences of their parents and grandparents, and this discursive process is crucial, in the novel, to the development of class consciousness. In adulthood, David Ramsay recalls his father's drowning in a fishing accident and, suffering from his own hardships and frustrations, he is suddenly able to articulate the class content of the tragedy: 'Yes: the farmers had killed his father long before he had been drowned' (212). This apprehension of the injustice of his father's death motivates a quest for revenge, recognising in his father abilities that went unfulfilled:

---

86   Blackett 2002, p. 92.
87   Note the sudden, violent intrusion of the First World War into Gibbon's Kinraddie community, Gibbon 1998, pp. 148–51.
88   Marx and Engels 1988, p. 83.

His was a different courage – the courage of the mind and the spirit – the kind o' courage that Rabbie Burns had – only he hadna Rabbie's gifts – and that's what hurts: when you have the vision but havena the gifts – when you know a thing should be, but just canna do it. I know ... I've had my visions ... Men will no' stand to be worked like slaves forever ... There's money and plenty in Glasgow. There's enough for a'body in Glasgow – and it's the men and women o' Glasgow that'll lead Scotland yet.

p. 244

David's feeling is that his father lacked the 'gifts' by which to effect a change, but suggests too that his own visionary sense is linked to the possibilities embodied by the industrial city. David himself, a member of the second of the three generations, is continually figured as a visionary who is limited by his situation. His struggle to understand reality is 'an unequal, unfruitful struggle: he was no Isaiah, no Hegel' (292), and thus he is a 'problematic' individual in Lukács's sense, for whom 'neither the goals nor the way leading to them can be directly given'.[89] David's profound uncertainty contrasts with Tom Gibson's rock-like faith. Like Scott's heroes, in Lukács's analysis, David 'possesses a certain, though never outstanding degree of practical intelligence, a certain moral fortitude and decency which even rises to a capacity for self-sacrifice, but which never grows into a sweeping human passion, is never the enraptured devotion to a great cause'.[90] Lukács attributes the mediocrity of Scott's central characters to his conservatism, which led him to resist the Romantic construction of the exceptional 'demonic' hero.[91] Certainly, in focusing on David and, later in the novel, his son Andy, Barke moves away from the focus in *Major Operation* on the exceptionally virtuous figure of Jock MacKelvie and the exceptionally unfortunate George Anderson (as well as Gibbon's exceptionally ruthless Ewan Tavendale), and towards an examination of 'the constant and typical manifestations of human life' that, for Lukács, were crucial to the 'great progressive reverberation' of realism.[92] A crucial formal moment in the novel comes with the frustration of an epiphanic experience:

He felt alone, isolated. There was no one who knew him or understood him – in relation to his deepest need for knowledge and understanding. He could not plead, he did not know for what to plead: he was inarticulate.

---

89   Lukács 1978, p. 60.
90   Lukács 1976, p. 32.
91   Lukács 1976, p. 33.
92   Lukács 2007, p. 56.

His fiddle had been broken long ago and there had never been money to buy another. He wanted, he longed for human expression – for companionship – for communion of spirit and heart and mind.

p. 293

David's economic position ensures that he can become neither a liberating hero of his class nor the chronicler of its struggles. The moment, which brings to David's consciousness the futility and anguish of life and the absence of adequate forms of expression, could lead him into either a political or a spiritual epiphany (like the political epiphanies in *May Day*), but it does not do so. He finds Glasgow incomprehensible, and his disarticulation leaves him vulnerable to uncritically assimilating the reactionary rhetoric of the press: a worker himself, he experiences a self-estrangement from his own economic position and from his fellow workers: 'The workers were ignorant, devoid of education and essential book learning. They were at the mercy of agitators and malcontents, financed by Russian gold. But Russia was breaking up, disintegrating' (471). Here Barke marks the point past which David's class consciousness will not advance. Barke deploys the technique of foreshadowing at this point, telling the reader that David could not know 'through what grey hell of suffering and torment the path of duty was to lead him' (471). David succeeds in understanding his father's experiences in politicised terms that were not available to his father himself; however, it falls to David's own sons to identify, articulate, and attempt to finally redress, the frustration, disarticulation and sheer overwork that have marred their father's life. This devolution through the generations of narrative responsibility constructs class consciousness in discursive terms, giving it the shape of an unfolding family story.

The book's final geographical shift to Glasgow marks the supersession of the sons over their parents as the main focus of narrative attention and provides the setting for their re-narration of their parents' experiences. The move 'inside the city walls' entails more precise detail of location: 'MacDougal Drive off the Crow Road in Jordanhill' (441), rather than the broader topographical descriptors like the 'Rhinns of Galloway' in the earlier sections (18). The Glasgow section moves the novel into the territory of *Major Operation*, and begins in a similar style with a 'Shipyard Symphony': 'the rivet hammers beat like crazed woodpeckers; a plate slammed on the deck with a roar of protest' (456). The sound is punctuated by the whistles and horns that divide the time of the industrial working day, announcing the final end of the cyclical time of the novel's beginning. This increase of detail and specialisation reflects increasing alienation, and it is countered by the radicalisation narrative of the family's son, Andy (named, like his brother Tom, after one of the novel's first generation). Andy's conversion to Communism, through long experience of unemployment, prompts him to reconsider his family's history and to recognise its claim on him: 'If they didn't understand the nature and significance of the system that had driven them like beasts for the greater part of their lives, he did' (543). As fascism in Europe comes into view, Andy's politics are reoriented towards Communism and the Popular Front; Jock MacKelvie reappears, having fought on the Jarama Front in Spain, to perform, as he does in *Major Operation*, the donor-like function of supplying political purpose to the bewildered Andy.[93] Echoing closely Barke's own public statements on the claims Spain made on the people of Scotland, MacKelvie makes a speech about the international volunteers, speaking

> of Austrians and Frenchman and Italians (how the Garibaldi battalion had routed the Italian Fascists at Guadalahara) – of Americans, Canadians, Poles, Norwegians – and Scots. It was a deathless record of how the best and bravest elements of the common people of the old world and the new world had, together with writers and scientists and intellectuals, gone to the defence of the heroic Spanish people and had led the counter offensive against the Fascist hordes.[94]
>
> p. 593

This figures, in ideal form, the Popular Front as popular internationalism, connecting the national traditions and identities of all classes and orienting them towards anti-fascism. The argument that the war was the front of struggle for fundamental values seems to have been felt as genuinely compelling by volunteers themselves. One volunteer, interviewed by Ian MacDougall in the 1980s, expressed the feeling that, 'I saw the War in Spain as part and parcel of the general offensive by the Fascist Powers against working class rights and

---

93   Denning describes this function in the fiction of his 'Novelists' International', noting that 'militants and organizers', rather than being central characters, tend to 'provid[e] guidance like the donor in folktales': Denning 2006, p. 719.

94   John Manson suggests that the model for Jock MacKelvie was the Glasgow Communist Party organiser, Peter Kerrigan: Manson 2006, p. 7. In Ian MacDougall's collection of reminiscences of Scottish volunteers, Kerrigan is mentioned by one as the catalyst for his decision, Kerrigan's arguments appearing to him, as an unemployed man, 'just plain common sense': David Anderson, qtd. MacDougall 1986, p. 89. Kerrigan reported from Spain for the *Daily Worker*; see, for example, his hyperbolic reporting of the Battle of Jarama as an 'epic of valour unequalled in all history': Kerrigan 1937.

liberties all over the world, including in our own country'.[95] However, where for George Anderson MacKelvie's rhetorical operations enforced a repudiation of his past, the effect of MacKelvie's Popular Frontist intervention on Andy is a radical reframing of his sense of his own and his family's history:

> He felt that all his life had moved towards the making of this momentous decision. Only now was his life having point and significance. But not only his own life. Now the life of his father and his mother might be fulfilled. They had toiled and laboured from the Galloway fields to the city itself – from one century into another. How often had he thought of the senselessness and futility of their days! They had been the victims of the greed and brutality, the passionless indifference of British Capitalism.
>
> p. 596

This is a crucial passage in which Andy both restates and answers his father's earlier cry of frustration, when David had 'thought how generation upon generation had come and gone, toiling and struggling and dying ... it would go on – for the world was without end ... But how could it go on – for ever?' (292). There is a movement from the novel's great stress on the hardship, resilience and struggle for self-definition of a family – all of which could combine to form what Williams calls the 'characteristic nationalist emphasis' of such texts as *A Scots Quair* – to an internationalist politics, and back again, with a renewed sense of clarity.[96] The difference between these two statements is one of perspective: instead of his father's perception of endless, unchanging struggle, Andy perceives the possibility of fulfilment and meaning to be realised through his actions. This might mark the acquisition of the perspective Lukács thought the Popular Front novel would attain, a perspective from which to see 'that the heroism of the struggle does not have to be an episode ... in the triumphal march of capitalist prose', and which also 'changes our attitude to the past'.[97] In projecting a continuum of struggle across history, Barke also moves the novel towards fulfilling Ralph Fox's imagining of a 'new picture of life', in which the 'daily resistance to the horrors of the mass-production regime' becomes 'res-

---

95   Donald Renton, qtd. in MacDougall 1986, p. 21. Other volunteers saw the war more clearly in the terms of class war: 'The reason I went to Spain was in the Hungry Thirties I was navvying at a bob an hour and if you straightened your back you were off the job. Finally, I got a job wi' a contractor. The gaffer was a pig ... I says, "Look, gie's the books. I'd rather go to Spain and shoot bastards like you"': Tommy Bloomfield, qtd. in MacDougall 1986, p. 47.
96   R. Williams 1975, p. 322.
97   Lukács 1976, p. 417.

istance to war, to Fascism', and in so doing 'creates heroes, new types of men and women'.[98] A perspective is implied from which an entire history becomes meaningful, and the struggles of the past no longer appear as isolated episodes but as meaningfully linked moments in an unfolding narrative. Although MacKelvie here appears to perform a Leninist function of bringing consciousness 'from without', suggesting that, unlike in previous generations, the family's evolving story can no longer develop in a self-contained way, it is nonetheless Andy's working over of his experience and his family's experience that makes the discourse of anti-fascism persuasive. Once that persuasion has been assented to, Andy's consciousness requires the 'criterion of practice' if it is to continue to develop, and he must leave his nation and community in pursuit of that 'fulfilment'.[99] In such a narrative, Andy's commitment to the International Brigades may be considered approximate to the 'epic action' that Lukács in 1936 wrote might re-enter the novel when a mass movement for socialism awakens 'the latent, previously suppressed, deformed or misapplied energies of the millions, brings out the best of them and leads them to accomplish deeds which reveal capabilities they themselves had never been aware of'.[100] Andy's immersion in practice is, in this sense, something of a mirror image of George Anderson's, which is predicated on the cancellation of the past, and leads inevitably to self-sacrifice. Spain, by contrast, seems to offer a genuinely transformative political subjectivity, changing not only Andy's sense of himself and the injustices he has suffered, but also the historical determinants of that injustice. It suggests a way to overcome the 'shame' that Barke felt had settled on the people of Scotland as a result of appeasement.[101]

But Andy also dies, as did many international volunteers; and moreover by the time Barke completed the novel the Republic was all but defeated.[102] It

---

98   Fox 1979, p. 121.

99   In *Major Operation*, George Anderson reaches this point on being discharged from hospital, when the theoretical lessons of MacKelvie must be furthered in practice; accordingly, the final book of the novel, which begins after the patients' discharge, is subtitled 'The Criterion of Practice', the phrase taken from Lenin's *Materialism and Empirio-Criticism*.

100   Lukács 1936a, pp. 73–4.

101   'The Scottish people must cleanse themselves of the shame, the bitter, humiliating shame of Chamberlain and Munich': Barke, TS, to Neil M. Gunn, 28 November 1938, Box 4A, James Barke Papers, Mitchell Library, Glasgow.

102   According to James K. Hopkins, of 437 Scottish volunteers, 64 from Glasgow died: Hopkins 1998, p. 112. The withdrawal of the International Brigades began in October 1938, shortly before Barke completed the novel, marking 'the Republic's failure … to transform the Spanish Civil War into a global crusade against fascism': Brendon 2000, pp. 347–8.

is tempting to read this deeply troubling historical reality into the recurring
references to 'faith' that appear in the final chapters and the attendant blur-
ring of a political discourse of revolution with a religious discourse of Apoca-
lypse. MacKelvie restores Andy's 'faith' in politics after the General Strike (595);
Andy's wife has 'faith' in his survival (600). Andy envisages a coming revolution that is also a day of judgement, 'when vengeance would be meted out to
those who had ground the faces of the poor' (596). Most of all, following Andy's
departure for Spain, a dual narrative focus on the Christian Socialist minister,
Tom, and the elderly Jean Ramsay offers, in the end, a vision of justice in a religious rather than a political mode. One important function that the turn to a
religious register performs is a weaving together of the family at the moment
when it is most fragmented: David has died, the daughters have left Scotland
for marriages abroad, Tom has moved away to a country parish and Andy has
left for Spain. The shared discourse of faith, and of the future that it promises,
in heaven if not on earth, attests to a common history even under these conditions of dispersal. It is useful to note the contrast with Lewis Grassic Gibbon's
characterisation of religion in *Scottish Scene*, echoed by Barke in *Major Operation*; described in typically corporeal terms as an institution '[a]s fantastically
irrelevant to contemporary Scottish affairs as the appendix is to the human
body', in need of excision in the name of 'social hygiene', and which furthermore conspired in the advance of fascism through its fostering of 'little parish
tyrannies'.[103] In a differentiating gesture characteristic of Popular Front cultural
politics, Barke implies a distinction between the popular content of Christian-
ity, as a form for popular expression, and the politics of its institutional forms.
But there is nonetheless a profound ambiguity to Tom's declaration that 'I feel
that in working for Socialism ... I am working for something that justifies their
whole existence – justifies all the suffering and hardship they have undergone'
(635). It is ambiguous in that it retrospectively recasts the events of the novel
as somehow legitimised, cancelling out the important moments when characters show themselves to be aware, however dimly, that their situation was not
necessary or justified. As one of the novel's survivors, Tom's narrative role is to
rearticulate his brother's death not within the confines of family history, but in
a narrative of human destiny (631).

Barke's choice of Jean as medium for his closing representation of the war
concludes her story at one level by connecting her with the historical narrative
to which she has always been indifferent, but it also returns the text to the

---

103   Gibbon 2002e, pp. 165–6. For Barke's rehearsal of the same association between Christian-
       ity and fascism in *Major Operation*, see Barke 1955 pp. 308–9.

mythic register in which it began. She imagines in Galloway, '[m]ilk: gallons and gallons of rich frothing milk – but no honey in all the land', a land of labour without respite that blurs into Spain, another country of exploited peasantry, the imagery suggestive of the bombing of Guernica: 'Some of them moaned in terror and some of them kneeled in the dust and made the sign of the Cross: for the heavens were darkened with the wings of death' (637–8). In Jean's last dream, the Galloway of her childhood and the land of Spain merge and become identical: the 'land of the leal' she feels herself approaching is therefore a homeland for her class, theirs by right of 'sweat and blood' (510). But in the scheme of the novel, historical and political knowledge is transmitted through generations so that when Jean hears the phrase, 'Blessed are the barren', taken from *Luke*, the implication is of a coming end of history. It is useful to compare this figurative return to the homeland with the more literal return that ends *A Scots Quair*. The concluding book of the trilogy, *Grey Granite*, ends with the breaking up of the family and of the household; Chris Guthrie closes up her boarding house in the city as her son leaves for London on the Hunger March, and returns to the farm where she was born. This return seems to end the conflicts she has survived but not resolved, leaving 'only the land, enduring, encompassing'.[104] There is no consoling return for Jean Ramsay; she dies in the city that, as Gustav Klaus notes, has never been a true home to the family, and the land she dreams of is a land at war.[105] Barke offers a mythic return to complete the novel's cyclical, epic-like structure which is both a resolution and a reminder of the crushed revolutionary hopes of 1938. Signs of the future are nonetheless present, though fragile; Andy's wife discovers she is pregnant (621); Tom considers returning to ministry in the city (623), for epics, as Denning suggests, 'may have sacrificial and redemptive deaths, but someone ... is left to tell the tale'.[106] The final sequence, however, and the novel's closing moments, locate Jean's folk beliefs and peasant values as the moral touchstone of the novel; it is these that it finally seeks to vindicate.

Conclusion

The novel, Fox argued, was 'the great folk art of our civilization', and in *The Land of the Leal* in particular, Barke strove to write a novel of the struggle

---

104   Gibbon 1998, p. 496.

105   Klaus 1998, p. 18.

106   Denning 1997, p. 199. Denning's argument is that Dos Passos's *U.S.A.* trilogy is not an epic since it 'glimpses no future'.

across history of the Scottish folk.[107] Much more than in *Major Operation*, the past is invoked as a source of resilience and defiance; full political subjectivity emerges not in breaking with the past but in understanding and rearticulating it. The use of the Spanish conflict to give a sense of unity to a history of loss, displacement and frustration inevitably places a huge strain on that event. Moreover, by the time the novel was completed, any possibility that the popular militancy of the war could stave off the threat of a global conflict had been crushed. That prospect of coming catastrophe is clearly felt in the novel's final pages. However, Barke's novel gives an important grounding in working-class historical experience to the ambitions of the Popular Front, which in other texts can feel distanced from those realities. In Rickword and Lindsay's work, the universalising rhetoric sometimes blurs the details of experience in uncomfortable ways. Rickword felt that abject states of historical oppression were beyond the reach of the contemporary imagination, and instead required an ethical rather than an empathetic position of filiation in which 'we are heirs to the fierce protest which swept [oppression] from our soil'.[108] The theme of inheritance and tradition is given concrete form in *The Land of the Leal* through the passing of memory and experience through the generations, identifying a living tradition of struggle that owed nothing to the nationalists' fetishisation of an irrecoverable past. For Barke, *The Land of the Leal* inevitably fell short of encompassing the history and the struggle that is its theme: 'the events of our generation', he wrote in his prefatory note, 'are on too vast a scale to come within the scope of our literary artists', but nonetheless the writer cannot simply await 'a more leisured age' in which the 'future Tolstoy will ... be in a position to complete the sequel to *War and Peace*'.[109] For Barke, Spain was a cause and an occasion in which to articulate, in novelistic form, a class history in new terms: the terms of the popular and progressive 'republican commonality' he identified in his *Left Review* article, and to offer a synoptic vision of the people in history, acting and being acted upon, that perhaps comes closest of any novel discussed here to the elusive 'standpoint of popular life' Lukács proposed.[110]

---

107   Fox 1979, p. 19.
108   Rickword 1941, p. 123.
109   Barke 1950, p. iv.
110   Lukács 1976, p. 344.

CHAPTER 6

Lewis Jones's Fiction

In the last chapter, I suggested that, in *The Land of the Leal* especially, James Barke attempted to write a novel in which the history of the Scottish working class and the anti-fascist struggle were inextricably connected. This chapter considers Lewis Jones's novels *Cwmardy* (1937) and its sequel *We Live* (1939), which bear a number of important similarities to *The Land of Leal*. Like Barke, Jones charts the development of political consciousness within a particular class and national fraction: in his case, the workers of the fictional Rhondda mining community of Cwmardy. Like Barke, too, Jones adopts a generational structure to trace this development: the novels follow the development of the young miner Len Roberts from childhood to labouring adulthood and prolonged unemployment; and, finally like Barke's Andy Ramsay, to death on the battlefield in Spain. In Jones's and Barke's work, there is a similar deep investment in the popular life of a provincial, proletarian community both as the symbol of what was at stake in the struggle against fascism and as a reserve of strength and resistance. An important distinction between the texts, however, is that in Jones's work the historical experience of migration is largely – though not completely – marginalised in favour of a portrayal of the community as a relatively stable social entity continually attempting to resist or absorb pressures originating from without. The central family in Barke's *The Land of the Leal* experience alienation as an unresolvable sense of homelessness stemming from the dispossession that uproots them from the stability of rural life and displaces them into the unsettled spatial and temporal regime of increasingly urbanised space. Jones's novels by contrast consider development within a settled community whose way of life, based on its sense of itself as an essentially closed social entity, is radically undermined by the threat, from within and from without, of boundless capitalism that transforms its experience of space, time and the objective world. As the community faces and endures the historical crises of the early twentieth century – the Cambrian Combine dispute of 1910/11, the First World War, the General Strike, the Depression and the rise of fascism – it is over the definition of 'home', over where the interests of the community really lie, and to what authority it is answerable, that its conflicts are played out. In a particular version of the Bildungsroman, Len comes to represent his 'people', but while the intimacy and intelligibility of the settled community initially seem to offer a vital counterweight to the abstracting, anonymising and atomising dynamics of capitalism, ultimately it is not in

the confines of the valley but on the battlefield of Spain that Len finds meaning. But Len's development is also stalled and incomplete in ways that raise
questions about the relationship between class, nation and modernity in the
Popular Front formation.

Lewis Jones (1897–1939) actively strove to be seen as a representative of
his class and community, and this position underwrites his novels' attempts
to represent the radical popular consciousness of the community in which
he lived, worked and fought.[1] Jones regularly contributed journalism to the
Daily Worker through the thirties detailing the desperate conditions in the
Rhondda, demonstrating a flair for the effective combination of documentary
evidence and telling anecdote.[2] When, in 1937, he was tried for threatening to
bring a demonstration to an unemployment office, the *Daily Worker* covered
the trial under the headline, 'A Whole People in the Dock', quoting Jones's
lawyer as saying that, '[i]t is not Lewis Jones, an individual, who is in the dock,
but a whole people and their constitutional rights'.[3] The project of writing
novels was, Jones reported, inspired by the Communist miners' leader Arthur
Horner, who suggested that 'the full meaning of life in the Welsh mining
areas could be expressed for the general reader more truthfully and vividly
if treated imaginatively'.[4] Jones attended the Comintern's Seventh Congress
at which Dimitrov announced the national, popular and historical emphases
of Popular Front ideological struggle; in this light, the relationships between
Jones's popular prestige and the novel-writing project he began late in 1935 is
of particular, even unique interest.[5] Jones's sense of the relationship between
his personal prestige and his novels' significance is clear in his letters to Douglas
Garman, who worked extensively with him on the manuscript of *Cwmardy*,
to the extent that Jones told Garman that 'it is misleading to name myself

---

1   Some of Jones's notable activities included industrial activism in South Wales and Notting-
    hamshire during the 1920s, resulting in three months' imprisonment during the General
    Strike; leading hunger marches from South Wales in 1932, 1934 and 1936; winning a seat on
    Glamorgan council as a Communist Party candidate in 1936; and energetic leadership of the
    unemployed throughout the thirties. The most detailed available account of his short but
    intense career is Dai Smith 1992.

2   See, for example, Jones 1934a and Jones 1934b.

3   *Daily Worker* 1937b, p. 5. Jones includes in *We Live* an incident in which the women of the valley
    invade the unemployment office at the conclusion of the mass demonstration, pp. 756–7.

4   Jones qtd. in H. Francis 2006, p. xii. Horner was President of the South Wales Miners' Feder-
    ation, the origins and development of which are fictionalised in the novels.

5   Jones's attendance at the Seventh Congress is referred to in H. Francis 2006, p. x, and Croft
    1990, p. 86. Dai Smith dates the beginning of Jones's work on *Cwmardy* to late 1935: Dai Smith
    1992, p. 35.

as the author because yourself and the other comrade have at least as much responsibility as I for it'.[6] Garman suggested that it was Jones's connection to popular life that gave the novel its 'epic quality', and which set him apart from other writers.[7] Lawrence & Wishart's advert for *Cwmardy* in the *Daily Worker* certainly sold it on the terms Jones proposes here: the advert sought to convince readers that the novel showed the way forward to a 'creation of a new literature, written of the people and by the people – for the people of Britain'.[8]

The reception of *Cwmardy* was, however, rather more muted in the left-wing press. Ralph Wright in the *Daily Worker* felt the need to reassure readers who might expect 'a certain narrowness, a certain lack of proportion, an inability to see the wood for the trees, and above all a certain weakness in the creation of individual characters' that the story in fact 'carries you along because you are interested in and, indeed, deeply moved by the characters who live it'.[9] Wright also praised the 'reality of living, turbulent, warm-hearted humanity'.[10] Meanwhile in *Left Review*, under the title 'A Working Class Epic', W.H. Williams praised the way Jones 'writes of an intimate experience, that is part of the fibre of his very being', in contrast to Orwell's account of mining in *The Road to Wigan Pier*.[11] Jones however professed himself disappointed with the reception of the novel:

> Even now I can't understand why so many really good comrades have missed the underlying political motive of the first book. Some of the genuine appreciations are really discouraging and sometimes I wonder if we haven't failed in what we set out to do with *Cwmardy*.[12]

---

6   Jones, undated facsimile letter to Garman, DG 6/4, Douglas Garman Papers, Department of Manuscripts and Special Collections, University of Nottingham. No date, but the same section refers to Harry Pollitt's review of *The Road to Wigan Pier*, published in the *Daily Worker* on 17 March 1937. Garman refers briefly to his work on the first novel in his notes for a talk on Jones: Garman, TS, 'A Working Class Writer. Lewis Jones', 24 February 1939, DG 3/1, Douglas Garman Papers, Department of Manuscripts and Special Collections, University of Nottingham.

7   Garman, TS, 'A Working Class Writer. Lewis Jones', 24 February 1939, DG 3/1, Douglas Garman Papers, Department of Manuscripts and Special Collections, University of Nottingham.

8   Lawrence & Wishart 1937.

9   Wright 1937, p. 7.

10   Ibid.

11   W.H. Williams 1937, pp. 428–9.

12   Jones, undated facsimile letter to Garman, DG 6/4, Douglas Garman Papers, Department of Manuscripts and Special Collections, University of Nottingham.

Jones is no more specific about what the 'underlying political motive' actually was, but a later letter expressing his concerns over the possible reception of *We Live* sheds some light on his ambition for the novels. He was worried that 'bourgeois' critics would not understand, or would not 'be permitted to explain' that it was 'definitely a *class* book in the fullest sense of the word'.[13] My readings of Jones's novels explore what this categorisation means, and, although I do not wish to suggest Jones was writing with a conscious theoretical sense of the novel's formal or ideological problems, I nonetheless argue that the task did require engagement with the relationship between politics and form. A further complaint of Jones's is also significant:

> The book also helps to prove that communists are essentially regenerative and creative. It gives our Party in s.w. a new intellectual status in the eyes of the masses here, precisely because I have been regarded as a leader of the party, a good chap and all that, but necessarily limited. We have not taught the workers that communists are concerned with and understand *every* phase of human existence, and all its 'cultural' aspects as well as the political. In other words we have not shown that communism is not a creed but that it is a *life*.[14]

The association between Communism and 'life' is a fundamental one in the scheme of both novels. The ambition to represent a whole way of life from a Communist point of view certainly seemed to resonate with Randall Swingler, who suggested in his *Daily Worker* review of *We Live* that Jones's first novel 'fitted more obviously perhaps than any other novel published in our time into what Ralph Fox called the epical tradition', and that the two novels should be read together as 'a sort of parable of the whole development of the working-class in England'.[15] Aside from Swingler's elision of 'England' and 'Britain', which misses the historical specificity of the novels' setting, he nonetheless identifies the novels' epic ambitions in their investment in popular life, and also, more saliently, in their identification of what is 'characteristic' to create 'a glorious affirmation of the people who made this book'.[16] The quality of affirmation inheres in Jones's shaping of his historical material to show that

---

13   Jones, undated facsimile letter to Garman, DG 6/4, Douglas Garman Papers, Department of Manuscripts and Special Collections, University of Nottingham. Emphasis in original.

14   Jones, undated facsimile letter to Garman, DG 6/4, Douglas Garman Papers, Department of Manuscripts and Special Collections, University of Nottingham. Emphasis in original.

15   Swingler 1939, p. 7.

16   Ibid.

even at moments of internal conflict and defeat, the utopian possibilities immanent in the class community's way of life are preserved.

As Hywel Francis has argued, the intensity of the pressures faced by the coalfield societies in industrial Wales was acute and distinctive. A particular developmental formation arose in localities rapidly and intensely industrialised in which the social forms of capitalist modernity existed alongside residual, pre-industrial social and cultural practices. Poverty and unemployment alienated large sections of the working class not just from wider society but 'to some extent from the traditional form of political activity of seeking greater working-class parliamentary representation'; instead, energy was regularly channelled into 'extra-parliamentary and extra-legal actions', generating an image, from within and from without, of an 'alternative society'.[17] The development of this alternative society, characterised by exercises of popular justice and direct action, is at the heart of Jones's novels. Francis notes furthermore that this culture of 'collective direct action' made it 'seemingly inevitable' that some would volunteer for Spain.[18] Over the course of the novels, the community's close-knit, defensive culture transforms into a powerful antifascist front through the emerging recognition of the identity of its interests with European communities threatened by fascism. Jones, indeed, was keen even before the official instantiation of the Popular Front line to project the Rhondda as a model of mass, united action: 'Sceptics regarding the possibilities of developing an all-embracing mass action on the basis of the united front', he wrote on the eve of a mass demonstration in 1935, 'should come to Red Rhondda to have their delusions shattered'.[19] 'Red Rhondda', he concluded, 'has laid a basis for the development of a Red Britain in the period confronting us'.[20] That the Valleys' communities, with their distinctive culture of unofficial, popular political action, which, Hywel Francis reports, 'tended to transcend political parties', could exemplify the emerging Communist vision of a culture of popular activism is a central message of Jones's work and the principle underlying his strategy of typification.[21]

Jones constructs the community's distinctive culture – its particular configuration of interconnecting ways of feeling and interacting – through antithetical discursive formations. The discursive formation that might be described as 'proletarian', associated with Len and his family, is marked by the routine

---

17   H. Francis 1984, p. 199.
18   H. Francis 1984, pp. 199–200.
19   Jones qtd. B. Francis 1935, p. 5.
20   Ibid.
21   H. Francis 1984, p. 200.

linkage of a series of associations: light, cleanliness, vision, honour, collectivity, change (development) and the comic are frequently evoked together in varying combinations. This associative grouping is set against an oppositional complex of associations which includes darkness, dirt, shame, blindness, objectification, stasis (frustrated development), fascism, tragedy and death. Cleanliness, for example, is associated with Len's sister Jane before her ultimately tragic sexual exploitation by the son of an official, but also with the strikes that attempt to 'clean' the pits of blackleg labour.[22] These oppositions seem, of course, conventionally encoded, but their meaning is not fixed, and much of the political development in the novels turns on the modification or mediation of these elements, wresting them away from damaging significations and repositioning them in the discourse of anti-fascism that is articulated by the end of *We Live*. The most significant mediation of this kind is of the term 'home'; a mediation needs to take place between the operative concepts of 'home' as what is immediately experienced, on one side, and the 'foreign' as the unseen or unexperienced on the other. The completion of this process is announced when Len addresses a foreign country – Spain – as 'home' (876), articulating the coextension of the class struggle in Cwmardy and the struggle against fascism in Spain.

The community perceives itself to be a closed social entity bound by its own moral code. Power can only be legitimate if it is visible, consensual and directly encountered, and thus the power of a distant government does not belong in the valley. The episodes in *Cwmardy* dealing with the 1910/11 lockout, strike and unrest that have become known as the Tonypandy Riots demonstrate the political significance of the clash of conceptions of 'belonging' in Jones's work, as well as offering a vivid depiction of the alternative society of Cwmardy in action to enforce its values against alien authority. A number of critics have pointed out that Jones revises the historical facts of the crisis, especially in relation to the role of South Wales Miners' Federation and the internal disputes over organisation that culminated in the publication in 1912 of the celebrated pamphlet, *The Miners' Next Step*.[23] The events of 1910–11 in the Rhondda were distinctive, as Dai Smith argues, because the events raised questions about the development of communities like Tonypandy, and about who 'controlled them', that could only be read as political questions requiring answers that

---

22   Jones 2006, pp. 220–1. Page references to this combined edition of the novels are hereafter given in parentheses in the text.

23   See for example Snee 1979, p. 184, and Dai Smith 1992, p. 40. It should however be noted that a section of the 'Strikers are sent into the valley' chapter appeared in *Left Review* under the title 'Tonypandy', which suggests Jones was willing for the episodes to be interpreted as representations of that historical event (Jones 1937).

countenanced the possibility of a different social order rather than reform or compromise.[24] *The Miners' Next Step* itself proposed a strikingly new politics that sought to end the Liberal hegemony in industrial Wales; its principal proposal was that '[t]he old policy of identity of interest between employers and ourselves be abolished, and a policy of open hostility installed'.[25] The conflict with the police is figured as a fight for the community's integrity as represented in the Square, which 'as always on important occasions, became the centre of attraction' (224). It is a matter of 'honour to the people of the valley that the Square belonged to them and that no one could turn them from it' (236). While in Barke's *The Land of the Leal*, the dispossession of the Scottish peasantry deprives them of the land which they nonetheless feel should be theirs by natural right, in Jones's novel the public square acts as a vital common space in which authority can be contested.[26]

At the dramatic centre of the conflict as Jones represents it is the looting of shops and the destruction of private property. It was this aspect of the events in Tonypandy that most disturbed and incensed the authorities at the time, and was used as evidence for the 'lawlessness' of the Rhondda.[27] The community's refusal to accept the sanctity of property presents a direct challenge to the discipline of the state, and the state responds with the methods of colonial violence used to subjugate 'lawless' regions elsewhere. The commander of the police treats the situation as an imperialist war, and is clearly based on Lionel Lindsay, chief constable of Glamorganshire police, whom Will Paynter – prominent Welsh Communist and volunteer in Spain – described in his autobiography as 'part of the Coalmasters' army of occupation in South Wales'.[28] Honour and belonging form the affective basis of resistance against this 'occupation': 'Gradually the police were driven from the Square, which was left in the possession of the strikers' (240). The victory is expedited by Len's burning of the power-house, making visible the advancing police (238) and providing the desperately needed '[l]ight to see the enemy' (237). It seems likely that Jones based this moment on a historical incident that occurred in his home village in November 1910 when 'officials were stoned out of the electric power-

---

24   Dai Smith 1984, p. 96.

25   Unofficial Reform Committee 1912, p. 25. For a discussion of the pamphlet's politics in relation to the tradition and development of syndicalism more widely, see Egan 1996, pp. 13–33.

26   As Jean Ramsay puts it, 'the sweat and blood o' the Gibsons are in they fields – they should be ours ten times ower'; Barke 1950, p. 510.

27   See, for example, *The Times* 1910, p. 12.

28   Paynter 1972, p. 38.

house built in 1905 at a cost of £25,000', and his manipulation of the event underscores Len's function of enlightening and extending the vision of his community.[29]

What is established by the end of the episode is Cwmardy's self-identification as a community under attack, indeed, in armed struggle, whose most basic principles and interests were fundamentally opposed to those of the government. This is the process Chris Williams describes as a 'societary redefinition' beginning in 1910, the outcome of which was that, by 1926, the 'Lib-Lab *gwerin* [folk] had now taken the form of a proletariat'.[30] The community thus repels the efforts to bind this 'lawless' fraction into the spatial order of the modern state. Rejecting police efforts to control the square, it instead uses this common space to publicly enact its own forms of justice. Jones suggests the ways that the residual folk practices and popular culture of the valley, with their distant echoes of rough music and the *ceffyl pren*, often brought by immigrants from the rural West, not only rebuts its alleged 'lawlessness' but also provide vital ways of redressing injustice and exploitation. Siân's humiliation of Evan the Overman in retaliation for his slandering of her daughter and his refusal to accept responsibility for her death is a key example. At this point the forces of shame, belonging and objectification powerfully coalesce. Siân claims the right to enact justice on Evan, a right expressed through her objectification of him: 'Don't anybody touch him … He do belong to me' (256). The 'shame-faced figure' of Evan is associated with the exploited body of Jane as Siân dresses him in her daughter's nightgown: 'Let your eyes see it' (256). The objectifier becomes objectified in a carnivalesque public reversal.

Shame, Vision and Reification

These episodes reflect a valorisation of the immediate and the visible. 'Alien' power is expelled; unseen injustice is publicly punished; abstract conceptions of property ownership are overcome by a sense of belonging rooted in the continuity of social life in a given place over time. The community mobilises its internal resources to resist the transformation of its social life into the normative forms of capitalist modernity. It is a matter of honour that invisible powers are resisted. When the miner's leader Ezra proposes a compromise, Len tells the miners that their wives would scorn the men's fear of 'a Home Secret-

---

29   Dai Smith 1984, p. 66.
30   C. Williams 1996, p. 127.

ary we have never seen' and who 'don't belong to us' (268), and, comparably, he resists Ezra's recruitment efforts on the outbreak of war, asking 'Do you believe I should kill men I have never seen?' (334). However, the basic dichotomy between the immediately perceived and the unseen and thus irrelevant, is progressively complicated through a struggle over ways of seeing that plays out in the negotiation of concepts of shame and objectification. Jones's handling of commodification suggests a quite complex sense of the relationship between capitalism and subjectivity, and very particularly of the way that the ambiguity of the commodity form itself undermines any appeal to the integrity of the immediately perceived. In *Cwmardy*, Len's mother Siân uses commodification as an insult to her husband, rhetorically reducing him to a cheap commodity: 'Call yourself a man! Why, I could buy your sort for ten a penny' (95–6), a description Len's father Jim bitterly repeats after a pit explosion: 'What do hundred men count for 'longside a hundred trams of coal? Men be cheap 'nough these days, and will soon be dear at ten a penny' (132), and at an earlier point, resignedly, 'What do us men count? We be cheaper than chickens' (116).[31] To be seen as – and to see oneself as – nothing more than a commodity is a constant threat in the novels' moral world, and these moments register awareness of the declining value of the human in capitalism's accelerating development.

The episode describing Jane's death in childbirth after she has been disowned by the manager's son is a key moment in Jones's use of sight in relation to the commodity form. The macabre scene in which Len views his sister's body makes clear the link between visuality and the critique of the commodity: on each of her eyes is 'a blackened penny' (81). The image of blackened pennies signifies Jane's status as a corrupted commodity; the displaced human potential represented in money, 'the alienated *ability of mankind*', is here figured as a corruption of the organs of sight.[32] Jane's eyeless baby represents the same corruption: its face 'a blob of paste' (79), carrying both the connotations of something incompletely or defectively produced, and, from 'paste', the connotation of the cheaply mass-produced commodity. When Len sees Jane's coffin, the commodity is figured as the site of displaced subjectivity: 'The shining shield near its top stared at him like a lonely, glaring eye' (79). The tragedy of Jane's death is announced by the description of her as blinded: 'In her eyes grew the dull glazed look of a hunted animal that, even as it runs, knows there is no

---

31   A comic and ironic subversion of this figure of speech occurs when Jim evades justice by
     hiding in Will Smallbeer's chicken hutch during the 1910/11 strike, p. 235.
32   Marx 2000a, p. 118; emphasis in original.

escape' (71). Elsewhere, the violence of capital's appropriation of the body of
the worker is figured as the displacement of perception: when a young miner
loses an arm in an accident, a 'gleaming bone wink[s] wickedly through the
blood' (397). Displaced perception, in the scheme of Jones's novels, signifies
the complete effacement of the subject of labour by the object of labour – the
fragmentation of the human by the rationality of production. Objectified bodies can only be looked upon. The connection between this displacement of
the privileged sense of sight and the perpetuation of class violence is stated
clearly during the 1910/11 strike, when the gun brought by the officials to break
the strike 'seemed to leer through its bore at each of them in turn' (217). But
where, for the characters, blindness indicates the effacement of their subjectivity by the object of labour, here, the community's victorious defence of its own
social order is figured by an uncanny reversal in the image of the smashed shop
windows which, 'covered with corrugated iron sheets, looked like bandaged
eyes' (265). The community successfully strikes back at the power of capitalism to animate the commodity while objectifying (and figuratively blinding)
the human.

   The uncanniness of these sighted figures gives form to the ambiguity of
the commodity that arises from the radical duality of its nature. Despite its
appearance of objectivity, direct perception cannot reveal the commodity's
true nature since, 'the existence of the commodity-form, and the value-relation
of the products of labour within which it appears, have absolutely no connection with the physical nature of the commodity and the material relations
arising out of this'.[33] The unseen truth of this form is therefore an alien, disturbing presence within the apparently intelligible and unmediated social world of
Cwmardy, a community that Len experiences early in his life as a fully 'knowable' community, in Raymond Williams's sense.[34] His boyhood is marked by
the experience of measurable, bounded time and space, where home can be
reached in 'ten strides' and 'a few minutes' (14). The essential intelligibility of
the community persists through *Cwmardy* and fosters resistance to the state's
attempts to recruit the community in the service of defending imperialism,
as exemplified by Len's mother Siân's dismissal of the entire enterprise: 'For
King and country indeed! I have never seen no king, and the only country I
know is inside the four walls of this house and between the three mountains of
our valley' (330). As in the 1910/11 strike scenes, the belief in the integrity of a
community based on continuous inhabitation of a defined space is vital to the

---

33   Marx 1990, p. 165.
34   R. Williams 1975, pp. 202–3.

community's survival. But from the outset, the closed, intelligible community is shadowed by the disturbing, unknowable and unbounded forces of modernity. When Len begins to work, a milestone that he considers his initiation into manhood, his first experience is of the 'uncanny' intuition that 'the pit had a life of its own' (148), as well as a horror of the infinite distance and endless time of labour (151). The pit appears possessed of its own expanding and insatiable nature, transforming daily life so that 'quietly and stealthily, the pit became the dominating factor in his life' (159). Daily Len joins the 'never-ending silent flow of men to the pit' and travels 'the same ever-lengthening pit roadway' (159); time and space extend indefinitely with no sense of progression. Here Jones suggests the reification of time described by Lukács in 1922: 'time sheds its qualitative, variable, flowing nature; it freezes into an exactly delimited, quantifiable continuum filled with quantifiable "things" ... in short, it becomes space'.[35] Scenes of both economic and sexual exploitation are marked by a heightened sense of limitless time and space: in the pit, 'the men were immersed in a universe of coal, sweat, and clamour. If anything happened to stop the machinery they felt that the world would become suddenly void' (395), while the hours of Jane's labour feel to Len as if they will never end while '[e]very second became an embodied nightmare' (73).

Forms and Modes

Len becomes aware that the commodity form is the dominant form in his life: he understands that his life is without value in the scheme of exploitation: '[The officials] measure coal without giving a thought to our flesh. They think, they dream, they live for coal, while we die for it. Coal – that's the thing' (184). His development is determined by a quest to find order and meaning as the community is increasingly pressured by the crises of the early twentieth century. While at first the community seemed to offer a definite form against the abstraction of capitalism, it is only through recognising its true nature – that which is visible and that which the visible form of the commodity must repress – that its place on the world stage can be understood. Len becomes aware of this duality in himself as something 'moulded in the pit by his fellow workmen', and 'without them he knew his world would be empty' (537); it is both the indefinite form of work and the definite forms of sociality and solidarity that have shaped his life (that is, both the commodity and its repressed

---

35   Lukács 1975, p. 90.

history). The version of 'belonging' evoked by Len is central to both of Jones's novels and informs the texts' account of how the class community can resist the dehumanisation of commodification and instead affirm the possibility of a different society.

The 'phantom objectivity' of the commodity form, as Lukács calls it, seems to inform Jones's narrative strategies and deployments of generic convention.[36] Courtroom scenes dramatise the different relationships that the workers and the capitalist class have with material objects. In the Tonypandy episode, the law is clearly figured as defending property, but Jones also demonstrates that working-class knowledge and experience are not recognised by legal epistemology. At the inquest following a fatal explosion in the mine in *Cwmardy*, Jim describes how 'it was awful, mun, to see your butties lying cold like that' (126), to which the lawyer defending the mine owners responds, 'we want to know what you saw, not what you felt' (126). Jim's insistence that the dead miner's lamp has been tampered with is based on his practical knowledge that 'the first thing a miner will do whenever he get a lamp in his hand is to twist the pot … It do come natural to us' (128). Jim's knowledge gained in labour – the history of production the commodity conceals – rather than the acceptance of the object in its appearance of 'phantom objectivity' is inadmissible in the court.[37] A second, more curious, example of this procedure occurs in the seemingly self-contained 'Night on the Mountain' episode in *We Live*, in which a young miner is found dying by Len and Mary. The episode develops like a murder mystery, complete with a crucial clue, a 'button shining' (560), and an incomplete deathbed accusation, 'it was a b–' (571). Jones again uses a courtroom scene to illustrate the way that the construction of evidence in law blocks the achievement of justice and masks class violence. Mary is told, 'We want to know what you saw, not what you think' (575). She is not permitted to make the association

---

36   Lukács 1975, p. 83.

37   These scenes would undoubtedly have resonance for contemporary readers as a result of the widely reported and widely condemned inquiry into the Gresford colliery disaster, which killed 266 North Wales miners in September 1934. The inquiry criticised managers and inspectors but ultimately absolved them of direct responsibility, and allegations were made that (as in *Cwmardy*) evidence had been tampered with and records destroyed. See, among many examples of the *Daily Worker*'s coverage: *Daily Worker* 1936b; and Fred Pateman's reflection on the inquiry's report: Pateman 1937. In his contribution to the *Fact* issue on documentary, Arthur Calder-Marshall cited the testimony of one miner at the inquiry, John Edward Samuel, as exemplifying the type of language that documentary fiction should aspire to, 'a command of language and vividness of description, similar to Hemingway or Dos Passos', Calder-Marshall 1937a, p. 39.

between the silver button and the policemen who appear with increasing frequency in *We Live*.

Such narrative incompletion is not, however, necessarily allied to defeat, and at other points a refusal of convention opens an important narrative space. The shift between the mock-heroic and the heroic modes that describe Jim and Len's respective war exploits is a useful example. Jim, like Siân, is a comic force in the novel and his bragging about his own heroic feats in the wars he has fought is a source of humour (10; 241). Jones resists the potential for a tragic narrative to be motivated by Jim's drunken enlistment for the Great War and instead resolves the subplot in an almost bathetic manner, with Jim returning home apparently unscathed (388–9). This move keeps Jim within the associative grouping of comedy and survival in the narrative. In his earliest published piece of fiction, 'Young Dai', published in 1932, Jones's plot moves at a tangent to that of *Cwmardy*, telling the story of a miner who, unlike Len, did catch 'the germ' and enlist in 1914.[38] The story is told in an anecdotal, laconic manner by a collective working-class voice that comments with indifference on Young Dai's decision: 'It was obvious to all of us that he had caught the germ'.[39] Dai's misfortunes in the ensuring years are recounted, before Jones states the thematic development elaborated in *Cwmardy*: 'His nephew has also caught the germ 18 years after Old Dai had it. He wants to fight now. But he knows his enemy'.[40] In *Cwmardy* and *We Live* this movement of transition from imperialist to anti-fascist war is narrated from within the relationship between father and son, but unlike Dai, Big Jim is not harmed by his experiences. This gesture keeps open a necessary hope, allowing even the experience of war to be assimilated in the comic and vital structure of proletarian feeling in the novel. While Graham Holderness has described Jones's novels as 'naturalistic', this is to underrate the political significance of Jones's compulsive depiction of the ways that subjectivity and the commodity interplay.[41] One might therefore attribute to Jones more sensitivity to the politics of form than he is normally afforded.[42]

---

38   Jones 1932, p. 6.

39   Ibid.

40   Ibid.

41   Holderness 1984, pp. 27–8.

42   Frank Kermode, for example, implies that Jones was not, in effect, in control of the modes he was using, as evidenced by what Kermode considers a tendency towards 'posh over-writing' and 'fancy creative-writing-course prose' (Kermode 1988, p. 89). Kermode's wider point is a more nuanced one about working-class fiction's relationship with bourgeois

Spain and Home

The intensifying pressures on the community's way of seeing are traced in
We Live, which begins in 1924, six years after the end of the First World War
that concluded *Cwmardy*. The novel charts the increasingly acute tensions
between the politics of the older generation, characterised by a prioritisation
of immediate struggles and a rejection of what is considered to be outside the
community, and a newer militant politics oriented towards wider alliances and
solidarities. Len's developing insight is always tempered by uncertainty, and
this quality distinguishes him from Ezra whose vision becomes, dialectically,
a form of blindness as his power recedes and the demands of history outpace
him: 'I know the struggle from A to Z ... What I have done I have done with
my eyes open and the people have listened to me' (522). Ezra's decline is
hastened by his misrecognition of Communism as a foreign theory, predicated
on his misunderstanding of 'home' as what is immediately experienced (674).
The final confrontation between Len and Ezra occurs in the shadow of the
rise of fascism; Len looks over the valley at the point 'when the whole world
was centred on Leipzig' with his 'thoughts fixed on Dimitrov', and from this
vantage point – a position of superior insight both literally and figuratively –
he watches Ezra entering the house of the mine owner (671). The revelation of
Ezra's betrayal announces that the community can no longer distinguish simply
between what does and does not belong in Cwmardy. Siân's vision has to give
way to the realisation that the 'home' is not independent of the wider totality,
and that its interests cannot be defended within the limits she indicates. On
hearing of Len's plan to join the International Brigade, she is dismissive of its
relevance to her family: 'Huh! Spaniards indeed! I have never seened one of
them and don't owe them a single penny' (849). Siân's conflation of experience
('never seened') and economic relations ('single penny') is no longer adequate
as a way of delineating class interests.

It is useful, at this point, to consider Jones's novels in light of Jed Esty's study
of the problematic or incomplete Bildungsroman of late imperialism. While,
Esty argues, in the classic novel of development, the 'soul-nation allegory' suggests that the nation gives mature, finished form to modern societies just as
adulthood gives finished form to the modern subject, imperial crisis disturbed
the transition from immature colony to mature nation, and hence colonial
societies were locked in a state of permanent transition registered through

---

standards of value, but it nonetheless depends on an assumption that Jones's own relationships with those standards were largely unconscious.

the 'figure of youth, increasingly untethered in the late Victorian era from the model and telos of adulthood' that 'seems to symbolize the dilated/stunted adolescence of a never-quite-modernized periphery'.[43] The Bildungsroman functioned to mediate between the open-ended temporality of capitalism and the bounded countertemporality of the nation.[44] The nation, Esty argues, provided 'an emergent language of historical continuity or social identity amid the rapid and sweeping changes of industrialization'.[45] In many ways Len represents something resembling the characteristic subject of the Bildungsroman: sensitive, slightly detached, dreamy, physically weak, 'queer' (20), Jones's central character feels acutely the tension between the stability of community and the unceasing revolution of modernity. His sense of a life that has no inner form or meaning, that is shapeless under capital's regime of endless expansion, causes in adolescence a serious illness (163) and preconditions his eventual acceptance of the Marxist message of the novel's ideological donor figure, the educated shopkeeper's son, Ron. But while Len is used to focalise questions of development in the novels, he does not reach the condition of maturity and social accommodation that is the signature resolution of the classic Bildungsroman. He continues to be physically overshadowed by his father, and his sexual development is disturbed by a continuing association between sex and death originating in his sister's death, so that Len and Mary's sexual relations are continually figured as deathly (as when they are 'buried in each other', 493). The primal trauma of his sister's exploitation stunts his development and ensures he cannot achieve conventional (bourgeois) masculine maturity as father and head of a household. His wife Mary is comparably emotionally inhibited and physically weakened. The family, as Raymond Williams points out, is the most accessible fictional centre for the working-class novelist, and would, of course, provide Jones with an obvious structure in which to formalise his alignment of Communism with life and creation.[46] But Jones refuses to separate the family from the relations of exploitation that determine life in Cwmardy. The family of Evan the Overman is fated to fail as a structure through which life can be reproduced as a consequence of Evan's implication in practices of exploitation: Evan's son is another man's child – 'see if you can find the likeness', Siân tells him (66) – and Jane and her baby both die. Patrilineal structures are shown to be dependent on and liable to debasement by the economic system Evan exploits.

---

43   Esty 2012, p. 137.
44   Esty 2012, p. 5.
45   Esty 2012, p. 4.
46   R. Williams 1982, pp. 116–17.

The refusal to integrate Len into the 'organic' social form of the family is a consequence of Jones's desire, particularly evident in the final chapters of *We Live*, to deflect attention onto the fate of the community rather than of the individual, in order to demonstrate that the forms that stunt the growth of singular lives can only be overcome by collective action. Through the actions of the Communist characters, political consciousness grows in the community, culminating in a mass march in 1935.[47] The constant threat of dehumanisation is ultimately met not with individual vocation but with Len's recognition that his 'existence and power as an individual was buried in that of the mass now pregnant with motion behind him' (747). Jones's figuration of the march is significant because it meets the endless proliferation of modernity with seemingly limitless popular power that overtakes spatial and temporal organisation: 'Time and distance were obliterated by the cavalcade of people, whose feet made the roads invisible' (747–8). The people are now innumerable, no longer the fragmented, quantifiable subjects of modernity or the sociable but numerically weak members of a peripheral community. The march achieves a plenitude and coherence in time and space that capitalist modernity's constantly mobilising and expanding dynamics do not allow. Ultimately, it is the community's social and political development that is the subject of the novels, and the march is the point at which it finds itself capable of a more radical gesture than the localised attacks on the visible signs of exploitation that preceded it. While Len himself is a figure of incomplete development, his final glance at his community is one of pride in *its* maturation from 'a tiny village' to an industrial town of 'hundreds of streets and big buildings with bright windows' (863).

Len's death in Spain is both an ending and the refusal of an ending. He conceives of his participation in Spain as giving form and purpose to his disenfranchised, unfulfilled life; though he has lived as 'a man who had always been unemployed – a man who wandered from meeting to meeting and street to street looking for something he never seemed to find' – the children of Cwmardy will remember him and think, 'We knew Len. He fought for us in Spain' (855–6). While this suggests the essentially novelistic quality Lukács calls 'the story of the soul that goes to find itself',[48] Len's letter from Spain, received after his death, announces that he has not found his true self in the socially different context of a foreign land but has instead returned home:

---

47 The march is based on the ones Jones led in the Rhondda in early 1935. These marches were reported in the *Daily Worker*: B. Francis 1935.

48 Lukács 1978, p. 89.

Yes, my comrade, this is not a foreign land on which we are fighting. It is home. Those are not strangers who are dying. They are our butties. It is not a war only of nation against nation, but of progress against reaction, and I glory in the fact that Cwmardy has its sons upon the battle-field, fighting here as they used to fight on the Square, the only difference being that we now have guns instead of sticks.

    p. 876

In this peroration, 'Home' and 'the Square' have become not just spatial designators but intensely political, even utopian, ideas, the integrity of which have been fought for throughout the preceding episodes in the novels. As the novel constructs it, the war is a class war in which the false differentiation of nationhood ('strangers') gives way to class solidarity ('butties').

Len is a figure of curtailed development whose death marks a historical impasse for Communist politics in Europe in so far as it (perhaps unintentionally) allegorises the imminent collapse of the Republic and the withdrawal of the Brigades. But it marks him, too, as a figure of permanent transition, of unrealised revolution. Len's failure to achieve socially integrated adulthood signifies Jones's refusal to accept that conditions in the Valleys could be lived with as they were. But the novels' often comic and burlesque narration of a community developing in history also speaks against the assumption made by other Welsh writers that the industrialisation of South Wales and the subsequent economic collapse had been an unmitigated tragedy that was entering its final stages during the late thirties. Idris Davies's 1938 poem *Gwalia Deserta* imagines Wales ('Gwalia', the archaism making clear Davies's elegiac intent) as a land ruined by an unspecified and alien 'they', who 'slunk away and purchased/ The medals of the State', leaving 'the landscape of Gwalia stained for all time/ By the bloody hands of progress'.[49] T.S. Eliot described Davies's works of this period as 'the best poetic document I know about a particular epoch in a particular place'.[50] The Nationalist poet and politician Saunders Lewis, meanwhile, ruminating on the decade's many failures on the eve of war, saw in the 'human

---

49   Davies 1994, p. 11. There is, however, more to this poem than simple nostalgia, and an interesting study could be made of its conflicted attitudes to popular culture, the various angles from which it recalls the defeat of 1926, and its connections with better-known poetry of the decade (with Louis MacNeice's *Autumn Journal*, for example). At its more anecdotal narrative moments (for example, in section VIII) the tone is not dissimilar to Jones's.

50   Qtd. Stringer (ed.), p. 157.

wreckage' of the crisis-stricken Valleys a culture-less and denationalised waste-
land that 'once was Wales'.[51] Jones's novels stand counter to these projections of
catastrophe, asserting instead that the working-class community's resources of
survival and self-definition placed it at the heart of the struggle for the survival
of civilisation and for the possibility of a new society. The fragility of that community must be stressed; the crisis in South Wales was so severe that serious
proposals were made to clear the industrial Valleys of much of their population.[52] Jones saw the unruly, creative culture of collective direct action that
emerged under the extreme pressures of industrialisation as offering a living
example of the type of culture projected by the Popular Front, and his novels
both celebrate the integrity of that community and reflect the optimism and
despair of the closing years of the 1930s.

Conclusion

> Have had a letter from the boys in Spain in which they issue a challenge
> that they will have finished the Fascists there and be back home by the
> time the second book is published. That's the spirit for you.[53]

Jones died suddenly in January 1939, in the week that Barcelona fell to Franco's
forces. Dai Smith and Hywel Francis both suggest that Jones had intended, after
We Live, to write a third work in which the volunteers returned, victorious,
to lead a socialist revolution in the valley.[54] Barke's *The Land of the Leal* and
Jones's *We Live* were published almost simultaneously in 1939, and at least one
critic made the connection between them. Frank Swinnerton, writing in the
Observer, praised the sincerity of *We Live* despite its being 'crudely written';
he also commended the pastoral elements of *The Land of the Leal*, though
appeared puzzled by the connection between the urban and rural sections of
Barke's text. He concluded, however, that if Barke, like Jones, 'has to use the
Spanish War as a useful mechanism he has the excuse that it is part of the
history of our time and a fitting landmark in such a chronicle'.[55] But the novels
do more than appropriate the war as a plot mechanism. Len's letter in Spain

51   S. Lewis 1967, p. 246.
52   G.A. Williams 1991, p. 252.
53   Jones, undated facsimile letter to Garman, DG 6/4, Douglas Garman Papers, Department
      of Manuscripts and Special Collections, University of Nottingham.
54   Dai Smith 1992, p. 76; and H. Francis 1984, p. 103.
55   Swinnerton 1939.

echoes a letter from Will Paynter to Arthur Horner, President of the South Wales Miners' Federation, published in 1937:

> From it all emerges one thing at least, and that is that the International Brigade and the British Battalion as part of it, is not some noble and gallant band of crusaders come to succour a helpless people from an injustice, it is the logical expression of the conscious urge of democratic peoples for self-preservation.[56]

In his study of the British volunteers in Spain, James K. Hopkins has suggested that

> there was a logical, sequential development of issues in the lives of many British militants: first, looking for explanations for the unemployment and repression they experienced; second, seeing the rise of fascism on the continent as an issue that concerned them; and third, seizing the opportunity to strike back at oppression, if not in Great Britain, then in Spain.[57]

But Barke's and Jones's novels do not simply reflect but actively participate in the cultural production of that sequence, giving emotional weight and life to those connections – a more difficult and conflicted process than such a summary allows. Both writers' interventions in the cultural life of the volunteers extended beyond their depiction in fiction: Barke, Gustav Klaus reports, wrote a bagpipe march for the Scottish Ambulance Unit in Spain, while Hopkins claims that the Welsh Brigaders enthusiastically read *Cwmardy*.[58] What might be written out in the production of such sequential narratives are, as Williams suggests, 'the *disconnections* of a wide cultural and political life'.[59] These novels nevertheless represent remarkable examples of writers' efforts to articulate the relationship between the values, traditions and distinctive culture of communities marginalised in regional and class terms and the most urgent global historical realities of the decade. Their conclusions in heroic death and the epic motif of homecoming both confront and refuse to accept the death of the political hopes whose development they have narrated.

---

56   Published in *Miners' Monthly*, June 1937; qtd. Paynter 1972, pp. 69–70.
57   J.K. Hopkins 1998, p. 107.
58   Klaus 1998, p. 8; J.K. Hopkins 1998, p. 383.
59   Williams 2005, p. 225, emphasis in original.

Conclusion

The most compelling criticisms of the cultural productions of the Popular Front are those of John Coombes and Nick Hubble. Hubble characterises Popular Front aesthetics as Stalinised pastoral, entailing a suppression of difference in the name of solidarity.[1] Coombes, in a similar vein, finds little that was genuinely socially transformative in the Popular Front; instead, he considers that its coordinates were liberal, not Marxist: it affirmed a valorisation of bourgeois culture 'under the mask of "humanist" Marxism', and required intellectual commitment to only the most minimal demands.[2] These are important criticisms in so far as they identify real sites of tension in the novels and the wider formation of which they were a part. It is tempting, and would not be unjustified, to see the recovery of the progressive potential of the nation as a mediation of imperial crisis in the burgeoning of globalisation. In their wide-ranging efforts to reveal a repressed radical cultural history, Popular Front texts might be read as seeking to legitimate a leftist civic nationalism; a nationalism that might nourish and be nourished by a renewed realism with an 'epic' dimension. But that realism required a bracketing or deferral of the particular problems of twentieth-century modernity, and especially the problems of imperialism, that were registered by the shattered, relativised and irreparable forms of modernist textuality. And for all their epic resonances and their concentration of collective fates in the typical individual, the violent endings of so many of these texts – *May Day*, *Men of Forty-Eight*, *Major Operation*, *The Land of the Leal* and *We Live* – suggest the vanishing point of that prospect. A full accommodation with realist narratives of development and fulfilment eluded the Communist imagination, and there is neither fulfilment in revolutionary liberation nor rapprochement with the social order for the characters whose deaths conclude these novels.

The charge of pastoralism alleges an erasure of class difference and class struggle, but I have suggested here that, rather than passively reflecting the counter-revolutionary positions of Stalinism, there is without doubt in these novels a deep investment in problems of class formations and relationships, and moreover an interrogative and sometimes sceptical attitude to class alliance. While a reconciliation with the institutions of democracy might seem to Coombes to be 'bourgeois', the articulation of parliamentary democracy as an

---

1   Hubble 2009, p. 184.
2   Coombes 1980, p. 80.

element in a history of popular struggles performed crucial ideological work in identifying the common investments of wide sections of the population necessary for a mass movement to be built, and in this sense Coombes mistakes ends for means. Within the Popular Front formation, activism was mobilised towards a range of issues and causes, some with identifiable class bearings and some without; these included intellectual freedom and civil liberties, the militarisation of scientific research, unemployment, rent strikes, poverty, workplace safety and the means test, as well as anti-fascism at home and abroad.[3] The relative claims of a politics based in specific class interests and those of the need for a national anti-fascist front had to be continually negotiated; the priority of the latter over the former was not, as Coombes and Hubble imply, taken as given. These negotiations find form in the novels; in, for example, Jack Lindsay's examinations of bourgeois dissidence in history and in James Barke's and Lewis Jones's positioning of regionally specific working-class experience as a factor in a particular historical conjuncture.

The book contributes in its own way to scholarly traditions that seek to recover and critically re-evaluate works suffering critical neglect. In seeking to restore to view some of the components of this still fragmented and incomplete history, there are, inevitably, many omissions. The most obvious of these is the lack of discussion of the contributions of women writers. The themes and analytic categories deployed here could certainly be extended to discussions of the thirties novels of Virginia Woolf, Storm Jameson, Sylvia Townsend Warner and Katharine Burdekin, among others. Productive work could certainly be done too on questions of the relationships between gender and political subjectivity in leftist fiction more generally. Lewis Grassic Gibbon is widely praised for his female protagonist Chris Guthrie in *A Scots Quair*, but even this resolves, in *Grey Granite*, into a reinvestment in the figure of the male militant, Ewan Tavendale, in whom the novel's apprehensive and ambivalent vision of the political future is concentrated.[4] Political activism, particularly Communist activism, tends to be a masculine mode in these novels. However, one of the symmetries between Jones's *We Live* and Barke's *The Land of the Leal* is the investment of political responsibility in the widows of the International Brigaders, pointing to a future in which women's political experience is central.

---

3 See Pollitt 1936, in which Pollitt raises a variety of these issues as part of an appeal to intellectuals.

4 The seminal intervention is Burton 1984.

It has perhaps become commonplace to evoke, on the subject of 'recovered' fiction, Raymond Williams's memorable image of 'the neglected works left in the wide margin of the century'.[5] Williams's more salient point, however, relates not to the inclusion and exclusion of particular texts in the critical field, or their relative statuses, but rather to how those procedures of selection are implicated in the construction of twentieth-century history. For Williams, the reduction of the cultural history of the early twentieth century to a narrowly selective and 'exploitable' modernist repertoire amounts to historical closure, a plotting of the century as defined by the transition from modernism to a post-modernism understood as, in some sense, post-historical.[6] The mid-century transition between those phases coincides with, and may be seen as a corollary of, another sequence of positions that E.P. Thompson calls the 'declension from disenchantment to acquiescent quietism' that defined the intellectual retreat of many intellectuals from Communism in particular and political commit-ment in general.[7] For Thompson, it was this 'default of the disenchanted which gave to Natopolitan ideology its form'; that is, a depoliticising, de-historicising conformism.[8] With these problems of history in mind, it is worth briefly pur-suing the main threads of this study beyond its limits in 1940 to consider the tributaries into which the energies of the Popular Front flowed. Of the writers considered here – Jones excepting – all would continue to be active in the political culture of the war years, though only Lindsay would stay the course with the Communist Party until the end of his life. John Sommerfield served with the RAF and channelled his literary energies into short fiction and docu-mentary, contributing several pieces dealing with military experience to John Lehmann's New Writing.[9] Arthur Calder-Marshall worked as a script-writer and editor for the Ministry of Information, collaborating on documentary and pro-paganda films.[10] James Barke continued to work in the Clydeholm Shipyard through the war, becoming a central figure in Glasgow Unity Theatre, for which he wrote plays about the wartime experiences of the Glasgow citizenry such as The Night of the Big Blitz and When the Boys Come Home, the latter both hop-

---

5   R. Williams 2007, p. 35.
6   R. Williams 2007, p. 34.
7   E.P. Thompson 1978, p. 231.
8   Ibid.
9   See, especially, Sommerfield 1943. Sommerfield's wartime short stories are collected in Sommerfield 1947.
10   Writing the script for Night Shift (1942), for example, a short documentary about arma-ments workers directed by J.D. Chambers and produced by Paul Rotha (Chambers 2013).

ing and warning that a return to pre-war conditions would not be tolerated.[11] Between 1944 and 1947, Edgell Rickword edited the leftist cultural journal, *Our Time*.[12] Jack Lindsay, with characteristic intensity, continued his prodigious output after he was called up, first writing novels and poetry while serving with the Signal Corps, then working as a script-writer for the Army Bureau of Current Affairs.[13] For Lindsay, the cultural front of the war effort in some senses vindicated the aspirations of the Popular Front; it 'supplied the situation with the element lacking in the 1930s – a broadly based popular movement turning to the national classics and attempting to find its own means of expression'.[14] Communists were active participants in state-sponsored initiatives such as the Council for the Encouragement of Music and Art, which sought to break down the barriers between mass audiences and traditionally elite cultural forms.[15] In varying ways, directly and indirectly, these figures were active presences in the making of post-war social democracy.

But after 1939, when the Party, acrimoniously, asserted its prior loyalty to Moscow and denounced the war as 'imperialist' in its early phase, the status of intellectuals allied with it would be bound to the modulations of Soviet political relations.[16] As the Cold War developed, the openness to ideological and cultural struggle that the Party had fostered in the Popular Front period and the war years gave way to increasing bureaucratic pressure.[17] Lindsay and Rickword were both victims of an incipient climate of destructive anti-intellectualism; Lindsay's work was denounced and Rickword was bullied into resigning the editorship of *Our Time*.[18] Realism, still felt in the texts discussed here to be an open form, supple enough to speak to a mass readership, ossified into Socialist Realism codified as a kind of aesthetic negation. The writers, including Lindsay, who contributed to a symposium on Socialist Realism held by the Party's National Cultural Committee in 1952 offered a collective self-criticism by way of a preface to the published proceedings, outlining their failure to assert the priority of political struggle and their distraction by such 'bourgeois' concerns as 'abstractionism, formalism, atonalism, existentialism, etc'.[19] But the cultural

---

11   Manson 2006, p. 9.
12   Hobday 1989, pp. 230–2.
13   Lindsay 1982, pp. 797–9.
14   Lindsay 1956, p. 61.
15   Croft 1990, pp. 337–8; Callaghan and Harker 2011, pp. 165–7.
16   The complexities of this moment are summarised in Callaghan and Harker 2011, pp. 145–8.
17   E.P. Thompson 1979, p. xxvi.
18   E.P. Thompson 1979, p. xxvi; Hobday 1989, pp. 242–3.
19   Rodney Hilton et al. 1952, p. 3.

and intellectual atmosphere of the Popular Front years left a lasting impression on the generation of socialist intellectuals who would flourish in the post-war years: for E.P. Thompson and Raymond Williams, the need to envisage a socialism not bound to the abstractions of Stalinism would generate many echoes of the thirties Popular Front emphases on national histories and popular traditions.[20] Like the 'Natopolitan' orthodoxy, the narrative of twentieth-century literary history as one of the inevitable supersession of apolitical and ahistorical postmodernism over a modernism rigidly temporalised in the pre-1945 period relies for its coherence in part on the suppression of the memory and history of the Popular Front and of the possibilities it suggested for a productive encounter between intellectuals, popular culture and socialist politics. The central aim of this book has been to elucidate a particular formation in which, with some success, that engagement was fostered and which resists the narrative of the mid-century as a point of retreat and failure. Further studies could trace the longer evolution of that formation through the cultural making of the post-war settlement and the development of the New Left.

The contradictions between an internationalist, humanist outlook and a political practice rooted in the realities of class, nation and community (which may always be haunted by exclusivity, essentialism, racism and fascism) remain unresolved, though nonetheless urgent. Even 50 years on from the original Popular Front moment, another intellectual formed in that atmosphere, Eric Hobsbawm, could claim that 'the people's front remains the socialist strategy that most frightens the enemy'.[21] The validity of that claim will not be considered here; nonetheless, this book has sought to restore to view the possibilities and challenges that such a strategy, for a brief time, presented at the interface between culture and politics.

---

20   For Thompson and Williams's formative experiences in the thirties, see Woodhams 2001, pp. 23–42.
21   Hobsbawm 1985, p. 249.

References

All-London First of May Demonstration Committee 1935, *May Day 1935: Official Souvenir Programme*.

Allan, Dot 2010 [1934], *Makeshift and Hunger March*, Glasgow: Association for Scottish Literary Studies.

Allan, John R., James Barke, Ivor Brown, N. Brysson Morrison, Catherine Carswell, Edwin Muir, et al. 1938, 'Letters to the Editor: The Refugees in Spain', *Manchester Guardian*, 13 July: 18.

Anderson, Benedict 2006 [1983], *Imagined Communities: Reflections on the Origin and Spread of Nationalism*, London: Verso.

Anderson, Perry 1968, 'Components of the National Culture', *New Left Review*, I, 50: 3–57.

Anderson, Perry 1992, *English Questions*, London: Verso.

Aragon, Louis 1936, 'The Return to Reality: An Impassioned Speech by the Noted French Poet Louis Aragon', *International Literature*, 1936, 1: 100–6.

Auden, W.H. 1977, 'September 1, 1939', in *The English Auden: Poems, Essays and Dramatic Writings 1927–1939*, edited by Edward Mendelson, London: Faber and Faber.

Bakhtin, Mikhail 1981, *The Dialogic Imagination: Four Essays*, edited and translated by Michael Holquist and Caryl Emerson, Austin: University of Texas Press.

Barke, James 1936a, 'Lewis Grassic Gibbon', *Left Review*, I, 5: 220–5.

Barke, James 1936b, 'The Scottish National Question', *Left Review*, II, 13: 738–44.

Barke, James 1950 [1939], *The Land of the Leal*, London: Collins.

Barke, James 1955 [1936], *Major Operation*, London: Collins.

Belsey, Catherine 2002 [1980], *Critical Practice*, London: Routledge.

Benjamin, Walter 2005a [1932], 'Excavation and Memory', in *Selected Writings: Volume Two, Part 2, 1931–1934*, edited by Michael W. Jennings et al., Cambridge, MA: Harvard University Press.

Benjamin, Walter 2005b [1930], 'The Crisis of the Novel', in *Selected Writings: Volume 2, Part 1, 1927–1930*, edited by Michael W. Jennings et al., Cambridge, MA: Harvard University Press.

Benjamin, Walter 2007, 'The Work of Art in the Age of Mechanical Reproduction', in *Illuminations: Essays and Reflections*, translated by Harry Zohn, New York: Random House.

Bergonzi, Bernard 1978, *Reading the Thirties: Texts and Contexts*, Basingstoke: Macmillan.

Bernstein, Jay 1984, *The Philosophy of the Novel: Lukács, Marxism and the Dialectics of Form*, Minneapolis: University of Minnesota Press.

Blackett, R.J.M. 2002, *Divided Hearts: Britain and the American Civil War*, Baton Rouge: Louisiana State University Press.

Bleiman, Mikhail 1934, 'Jules Romains and John Doss Passos', *International Literature*, 1934, 4: 98–106.

Bounds, Philip 2012, *British Communists and the Politics of Literature 1928–1939*, Pontypool: Merlin.

Bowker, Gordon 1993, *Pursued by Furies: The Life of Malcolm Lowry*, London: HarperCollins.

Bramley, Ted 1936, 'Communism Grows from England's Soil', *Daily Worker*, 14 September: 4.

Bramley, Ted 2011 [1936], 'Radical Englishness'. Excerpt from *International Press Correspondence* 15, 44 (29 September 1936), in John Callaghan and Ben Harker, *British Communism: A Documentary History*, Manchester: Manchester University Press.

Brecht, Bertolt 1966, *Galileo*, New York: Grove Press.

Brecht, Bertolt 2003, *Brecht on Art and Politics*, edited by Tom Kuhn, London: Methuen.

Brecht, Bertolt 2007 [1980], 'Against Georg Lukács', translated by Stuart Hood, in Theodor Adorno et al., *Aesthetics and Politics*, London: Verso.

Brendon, Piers 2000, *The Dark Valley: A Panorama of the 1930s*, London: Jonathan Cape.

Brown, Alec 1934, 'Controversy', *Left Review*, 1, 3: 76–7.

Buchanan, Tom 2002, 'Anti-fascism and Democracy in the 1930s', *European History Quarterly*, 32: 39–57.

Buck-Morss, Susan 1995, 'Envisioning Capital: Political Economy on Display', *Critical Inquiry*, 21, 2: 434–67.

Bukharin, Nikolai 1935, 'Poetry, Poetics and The Problems of Poetry in the USSR', in A.A. Zhdanov et al., *Problems of Soviet Literature: Reports and Speeches at the First Soviet Writers' Congress*, London: Martin Lawrence.

Burdekin, Katharine 1985 [1937], *Swastika Night*, New York: Feminist Press.

Burke, Edmund 1800, *The Annual Register: or a View of the History, Politics and Literature for the Year 1768*, 6th edition, London.

Burton, Deirdre 1984, 'A Feminist Reading of Lewis Grassic Gibbon's *A Scots Quair*', in *The British Working-Class Novel in the Twentieth Century*, edited by Jeremy Hawthorn, London: Edward Arnold.

Calder, Angus 1982, 'A Mania for Self-Reliance: Grassic Gibbon's *Scots Quair*', in *The Uses of Fiction: Essays on the Modern Novel in Honour of Arnold Kettle*, edited by Douglas Jefferson and Graham Martin, Milton Keynes: Open University Press.

Calder-Marshall, Arthur 1935a, *Dead Centre*, London: Jonathan Cape.

Calder-Marshall, Arthur 1935b 'Fiction To-Day', in *The Arts To-day*, edited by Geoffrey Grigson, London: The Bodley Head.

Calder-Marshall, Arthur 1937a, 'Fiction', *Fact*, 4: 38–44.

Calder-Marshall, Arthur 1937b, *Pie in the Sky*, London: Jonathan Cape.

Calder-Marshall, Arthur 1937c, *The Changing Scene*, London: Chapman & Hall.

Calder-Marshall, Arthur 1939, 'Pickle My Bones', in *Ten under Thirty*, edited by Michael Harrison, London: Rich & Cowan.

Calder-Marshall, Arthur 1941, 'The Pink Decade', *New Statesman and Nation*, 15 February: 157–8.

Calder-Marshall, Arthur 1985, 'A Visit from the Calder-Marshalls', *Malcolm Lowry Remembered*, edited by Gordon Bowker, London: Ariel/BBC.

Calder-Marshall, Arthur 1991, *The Magic of My Youth*, London: Cardinal.

Callaghan, John and Ben Harker 2011, *British Communism: A Documentary History*, Manchester: Manchester University Press.

Caudwell, Christopher 1946 [1937], *Illusion and Reality*, London, Lawrence & Wishart.

Caudwell, Christopher 1970, *Romance and Realism: A Study in English Bourgeois Realism*, edited by Samuel Hynes, Princeton: Princeton University Press.

Central Committee of the All-Union Communist Party 2002 [1932], 'Decree on the Reconstruction of Literary and Artistic Organizations', in *Art in Theory 1900–2000*, edited by Charles Harrison and Paul J. Wood, Oxford: Blackwell.

Chambers, J.D. (dir.) 2013 [1942], *Night Shift*, on *Land of Promise: The British Documentary Movement 1930–1950*, Disc Two, BFI DVD.

Chase, Malcolm 2007, *Chartism: A New History*, Manchester: Manchester University Press.

Chinitz, David 2003, *T.S. Eliot and the Cultural Divide*, Chicago: University of Chicago Press.

Clark, Katerina 1995, 'Socialist Realism *with* Shores: The Conventions for the Positive Hero', in *Socialist Realism Without Shores*, edited by Thomas Lahusen and Evgeny Dobrenko, Durham, NC: Duke University Press.

Clark, Katerina and Evgeny Dobrenko, with Andrei Artizov and Oleg Naumov 2007, *Soviet Culture and Power: A History in Documents 1917–1953*, New Haven: Yale University Press.

Cockburn, Claud 1973, *The Devil's Decade*, London: Sidgwick and Jackson.

Communist Party of Great Britain 1935, *For Soviet Britain: The Programme of the Communist Party Adopted at the XIII Congress, February 2nd 1935*. Online at http://www.marxists.org/history/international/comintern/sections/britain/congresses/XIII/soviet_britain.htm. Accessed 22/5/2014.

Communist Party of Great Britain (South Wales District) and Communist Party of Great Britain (North Wales District) 1938, *The Lore of the People*, Cardiff: Communist Party of Great Britain.

Connolly, James 1914, 'A Continental Revolution', *Forward*, 15 August 1914. Online at http://www.marxists.org/archive/connolly/1914/08/contrev.htm. Accessed 01/08/2016.

Connor, John T. 2014, 'Jack Lindsay, Socialist Humanism and the Communist Historical Novel', *Review of English Studies*, 66, 274: 342–63. Doi: 10.1093/res/hgu056

Coombes, John 1980, 'British Intellectuals and the Popular Front', in *Class, Culture and Social Change*, edited by Frank Gloversmith, Sussex: Harvester.

Coombes, John 1989, *Writing from the Left: Socialism, Liberalism and the Popular Front*, Hemel Hempstead: Harvester.

Cornford, John 1964 [1936], 'Full Moon at Tierz: Before the Storming of Huesca', in *Poetry of the Thirties*, edited by Robin Skelton, London: Penguin.

Cox, Idris 1932, 'The Welsh National Eisteddfod: "Peace" and Comfort in a Mythical World of Music & Drama: Hiding the Class Struggle's Reality', *Daily Worker*, 6 August: 2.

Cox, Idris 1939, 'Key Books Launch Out', *Daily Worker*, 4 January: 7.

Crafts, Nicholas and Peter Fearon (eds.) 2013, *The Great Depression of the 1930s: Lessons for Today*, Oxford: Oxford University Press.

Croft, Andy (ed.) 1998, *A Weapon in the Struggle: The Cultural History of the Communist Party in Britain*, London: Pluto Press.

Croft, Andy 1983, 'Returned Volunteer: The Novels of John Sommerfield', *The London Magazine*, 1 April: 61–70.

Croft, Andy 1990, *Red Letter Days: British Fiction in the 1930s*, London: Lawrence & Wishart.

Croft, Andy 1995, 'Authors Take Sides: Writers and the Communist Party, 1920–56', in *Opening the Books: Essays on the Social and Cultural History of the British Communist Party*, edited by Geoff Andrews, Nina Fishman and Kevin Morgan, London: Pluto.

Croft, Andy 2002, *Comrade Heart: A Life of Randall Swingler*. Manchester: Manchester University Press.

Cunningham, Valentine 1988, *British Writers of the Thirties*, Oxford: Oxford University Press.

Cunningham, Valentine 1997, 'The Anxiety of Influence; or, Tradition and the Thirties Talents', in *Rewriting the Thirties: Modernism and After*, edited by Keith Williams and Stephen Matthews, Harlow: Longman

Crossman, Richard (ed.) 2001 [1949], *The God that Failed*, New York: Colombia University Press.

Daily Worker 1934, 'Wednesday Book Feature', 19 September: 4.

Daily Worker 1935a, 'The Novel and the Struggle', 13 March: 4.

Daily Worker 1935b, Unsigned editorial response to F.M. Roy, 'Left Review Defended', 9 January: 8.

Daily Worker 1936a, 'Pageant of Colour and Drama: London to See Communists March', 18 September: 5.

Daily Worker 1936b, 'Perjury Allegations at Gresford Pit Inquiry', 9 June: 1.

Daily Worker 1937a, 'A Scots Quair', 21 March: 7

Daily Worker 1937b, 'A Whole People in the Dock', 30 November: 5.

Daily Worker 1937c, 'Italian Leader Dies in Prison: Gramsci Killed by Fascists', 30 April: 5–6.

Davies, Idris 1994, *The Complete Poems of Idris Davies*, edited by Dafydd Johnston, Cardiff: University of Wales Press.

Day Lewis, C. 1937, 'Introduction', in *The Mind in Chains: Socialism and the Cultural Revolution*, edited by C. Day Lewis, London: Frederick Muller.

Day Lewis, C. 1964a [1933], 'The Magnetic Mountain: 25', in *Poetry of the Thirties*, edited by Robin Skelton, London: Penguin.

Day Lewis, C. 1964b [1933], 'The Magnetic Mountain: 32', in *Poetry of the Thirties*, edited by Robin Skelton, London: Penguin.

Dellinger, Mary Ann 2013, 'The Mythopoeia of Dolores Ibárrui, *Pasionaria*', in *Memory and Cultural History of the Spanish Civil War*, edited by Aurora G. Morcillo, Leiden: Brill.

Denning, Michael 1997, *The Cultural Front: The Laboring of American Culture in the Twentieth Century*, London: Verso.

Denning, Michael 2006, 'The Novelists' International', in *The Novel: Volume 1, History, Geography, and Culture*, edited by Franco Moretti, Princeton: Princeton University Press.

Dimitrov, Georgi 1935a, 'Georgi Dimitrov to Writers: A Speech Before the Soviet Writers Association', *Left Review*, I, 10: 343–6.

Dimitrov, Georgi 1935b, 'Revolutionary Literature in the Struggle against Fascism', *International Literature*, 1935, 4: 90–4.

Dimitrov, Georgi 1935c, *The Working Class Against Fascism*, London: Martin Lawrence.

Dinamov, Sergei 1935, 'No Mercy to Terrorists and Traitors: A Statement to All Writers', *International Literature*, 1935, 1: 85–103.

Douglas Garman Papers, Department of Manuscripts and Special Collections, University of Nottingham, Kings Meadow Campus, Lenton Lane, Nottingham, UK, NG7 2NR.

Dutt, Rajani 1935, 'Notes of the Month', *Labour Monthly*, 17, 1: 5–19.

Eagleton, Terry and Drew Milne 1996, introduction to Caudwell, 'English Poets: The Period of Primitive Accumulation', in *Marxist Literary Theory: A Reader*, edited by Terry Eagleton and Drew Milne, Oxford: Blackwell.

Edwards, Ness 1939, 'Rehearsal for Social Revolution: Chartism', *Daily Worker*, 8 November: 2.

Egan, David 1996, '"A Cult of their Own": Syndicalism and *The Miners' Next Step*', in *Miners, Unions and Politics, 1910–1947*, edited by Alan Campbell, Nina Fishman and David Howell, Aldershot: Scholar Press.

Eliot, T.S. 1998 [1923], 'Ulysses, Order and Myth', in *Modernism: An Anthology of Sources and Documents*, edited by Vassiliki Kolocotroni et al., Edinburgh: Edinburgh University Press.

Empson, William 1968 [1935], *Some Versions of Pastoral*, London: Chatto & Windus.

Engels, Friedrich 1933, 'Letters and Documents: Marx and Engels on Balzac', *International Literature*, 1933, 3: 113–24.

Engels, Friedrich 1934, 'Letters and Documents: Engels against Mechanicism and Vulgarisation of Marxism and Literary Criticism', *International Literature*, 1934, 4: 80–9.

Esty, Jed 2004, *A Shrinking Island: Modernism and National Culture in England*, Princeton: Princeton University Press.

Esty, Jed 2012, *Unseasonable Youth: Modernism, Colonialism, and the Fiction of Development*, Oxford: Oxford University Press.

Ewins, Kristin 2015, '"Revolutionizing a Mode of Life": Leftist Middlebrow Fiction by Women in the 1930s', *ELH*, 82, 1: 251–79, doi: 10.1353/elh.2015.0003.

Ferguson, Aitken 1936, 'A Marcher's Novel', *Labour Monthly*, 18, 10: 643–4.

Findlay Henderson, James 1936, 'Lady Macbeth of Mzensk', *Left Review*, II, 6: 272–3.

Fisher, David James 1988, *Romain Rolland and the Politics of Intellectual Engagement*, Berkeley: University of California Press.

Forgacs, David 1989, 'Gramsci and Marxism in Britain', *New Left Review*, I, 176: 70–88.

Fox, Ralph 1935, 'The Fight of Communism on the Front of Culture', *Daily Worker*, 11 September: 4.

Fox, Ralph 1979 [1937], *The Novel and the People*, London: Lawrence & Wishart.

Francis, Ben 1935, 'Red Rhondda's Might Protest', *Daily Worker*, 23 February: 5.

Francis, Hywel 1984, *Miners Against Fascism: Wales and the Spanish Civil War*, London: Lawrence & Wishart.

Francis, Hywel 2006, 'Foreword', in Lewis Jones, *Cwmardy & We Live*, Cardigan: Parthian Library of Wales.

Fyrth, Jim 1985, 'Introduction: In the Thirties', in *Britain, Fascism and the Popular Front*, edited by Jim Fyrth, London: Lawrence & Wishart.

Garman, Douglas 1934a, 'Controversy', *Left Review*, I, 1: 180–2.

Garman, Douglas 1934b, 'What? ... The Devil?', *Left Review*, I, 1: 34–6.

Gibbon, Lewis Grassic 1935, 'Controversy: From Lewis Grassic Gibbon', *Left Review*, I, 5: 178–9.

Gibbon, Lewis Grassic 1998, *A Scots Quair*, London: Penguin.

Gibbon, Lewis Grassic 2002a, 'Aberdeen', in *Smeddum*, Edinburgh: Canongate.

Gibbon, Lewis Grassic 2002b, 'Glasgow', in *Smeddum*, Edinburgh: Canongate.

Gibbon, Lewis Grassic 2002c, 'The Land', in *Smeddum*, Edinburgh: Canongate.

Gibbon, Lewis Grassic 2002d, 'Literary Lights', in *Smeddum*, Edinburgh: Canongate.

Gibbon, Lewis Grassic 2002e, 'Religion', in *Smeddum*, Edinburgh: Canongate.

Gibbon, Lewis Grassic 2002f, 'The Wrecker: James Ramsay MacDonald', in *Smeddum*, Edinburgh: Canongate.

Gorky, Maxim 1935, 'Soviet Literature', in A.A. Zhdanov et al., *Problems of Soviet Literature: Reports and Speeches at the First Soviet Writers' Congress*, London: Martin Lawrence.

Gramsci, Antonio 1971, *Selections from the Prison Notebooks*, translated by Quintin Hoare and Geoffrey Nowell Smith, London: Lawrence & Wishart.

Greene, Graham 1980 [1934], *It's A Battlefield*, London: Penguin.

Gruliow, Leo 1939, 'The Russian Edition of "International Literature"', *International Literature*, 1939, 1: 123–4.

Gunn, Neil. M. 1936, 'Scotland a Nation', *Left Review*, II, 13: 734–8.

Harker, Ben 2009, 'Mediating the 1930s: Documentary and Politics in Theatre Union's *Last Edition* (1940)', in *Get Real: Documentary Theatre Past and Present*, edited by Alison Forsyth and Chris Megson, Basingstoke: Palgrave.

Harker, Ben 2011a, '"Communism is English": Edgell Rickword, Jack Lindsay, and the Cultural Politics of the Popular Front', *Literature and History*, Third Series, 20, 2: 16–34.

Harker, Ben 2011b, '"On different levels ourselves went forward": Pageantry, Class Politics and Narrative Form in Virginia Woolf's Late Writing', *ELH*, 78, 2: 433–56, doi: 10.1353/elh.2011.0019.

Harker, Ben 2013, '"The Trumpet of the Night": Interwar Communists on BBC Radio', *History Workshop Journal*, 75, 1: 81–100, doi: 10.1093/hwj/dbs035.

Harvey, David 2010, *The Enigma of Capital and the Crises of Capitalism*, Oxford: Oxford University Press.

Hawthorn, Jeremy 1979, 'Preface', in Ralph Fox, *The Novel and the People*, London: Lawrence & Wishart.

Heinemann, Margot 1988, '*Left Review*, *New Writing* and the Broad Alliance against Fascism', in *Visions and Blueprints: Avant-garde Culture and Radical Politics in Early Twentieth-Century Europe*, edited by Edward Timms and Peter Collier, Manchester: Manchester University Press.

Hill, Christopher 1939, 'Our England', *Labour Monthly*, 21, 2: 126–7.

Hill, Christopher 1955 [1940], *The English Revolution 1640*, London: Lawrence & Wishart.

Hill, Christopher 1975 [1972], *The World Turned Upside Down: Radical Ideas during the English Revolution*, London: Penguin.

Hilliard, Christopher 2006a, 'Producers by Hand and by Brain: Working-Class Writers and Left-Wing Publishers in 1930s Britain', *The Journal of Modern History*, 78:1: 37–64, doi: 10.1086/499794.

Hilliard, Christopher 2006b, *To Exercise Our Talents: The Democratization of Writing in Britain*, Cambridge, MA: Harvard University Press.

Hilton, Rodney, James Klugman, Arnold Kettle, Sam Aaronovitch, Jack Lindsay and Alick West 1953, *Essays on Socialist Realism and The British Cultural Tradition*, London: Fore Publications.

Hobday, Charles 1989, *Edgell Rickword: A Poet at War*, Manchester: Carcanet.

Hobsbawm, Eric 1985, 'Fifty Years of People's Fronts', in *Britain, Fascism and the Popular Front*, edited by Jim Fyrth, London: Lawrence & Wishart.

Hobsbawm, Eric 1995, *The Age of Extremes: The Short Twentieth Century*, London: Abacus.

Hobsbawm, Eric 1997, *Age of Capital 1848–1875*, London: Abacus.

Holderness, Graham 1984, 'Miners and the Novel: From Bourgeois to Proletarian Fiction', in *The British Working-Class Novel in the Twentieth Century*, edited by Jeremy Hawthorn, London: Edward Arnold.

Hopkins, Chris 2006, *English Fiction in the 1930s: Language, Genre, History*, London: Continuum.

Hopkins, James K. 1998, *Into the Heart of the Fire: The British in the Spanish Civil War*, Redwood City: Stanford University Press.

Horkheimer, Max and Theodor Adorno 2002 [1947], *Dialectic of Enlightenment*, translated by Edmund Jephcott, Redwood City: Stanford University Press.

Hubble, Nick 2006, *Mass-Observation and Everyday Life: Culture, History, Theory*, Basingstoke: Palgrave.

Hubble, Nick 2009, 'The Intermodern Assumption of the Future: William Empson, Charles Madge and Mass-Observation', in *Intermodernism*, edited by Kristin Bluemel, Edinburgh: Edinburgh University Press.

Hubble, Nick 2012, 'John Sommerfield and Mass Observation', *The Space Between*, VIII, 1: 131–51.

Hutt, Allen 1935, 'Flint and Steel English', *Left Review*, I, 4: 130–5.

Hutt, Allen 1976, *The Auden Generation*, London: Pimlico.

Iannucci, Amilcare A. 2010 [2000], 'Dante and Film', in *The Dante Encyclopedia*, edited by Richard Lansing, New York: Routledge.

International Association of Writers in Defence of Culture 1937, 'Manifesto', *Left* Review, III, 7: 445–6.

International Literature 1936, 'Chaos Instead of Music', 1936, 6: 77–9.

Jackson, T.A. 1939, 'Walter Scott and his Historical Significance', *International Literature*, 1939, 8–9: 68–76.

James Barke Papers, Special Collections, The Mitchell Library, North Street, Glasgow, G3 7DN. All materials ©CSG CIC Glasgow Museums and Libraries Collection: The Mitchell Library, Special Collections.

James, C.L.R. 2001 [1938], *The Black Jacobins: Toussaint L'ouverture and the San Domingo Revolution*, London: Penguin.

Jameson, Fredric 1990, 'Modernism and Imperialism', in *Nationalism, Colonialism and Literature*, by Terry Eagleton, Fredric Jameson and Edward Said, Minneapolis: University of Minnesota Press.

Jameson, Fredric 1991, *Postmodernism, Or, The Cultural Logic of Late Capitalism*, London: Verso.

Jameson, Fredric 2002 [1981], *The Political Unconscious: Narrative as Socially Symbolic Act*, London: Verso.

Jameson, Fredric 2007a [1980], 'Reflections in Conclusion', in Theodor Adorno et al., *Aesthetics and Politics*, London: Verso.

Jameson, Fredric 2007b, 'The Poetics of Totality', in *The Modernist Papers*, London: Verso.

Jameson, Storm 1998 [1937], 'Documents', *Fact*, 4, reprinted in *Modernism: An Anthology of Sources and Documents*, edited by Vassiliki Kolocotroni et al., Edinburgh: Edinburgh University Press.

Jameson, Storm 2004 [1937], *In The Second Year*, edited by Stan Smith, Nottingham: Trent Editions.

Joannou, Mary (ed.) 1999, *Women Writers of the 1930s: Gender, Politics and History*, Edinburgh: Edinburgh University Press.

Joannou, Mary 1999, 'The Woman Writer in the 1930s – On Not Being Mrs Giles of Durham City', in *Women Writers of the 1930s: Gender, Politics and History*, edited by Mary Joannou, Edinburgh: Edinburgh University Press.

Johnson, Richard 1982, *The Will to Believe: Novelists of the Nineteen-Thirties*, Oxford: Oxford University Press.

Jones, Lewis 1932, 'Young Dai', *Daily Worker*, 1 July: 6.

Jones, Lewis 1934a, '75 Per Cent. of People Workless: Mighty Steel Works and Mines Now Derelict', *Daily Worker*, 11 May: 4.

Jones, Lewis 1934b, 'The Rhondda in 1934', *Daily Worker*, 19 May: 1.

Jones, Lewis 1937, 'Tonypandy', *Left Review*, III, 3: 157–9.

Jones, Lewis 2006 [1937 and 1939], *Cwmardy and We Live*, Cardigan: Parthian Library of Wales.

Kermode, Frank 1988, *History and Value: The Clarendon Lectures and the Northcliffe Lectures 1987*, Oxford: Clarendon.

Kerrigan, Peter 1937, 'Epic of Anglo-Irish Battalion in Madrid's Greatest Battle', *Daily Worker*, 6 March: 1

Kershaw, Angela 2007, *Forgotten Engagements: Women, Literature and the Left in 1930s France*, Amsterdam: Rodopi.

Kirk, Tim and Anthony McElligott 2004, 'Introduction: Community, Authority and Resistance to Fascism', in *Opposing Fascism: Community, Authority and Resistance in Europe*, edited by Tim Kirk and Anthony McElligott, Cambridge: Cambridge University Press.

Klaus, H. Gustav 1978, 'Socialist Fiction in the 1930s: Some Preliminary Observations', in *The 1930s: A Challenge to Orthodoxy*, edited by John Lucas, Sussex: Harvester.

Klaus, H. Gustav 1985, *The Literature of Labour*, Brighton: Harvester.

Klaus, H. Gustav 1998, 'James Barke: A Great-Hearted Writer, A Hater of Oppression, A True Scot', in *A Weapon in the Struggle: The Cultural History of the Communist Party in Britain*, edited by Andy Croft, London: Pluto Press.

Koestler, Arthur 1949, 'Arthur Koestler', in *The God that Failed*, edited by Richard Crossman, New York: Harper Colophon Books.

Kohlmann, Benjamin 2013, 'An Honest Decade: William Empson and the Ambiguities
of Writing in the 1930s', *ELH*, 80, 1: 221–49, doi: 10.1353/elh.2013.0006.

Kohlmann, Benjamin 2014, *Committed Styles: Modernism, Politics and Left-Wing Literature in the 1930s*, Oxford: Oxford University Press.

Laclau, Ernesto and Chantal Mouffe 2001 [1995], *Hegemony and Socialist Strategy:
Towards a Radical Democratic Politics*, London: Verso.

Laing, Stuart 1980, 'Presenting "Things as They Are": John Sommerfield's *May Day* and
Mass Observation', in *Class, Culture and Social Change: A New View of the 1930s*, edited
by Frank Gloversmith, Brighton: Harvester Press.

Lawrence & Wishart, Advertisement, '*Cwmardy* by Lewis Jones', *Daily Worker*, 2 July: 5.

Leites, A. 1933, 'Soviet Literature & Dos Passos', *International Literature*, 1933, 3–4: 103–
12.

Lehmann, John 1935, 'Grey Granite', *Left Review*, I, 5: 90–1.

Lehmann, John 1940, *New Writing in Europe*, London: Pelican.

Lennard, Ben 1936, 'Ten Years Back On May Day 1926', In All London First of May
Demonstration Committee, *May Day 1936: Souvenir Programme*.

Lewis, Pericles 2004, *Modernism, Nationalism, and the Novel*, Cambridge: Cambridge
University Press.

Lewis, Saunders 1967 [1939], 'Y Dilyw 1939'/'The Deluge 1939', translated by Anthony
Conran, in *The Penguin Book of Welsh Verse*, edited by Anthony Conran, Harmonds-
worth: Penguin.

Lindsay, Jack 1936, 'not english? A reminder for May Day', *Left Review*, II, 8: 353–8.

Lindsay, Jack 1937a, 'A Plea for Mass Declamation'. *Left Review*, III, 9: 511–17.

Lindsay, Jack 1937b, 'Man in Society', *Left Review*, II, 11: 837–40.

Lindsay, Jack 1937c, 'Marxism and the Novel', *Left Review*, III, 1: 51–3.

Lindsay, Jack 1937d, 'The Historical Novel', *New Masses*, XXII, 3 (12 July 1937): 15–16.

Lindsay, Jack 1937e, 'Three Novels', *Left Review*, II, 11: 915–16.

Lindsay, Jack 1938a, *1649: A Novel of a Year*, London: Methuen.

Lindsay, Jack 1938b, 'Neglected Aspects of Poetry (Part One)'. *Poetry and the People*, 1
(July 1938): 14–16.

Lindsay, Jack 1938c, 'The May Day Tradition', *Left Review*, III, 8: 963–8.

Lindsay, Jack 1939a, *A Short History of Culture*, London: Gollancz.

Lindsay, Jack 1939b, *England My England*, London: Key Books.

Lindsay, Jack 1939c, *Lost Birthright*, Bath: Portway Reprints, n.d.

Lindsay, Jack 1948, *Men of Forty-Eight*, London: Methuen.

Lindsay, Jack 1956, *After the Thirties*, London: Lawrence & Wishart.

Lindsay, Jack 1969 [1937], *John Bunyan: Maker of Myths*, New York: Augustus M. Kel-
ley.

Lindsay, Jack 1976, 'Towards a Marxist Aesthetic', in *Decay and Renewal: Critical Essays on Twentieth Century Writing*, London: Lawrence & Wishart.

Lindsay, Jack 1981, *The Crisis in Marxism*, Bradford-on-Avon: Moonraker Press.

Lindsay, Jack 1982, *Life Rarely Tells*, London: Penguin.

Lindsay, Jack 1984, 'A Note on My Dialectic', in *Culture and History: Essays Presented to Jack Lindsay*, edited by Bernard Smith, Sydney: Hale & Iremonger.

Literature of the World Revolution 1931, 'Reports on the Second International Conference of Revolutionary Writers', Special Number: 226–7.

Lodder, Christina 2013, 'From Futurist Iconoclasm to Socialist Construction: *Futuristy. Pervyi zhurnal russkikh futuristov* (1914); *Lef: Levyi fron iskusstv* (1923–5); *Novyi Lef* (1927–8); and *Internatsional'naya literature* (1933–45)', in *The Oxford Critical and Cultural History of Modernist Magazines: Volume III, Europe 1880–1940 Part I*, edited by Peter Brooker et al., Oxford: Oxford University Press.

Lukács, Georg 1936a, 'Essay on the Novel', *International Literature*, 1936, 5: 68–74.

Lukács, Georg 1936b, 'The Intellectual Physiognomy of Literature Characters', *International Literature*, 1936, 8: 56–83.

Lukács, Georg 1937, 'Narration vs. Description' [Part 1], *International Literature*, 1937, 6: 96–112.

Lukács, Georg 1938a, 'Walter Scott and the Historical Novel' [Part 1]. *International Literature*, 1938, 4: 61–86.

Lukács, Georg 1938b, 'Walter Scott and the Historical Novel' [Part 2]. *International Literature*, 1938, 9: 73–84.

Lukács, Georg 1970, *Writer and Critic and Other Essays*, translated and edited by Arthur Kahn, London: Merlin.

Lukács, Georg 1974, *Soul and Form*, translated by Anna Bostock, Cambridge, MA: MIT Press.

Lukács, Georg 1975, *History and Class Consciousness: Studies in Marxist Dialectics*, translated by Rodney Livingstone, London: Merlin.

Lukács, Georg 1976, *The Historical Novel*, translated by Hannah Mitchell and Stanley Mitchell, London: Penguin.

Lukács, Georg 1978, *The Theory of the Novel: A Historico-Philosophical Essay on the Forms of Great Epic Literature*, translated by Anna Bostock, London: Merlin.

Lukács, Georg 2007 [1980], 'Realism in the Balance', translated by Rodney Livingstone, in Theodor Adorno et al., *Aesthetics and Politics*, London: Verso.

MacDougall, Ian (ed.) 1986, *Voices from the Spanish Civil War: Personal Recollections of Scottish Volunteers in Republican Spain, 1936–39*, Edinburgh: Polygon.

Madge, Charles 1936, 'America's Lead', *Left Review*, II, 8: 404–6.

Madge, Charles 1937, 'Press, Radio & Social Consciousness', in *The Mind in Chains: Socialism and the Cultural Revolution*, edited by C. Day Lewis, London: Frederick Muller.

Manchester Guardian 1936, 'A Popular Front', 21 August: 8.

Manchester Guardian 1936b, 'Speech to National Liberal Demonstration', 27 September: 25.

Manson, John 2006, 'Did James Barke Join the Communist Party?', *Communist History Network Newsletter*, no. 19 (Spring 2006): 5–11.

Manson, John 2008, 'Grassic Gibbon's Internationale', *Communist History Network Newsletter*, no. 22 (Spring 2008): 44–50.

Marks, Peter 1997, 'Illusion and Reality: The Spectre of Socialist Realism in Thirties Literature', in *Rewriting the Thirties: Modernism and After*, edited by in Keith Williams and Stephen Matthews, Harlow: Longman.

Marshall, Bert 1937, 'Yessenin & Mayakovsky', *Left Review*, III, 11: 561–5.

'Martin Marprelate' 1938, 'A Novel in a Thousand', *Daily Worker*, 25 May 1938: 7.

Marx, Karl and Friedrich Engels 1988, *The Communist Manifesto*, London: Penguin Classics.

Marx, Karl 1973 [1852], *The Eighteenth Brumaire of Louis Bonaparte*, in *Surveys from Exile: Political Writings Volume II*, edited by David Fernbach, London: Penguin.

Marx, Karl 1990 [1976], *Capital: Volume I*, London: Penguin Classics.

Marx, Karl 2000a [1848], *Economic and Philosophic Manuscripts of 1844*, in *Selected Writings*, edited by David McLellan, 2nd edition, Oxford: Oxford University Press.

Marx, Karl 2000b [1844], *On the Jewish Question*, in *Selected Writings*, edited by David McLellan, 2nd edition, Oxford: Oxford University Press.

Marx, Karl 2000c [1850], *The Class Struggles in France, 1848–50*, in *Selected Writings*, edited by David McLellan, 2nd edition, Oxford: Oxford University Press.

Mass-Observation 1938, *First Year's Work, 1937–38*, London: Lindsay Drummond.

Mass-Observation 1943, *The Pub and the People: A Worktown Study*, London: Victor Gollancz.

Mengham, Rod 2004, 'The Thirties: Politics, Authority, Perspective', in *The Cambridge History of Twentieth Century Literature*, edited by Laura Marcus, Cambridge: Cambridge University Press.

Miller, Tyrus 2010, 'The Strings are False: Bathos, Pastoral and Social Reflexivity in 1930s British Poetry', in *On Bathos: Literature, Art, Music*, edited by Peter Nicholls, London: Continuum.

Montefiore, Janet 1996, *Men and Women Writers of the 1930s: The Dangerous Flood of History*, London: Routledge.

Morgan, Kevin 1989, *Against Fascism and War: Ruptures and Continuities in British Communist Politics, 1935–1941*, Manchester: Manchester University Press.

Morgan, Kevin 1995, 'The Communist Party and the *Daily Worker*, 1930–56', in *Opening the Books: Essays on the Social and Cultural History of the British Communist Party*, edited by Kevin Morgan, Nina Fishman and Geoff Andrews, London: Pluto.

Morgan, Kevin, Gidon Cohen and Andrew Flinn 2007, *Communists and British Society*, London: Rivers Oram.

Morton, A.L. 1934, 'Flesh and Bone of Revolution' [signed 'ALM'], *Daily Worker*, 1 August: 4.

Morton, A.L. 1992 [1938], *A People's History of England*, London: Lawrence & Wishart.

Mulhern, Francis 1974, 'The Marxist Aesthetics of Christopher Caudwell', *New Left Review*, I, 85: 37–58.

Mulhern, Francis 1979, *The Moment of 'Scrutiny'*, London: New Left Books.

Mulhern, Francis 2000, *Culture/Metaculture*, London: Routledge New Critical Idiom.

Myant, Martin 1985, '1935: The Turning Point', in *Britain, Fascism and the Popular Front*, edited by Jim Fyrth, London: Lawrence & Wishart.

Nairn, Tom 1981, *The Break-up of Britain: Crisis and Neo-Nationalism*, London: Verso.

Olesha, Yuri 1936, 'About Formalism', *International Literature*, 1936, 6: 86–92.

Ormond, Philip 1937, 'When London Workers Beat Up a Butcher General', *Daily Worker*, 11 March: 4.

Ortega, Ramón López 1981, 'Language and Point of View in Lewis Grassic Gibbon's *A Scots Quair*', *Studies in Scottish Literature*, 16, 1: 148–59.

Orwell, George 1970a [1940], 'Inside the Whale', in *The Collected Essays, Journalism and Letters*, Volume I, edited by Sonia Orwell and Ian Angus, London: Penguin.

Orwell, George 1970b [1938], 'Review, *Workers' Front* by Fenner Brockway', in *The Collected Essays, Journalism and Letters*, Volume I, edited by Sonia Orwell and Ian Angus, London: Penguin.

Page Arnot, Robin 1936, 'The English Tradition', *Labour Monthly*, 18, 11: 693–700.

Parker, David (ed.) 2008, *Ideology, Absolutism and the English Revolution: Debates of the Communist Party Historians, 1940–56*, London: Lawrence & Wishart.

Pateman, Fred 1937, 'Human Life Must Be Put Before Profit', *Daily Worker*, 23 February: 4.

Paynter, Will 1972, *My Generation*, London: Allen & Unwin.

Pimlott, Ben 1977, *Labour and the Left in the 1930s*, Cambridge: Cambridge University Press.

Pinkney, Tony 1989, 'Editor's Introduction: Modernism and Cultural Theory', in Raymond Williams, *Politics of Modernism*, London: Verso.

Pollitt, Harry 1936, 'Building the People's Front', *Left Review*, II, 15: 797–803.

Pollitt, Harry 1938, *For Peace and Plenty: Report of the Fifteenth Congress of the Communist Party of Great Britain, September 1938*. Online at https://www.marxists.org/archive/pollitt/1938/09/congress-report.htm. Accessed 01/08/2016.

Powell, David 2002, *Nationhood and Identity: The British State*, New York: I.B. Tauris.

Priestley, J.B. 1939, 'March of the People', *Daily Worker*, 24 May: 7.

Radek, Karl 1935, 'Contemporary World Literature and the Tasks of Proletarian Art', in A.A. Zhdanov et al., *Problems of Soviet Literature: Reports and Speeches at the First Soviet Writers' Congress*, London: Martin Lawrence.

Reckitt, Eve C. 1936, 'Ten Years Ago', *Left Review*, II, 8: 352–3.

Redfern, Neil 2005, *Class or Nation: Communists, Imperialism and Two World Wars*, New York: I.B. Tauris.

Rees, John 2000, 'Introduction', in Georg Lukács, *A Defence of History and Class Consciousness: Tailism and the Dialectic*, London: Verso.

Rickword, Edgell 1936a, 'Stalin on the National Question', *Left Review*, II, 13: 745–50.

Rickword, Edgell 1936b, *War and Culture*. London: Peace Library Pamphlets, No. 7.

Rickword, Edgell 1937a, 'Culture, Progress and English Tradition', in *The Mind in Chains: Socialism and the Cultural Revolution*, edited by C. Day Lewis, London: Frederick Muller.

Rickword, Edgell 1937b 'In Defence of Culture', *Left Review*, III, 7: 383.

Rickword, Edgell 1941 [1939], 'Introduction: On English Freedom', in *Spokesmen for Liberty: A Record of Democracy Through Twelve Centuries*, edited by Edgell Rickword and Jack Lindsay, London: Lawrence & Wishart.

Rickword, Edgell 1978a [1937], 'André Malraux: Action and Humanism', in *Literature in Society: Essays and Opinions (II): 1931–1978*, Manchester: Carcanet.

Rickword, Edgell 1978b [1940], 'Milton: The Revolutionary Intellectual', in *Literature in Society: Essays and Opinions (II): 1931–1978*, Manchester: Carcanet.

Rickword, Edgell 1978c [1934], 'Straws for the Weary: Antecedents to Fascism', in *Literature in Society: Essays and Opinions (II): 1931–1978*, Manchester: Carcanet.

Rickword, Edgell and Jack Lindsay (eds.) 1941 [1939], *Spokesmen for Liberty*, London: Lawrence & Wishart.

'R.K.' 1939, 'Here History Lives', *Daily Worker*, 21 June: 7

Rogers, Gayle 2012, *Modernism and the New Spain: Britain, Cosmopolitan Europe, and Literary History*, Oxford: Oxford University Press.

Rudé, George 1995 [1964], *The Crowd in History: A Study of Popular Disturbances in France and England, 1730–1848*, London: Serif.

Ruttmann, Walter (dir.) 1927, *Berlin: Die Sinfonie der Großstadt/ Symphony of a Great City*, Fox Film Corporation.

Samuel, Raphael 1980, 'British Marxist Historians, 1880–1980. Part One', *New Left Review*, I, 120: 21–96.

Saville, John 1977, 'May Day 1937', in *Essays in Labour History: 1918–1939*, edited by Asa Briggs and John Saville, London: Taylor & Francis.

Schwarz, Bill 1982, '"The People" In History: The Communist Party Historians Group, 1946–56', in *Making Histories: Studies in History Writing & Politics*, edited by Richard Johnson et al., London: Hutchinson and Centre for Contemporary Cultural Studies.

Shepherd, W.G. 1935, 'The Fate of France and of Europe', *Daily Worker*, 8 August: 2.

Short, Ben 1936, 'Lady Macbeth of Mzensk', *Daily Worker*, 20 March: 4.

Slater, Montagu 1935a, 'The Turning Point', *Left Review*, II, 1: 15–23.

Slater, Montagu 1935b, 'Writers' International', *Left Review*, I, 4: 125–8

Slater, Montagu 1936, 'Poems, Stories, Criticism, from Working-Class America', *Daily Worker*, 11 March: 7.

Smith, Adam 2007 [1776], *The Wealth of Nations*, Petersfield: Harriman House.

Smith, Ashley 1939, *A City Stirs*, London: Chapman Hall.

Smith, Dai 1984, *Wales! Wales?*, London: Allen & Unwin.

Smith, Dai 1992, *Lewis Jones*, Cardiff: University of Wales Press.

Smith, David 1978, *Socialist Propaganda in the Twentieth-Century British Novel*, London: Macmillan.

Smith, Stan 2008, '"Hard as the Metal of My Gun": John Cornford's Spain', *Journal of English Studies*, Vol. 5–6 (2005–8): 357–73.

Smith, Vern 1934, 'Soviet Authors in "Daily" Interview Tell What Writers' Congress Achieved', *Daily Worker* (USA), 24 September: 5.

Snee, Carole 1979, 'Working-Class Literature or Proletarian Writing?', in *Culture and Crisis in Britain in the Thirties*, edited by Jon Clark et al., London: Lawrence & Wishart.

Sommerfield, John 1930, *The Death of Christopher*, New York: Jonathan Cape.

Sommerfield, John 1935, 'Contributors' Conference: John Sommerfield', *Left Review*, I, 9: 367.

Sommerfield, John 1937a, 'John Summerfield [*sic*] Writes ...', *Daily Worker*, 17 March: 7.

Sommerfield, John 1937b, *Volunteer in Spain*, New York: Alfred A. Knopf.

Sommerfield, John 1938, *Trouble in Porter Street*, London: Fore Publications.

Sommerfield, John 1943, 'The Worm's Eye View', *The Penguin New Writing*, 17.

Sommerfield, John 1947, *The Survivors*, Letchworth: John Lehmann.

Sommerfield, John 1977, *The Imprinted*, London: London Magazine Editions.

Sommerfield, John 2010 [1936], *May Day*, London: London Books.

Sorel, Georges 1999 [1908], *Reflections on Violence*, edited by Jeremy Jennings, Cambridge: Cambridge University Press.

Spender, Stephen 1934, *Vienna*, London: Faber and Faber.

Spender, Stephen 1935, *The Destructive Element*, London: Jonathan Cape.

Spender, Stephen 1936, 'Music and Decay', *Left Review*, II, 15: 834–36.

Spender, Stephen 1937, *Forward from Liberalism*, London: Left Book Club.

Spender, Stephen 1948, 'Stephen Spender', in *The God that Failed*, edited by Richard Crossman, New York: Harper Colophon Books.

Spender, Stephen 1997 [1951], *World Within World*, London: Faber and Faber.

Stevenson, John 1990, *British Society 1914–45*, London: Penguin.

Strachey, John 1935, 'Paris Congress Speeches: John Strachey', *Left Review*, I, 11: 472.

Stradling, R.A. 2004, *Wales and the Spanish Civil War: The Dragon's Dearest Cause?*, Cardigan: University of Wales Press.

Stringer, Jenny (ed.) 1996, *The Oxford Companion to Twentieth Century Literature in English*, Oxford, Oxford University Press.

Swingler, Randall 1937, 'The Cultural Meaning of May Day', *Left Review*, III, 3: 130–3.

Swingler, Randall 1939, 'An Epic of the Rhondda', *Daily Worker*, 19 April: 7.

Swinnerton, Frank 1939, 'New Novels: Mr. LAG Strong and others', *The Observer*, May 7: 6.

Taunton, Matthew 2012, 'Russia and the British Intellectuals: The Significance of the Wells-Stalin Talk', in *Russia in Britain, 1880–1940*, edited by Rebecca Beasley and Philip Ross Bullock, Oxford: Oxford University Press.

The Times 1910, 'Welsh Strike Outrages: The Lawlessness of the Rhondda Valley', 22 November: 12.

Thompson, E.P. 1977, 'Caudwell', *Socialist Register*, edited by Ralph Miliband and John Saville.

Thompson, E.P. 1978, 'Outside the Whale' [1960], in *The Poverty of Theory and Other Essays*, London: Merlin.

Thompson, E.P. 1979, 'Edgell Rickword', *PN Review*, 6, 1: xxvi–xxviii.

Thompson, E.P. 2002 [1963], *The Making of the English Working Class*, New York: Vintage.

Thompson, Willie 1992, *The Good Old Cause*, London: Pluto.

Thorpe, Andy 2000, 'The Membership of the Communist Party of Great Britain, 1920–1945', *The Historical Journal*, 43, 3: 777–800.

Traverso, Enzo 2004, 'Intellectuals and Anti-Fascism: For a Critical Historization', *New Politics*, IX, 4. Online at http://newpol.org/content/intellectuals-and-anti-fascism-critical-historization. Accessed 03/01/2014.

Trotsky, Leon 1938, *The Transitional Programme*. Online at http://www.marxists.org/archive/trotsky/1938/tp/. Accessed 10/01/2014.

Trotsky, Leon 2004 [1937], *The Revolution Betrayed*, London: Dover.

Unofficial Reform Committee of the South Wales Miners' Federation 1912, *The Miners' Next Step*, Tonypandy: Robert Davies & Co.

Vance, Sylvia 1999, 'Lorca's Mantle: The Rise of Fascism and the Work of Storm Jameson', in *Women Writers of the 1930s: Gender, Politics and History*, edited by Maroula Joannou, Edinburgh: Edinburgh University Press.

Varoufakis, Yanis 2016, *And The Weak Suffer What They Must? Europe, Austerity and the Threat to Global Stability*, London: The Bodley Head.

Vishnevsky, Vselvod 1933, 'Soviet Literature and John Dos Passos', *International Literature*, 1933, 4–5: 106–10.

Wallis, Mick 1994, 'Pageantry and the Popular Front: Ideological Production in the Thirties', *New Theatre* Quarterly, 10, 38: 132–56.

Wallis, Mick 1995, 'The Popular Front Pageant: Its Emergence and Decline', *New Theatre Quarterly*, 11, 41: 17–32.

Wallis, Mick 1998, 'Heirs to the Pageant: Mass Spectacle and the Popular Front', in *A Weapon in the Struggle: The Cultural History of the Communist Party in Britain*, edited by Andy Croft, London: Pluto.

Walpole, Horace 1845, *Memoirs of the Reign of King George III, Volume 2*, London: Richard Bentley.

Warner, Rex 1937, 'Education', in *The Mind in Chains: Socialism and the Cultural Revolution*, edited by C. Day Lewis, London: Frederick Muller.

Warner, Rex 1938, *The Professor*, London: The Bodley Head.

Warner, Rex 1990 [1937], *The Wild Goose Chase*, London: Merlin Press.

Warner, Rex 2007 [1940], *The Aerodrome: A Love Story*, London: Vintage.

Warner, Sylvia Townsend 1938, 'Walter Scott', *International Literature*, 1938, 9: 100–1.

Warner, Sylvia Townsend 1987 [1936], *Summer Will Show*, London: Virago.

Watt, Ian 1957, *The Rise of the Novel: Studies in Defoe, Richardson and Fielding*, Berkeley: University of California Press.

Webb, Beatrice and Sidney Webb 1937 [1935], *Soviet Communism: A New Civilization*, London: Victory Gollancz.

Weinroth, Michelle 1996, *Reclaiming William Morris: Englishness, Sublimity, and the Rhetoric of Dissent*, Montreal: McGill-Queens Press.

Welsh, David 2010, *Underground Writing: The London Tube from George Gissing to Virginia Woolf*, Liverpool: Liverpool University Press.

West, Alick 1974 [1937], *Crisis and Criticism*, London: Lawrence & Wishart.

Williams, Chris 1996, '"The Hope of the British Proletariat": The South Wales Miners, 1910–1947', in *Miners, Unions and Politics, 1910–1947*, edited by Alan Campbell, Nina Fishman and David Howell, Aldershot: Scholar Press.

Williams, Gwyn Alf 1991, *When Was Wales? A History of the Welsh*, London: Penguin.

Williams, Keith 1991, 'Joyce's "Chinese Alphabet": *Ulysses* and the Proletarians', in *Irish Writing: Exile and Subversion*, edited by Paul Hyland, Basingstoke: Palgrave.

Williams, Keith 1996, *British Writers and the Media 1930–45*, Basingstoke: Macmillan.

Williams, Keith 1999, 'Back from the Future: Katharine Burdekin and Science Fiction in the 1930s', in *Women Writers of the 1930s: Gender, Politics and History*, edited by Maroula Joannou, Edinburgh: Edinburgh University Press.

Williams, Raymond 1975 [1973], *The Country and the City*, St Albans: Paladin.

Williams, Raymond 1977, *Marxism and Literature*, Oxford: Oxford University Press.

Williams, Raymond 1982, 'Working-Class, Proletarian, Socialist: Problems in Some Welsh Novels', in *The Socialist Novel in Britain*, edited by Gustav Klaus, New York: St Martin's Press.

Williams, Raymond 1984, *Writing in Society*, London: Verso.

Williams, Raymond 1987 [1958], *Culture and Society: Coleridge to Orwell*, London: Hogarth Press.

Williams, Raymond 2005 [1980], *Culture and Materialism*, London: Verso.

Williams, Raymond 2007 [1989], *Politics of Modernism*, London: Verso.

Williams, W.H. 1937, 'A Working Class Epic', *Left Review*, III, 7: 428–9

Williams-Ellis, Amabel 1934a, 'Not So Easy', *Left Review*, I, 1: 39–41.

Williams-Ellis, Amabel 1934b, 'Soviet Writers Congress', *Left Review*, I, 2: 17–28.

Wintringham, Tom 1935, 'Artists in Uniform', *Left Review*, I, 5: 152–60.

Woodhams, Stephen 2001, *History in the Making: Raymond Williams, Edward Thompson and Radical Intellectuals 1936–1956*, London: Merlin.

Woolf, Virginia 1992 [1940], 'The Leaning Tower', in *A Woman's Essays*, edited by Rachel Bowlby, London: Penguin.

Woolf, Virginia 2006 [1938], *Three Guineas*, edited by Jane Marcus and Mark Hussey, New York: Harcourt.

Worley, Matthew 2002, *Class against Class: The Communist Party in Britain Between the Wars*, New York: I.B. Tauris.

Wright, Ralph 1937, 'Reality of Living', *Daily Worker*, 23 June: 7.

Writers' International, British Section 1934, 'The Statement', *Left Review*, I, 1: 38.

Wyn, Iolo 1938, 'The Meaning of the Eisteddfod: The People's University', *Daily Worker*, August 1: 2.

Zhdanov, Andrei 1935, 'Soviet Literature – The Richest in Ideas, the Most Advanced Literature', A.A. Zhdanov et al., *Problems of Soviet Literature: Reports and Speeches at the First Soviet Writers' Congress*, London: Martin Lawrence.

Index